ACCLAIM FOR CATHERINE CLINTON'S

# HARRIET TUBMAN

### THE ROAD TO FREEDOM

"A thrilling reading experience. It expands outward from Tubman's individual story to give a sweeping, historical vision of slavery and the abolitionist movement. Tubman comes across as a deeply autonomous person who trusted in her brains, her religious faith, and her considerable muscle and moxie to get her where she needed to go in life. . . . As measured and scrupulous a historian as Clinton is, she can't help but create an inspirational biography in *Harriet Tubman*."

— Maureen Corrigan,
National Public Radio's *Fresh Air*

"Historian Catherine Clinton is uniquely positioned to provide an informed account of Tubman's life. . . . Her work demonstrates the importance of biography in understanding the range of the American experience."

— Leslie Harris, *Chicago Tribune*

"Catherine Clinton's Harriet Tubman is no mythical grandmother leading fugitive slaves to freedom. She's a flesh-and-blood warrior."

— Robin Dougherty, *Boston Globe*

"It wasn't until now, until Catherine Clinton took on Harriet Tubman's history, that we could begin to grasp Tubman in all her rich dimensions. The elementary school version may be more palatable, but the real Tubman is far more inspiring."         — Mary Ethridge, *Akron Beacon Journal*

"*Harriet Tubman* draws on the extensive historical writing of recent years about slavery and the Civil War to place Tubman's life within its times."

— Drew Gilpin Faust, *New York Times Book Review*

"It is astonishing that it has taken until today for Harriet Tubman, a central figure in the struggle against slavery, to find a modern biographer. But Catherine Clinton, an accomplished scholar of southern history, has now given Tubman the insightful, up-to-date treatment she so richly deserves."

— Eric Foner, Professor of History, Columbia University

"A riveting narrative."

— Carl Rollyson, *New York Sun*

"Catherine Clinton's *Harriet Tubman* is such a wonderful blend of history and biography that it reads like a novel. Harriet Tubman could not have found a more perfect biographer — this book is a triumph."

— Doris Kearns Goodwin, Pulitzer Prize–winning historian

"Clinton has an extraordinary knack of compressing complex history into an informing brief paragraph or a single sentence, making this 'first full-scale biography' of Tubman a revelation. . . . In her hands, a familiar legend acquires human dimension with no diminution of its majesty and power."

— *Publishers Weekly* (starred review)

"In this important and timely work, Catherine Clinton rescues Harriet Tubman from empty symbolism, restoring her full humanity, while showcasing her incomparable efforts on behalf of enslaved African Americans. It should be read by all who have an interest in the making of the American nation."

— Annette Gordon-Reed, author of
*Thomas Jefferson and Sally Hemings:
An American Controversy*

"Clinton's chronicle shines in its description of the lesser-known intricacies of the abolitionist movement."

— Alex Dolan, *San Francisco Chronicle*

"Clinton does an excellent job not only of cobbling together a revealing biography from sparse resources but also of rescuing Tubman from the woefully inaccurate, pop-culture, Washington-chopped-down-the-cherry-tree level of 'scholarship' found in elementary school textbooks. . . . In this fascinating, highly informative work Catherine Clinton has both fleshed out this legendary woman and provided us with a memorably rich cultural history of the loathsome 'Land of Egypt.'"

— Chris Patsilelis, *Houston Chronicle*

"Harriet Tubman was the Moses of her people, who led hundreds of African-Americans on the Underground Railroad from Southern slavery to freedom, yet today she is almost forgotten. Now, in this lively biography, based on thorough research in the sources, Catherine Clinton has restored this indomitable woman to her rightful place as one of the true heroes of American history."

— David Herbert Donald, Charles Warren
Professor of American History Emeritus,
Harvard University

"Clinton has written a profoundly lucid account of Tubman's life, illuminating the inner workings of the Underground Railroad in the process. . . . Tubman died in 1913, the year Rosa Parks was born. Because she was born into slavery, we will never know exactly how long she lived. Thanks to this biography, though, we can now fully appreciate her legacy."

— John Freeman, *Hartford Courant*

"At last Harriet Tubman, the great American hero, has received the stunning and major biography that she has so long deserved. *Harriet Tubman: The Road to Freedom* is absolutely thrilling."

— Gail Buckley, author of *American Patriots:
The Story of Blacks in the Military from the
Revolution to Desert Storm*

"A concise and readable biography that vividly updates the story of Tubman's life."

— *Library Journal*

*Also by Catherine Clinton*

## THE PLANTATION MISTRESS:
### WOMAN'S WORLD IN THE OLD SOUTH

## THE OTHER CIVIL WAR:
### AMERICAN WOMEN IN THE NINETEENTH CENTURY

## HALF SISTERS OF HISTORY:
### SOUTHERN WOMEN AND THE AMERICAN PAST

## TARA REVISITED:
### WOMEN, WAR, AND THE PLANTATION LEGEND

## I, TOO, SING AMERICA:
### THREE CENTURIES OF AFRICAN AMERICAN POETRY

## CIVIL WAR STORIES

## FANNY KEMBLE'S CIVIL WARS

## FANNY KEMBLE'S JOURNALS

## A POEM OF HER OWN:
### VOICES OF AMERICAN WOMEN YESTERDAY AND TODAY

# HARRIET TUBMAN

## THE ROAD TO FREEDOM

Catherine Clinton

BACK BAY BOOKS
Little, Brown and Company
NEW YORK    BOSTON    LONDON

HUDSON BRANCH

*For*

*John Hope Franklin*

Back Bay Books / Little, Brown and Company
Hachette Book Group
1290 Avenue of the Americas, New York, NY 10104
littlebrown.com

Originally published in hardcover by Little, Brown and Company, February 2004
First Back Bay paperback edition, January 2005

Back Bay Books is an imprint of Little, Brown and Company, a division of Hachette Book Group, Inc. The Back Bay Books name and logo are trademarks of Hachette Book Group, Inc.

The publisher is not responsible for websites (or their content) that are not owned by the publisher.

*Library of Congress Cataloging-in-Publication Data*

Clinton, Catherine.
    Harriet Tubman : the road to freedom / by Catherine Clinton. — 1st ed.
        p.   cm.
    Includes bibliographical references and index.
    ISBN 978-0-316-14492-6 (hc) / 978-0-316-15594-6 (pb)
        1. Tubman, Harriet, 1820?–1913.   2. Slaves — United States — Biography.
    3. African American women — Biography.   4. Underground railroad.   5. Antislavery
    movements — United States — History — 19th century.   I. Title.

E444.T82C57 2004
973.7'115 — dc21
[B]                                                                          2003056185

15

Book Design by Robett G. Lowe

OPM

Printed in the United States of America

# Contents

# Contents

*Preface*

# Remembering Harriet Tubman

◄○►

ONE HUNDRED YEARS AGO in the small upstate New York town of Auburn, a charity home named after antislavery martyr John Brown was planned. The modest, two-story brick structure was not remarkable in any other way, except that it would fulfill a lifelong dream of the ex-slave who had settled there in the decade before the Civil War: Harriet Tubman. Certainly she would have preferred that in the new twentieth century her rising and flourishing nation might provide for the aged and indigent, the orphaned and disabled, of whatever color. But while so much had changed since she was born into bondage in Maryland in 1825, Harriet Tubman knew how America had also stayed the same. There would always be those in need, and even as she approached the age of eighty, Tubman continued to extend a helping hand. She would never give up the struggle for racial justice. If she could not fulfill her dream of establishing the home, which all blacks deserved, then she would die trying.

After first striking out for freedom as a young enslaved woman in 1849, Tubman returned south again and again to help scores of slaves escape with the help of the Underground Railroad. When the Civil War broke out, the struggle went "above ground," and Tubman was an active participant in the fight to defeat the Confederacy. Once the Rebels finally surrendered, however, Tubman knew the fight was not over. She had given so much to her country — but she knew it would be a continuing battle for blacks to be granted rights associated with genuine freedom. And as a woman, Tubman recognized that the struggle for women's rights would be an even harder road ahead.

In 1865 Tubman returned to her adopted home, Auburn, New York, which had sheltered and protected her and her extended family since before the war. She wanted to carry on her campaigns for justice within this community and decided to maintain an informal shelter in the house she had bought from a patron, Secretary of State William Seward. Over time, she was able to expand her horizons and purchased an even larger parcel of land in hopes of establishing a separate charity institution. With the help of her church, this dream was eventually realized. In 1908 the Harriet Tubman Home was dedicated. Five years later, Harriet Tubman was dead.

Harriet Tubman had been a liberator, a woman who stood up to the slave power, and a warrior whose actions spoke louder than words. Unlike most women born into slavery, she seized the road to freedom — not just for herself, but also for her family and others during her decade-long association with the Underground Railroad. This bravery earned her a fierce contemporary reputation. She was on the slaveholders' most wanted list with reportedly a steep price on her head. Posters with a description of "Moses," as she was called, were prominently plastered throughout the upper South until the Civil War broke out.

During the war, in addition to nursing soldiers and assisting slave refugees in the coastal South, she took on a military role, organizing scouts and spies. Tubman led rescue missions to free slaves deep into occupied South Carolina. Her notoriety, her association with the infamous John Brown, her utter defiance of nearly every stereotype associated with those held in bondage, made her an anomaly. But the way in which she is remembered clearly has its own complexities, its own history, as well.

Harriet Tubman became a celebrity during her years with the Underground Railroad and was an acknowledged war hero for the small circle who followed her Union career. Yet the larger public rarely gained insight into her character or her motives, as she became in some ways a symbol rather than a flesh-and-blood figure by the end of the nineteenth century. At the turn of the twentieth century there were occasional articles and tributes published on this remarkable woman, but by the time of her death, in 1913, only those who had been directly associated with Tubman kept her memory alive.

In recent years, Americans have enjoyed a renewed appreciation of the champions of black freedom. Frederick Douglass is the subject of multiple biographers, and a lucrative historical book prize is named in his honor. The accomplishments of Martin Luther King Jr. are celebrated on a national holiday and analyzed in a continuing flood of scholarly and popular imprints. Sojourner Truth, Marian Anderson, Zora Neale Hurston, and even Rosa Parks have all commanded scholarly biographical attention, while Harriet Tubman has languished.[1] One authorized biography appeared more than a hundred years ago, and another was written by a journalist born in her adopted hometown of Auburn, New York. After multiple rejections, his manuscript was finally published by a black press in 1943.

For the most part, the life of Harriet Tubman has been confined to the storybook world of "following the drinking gourd" and freedom quilts. These accounts are more folkloric than analytical, more riddled with inaccuracies than concerned with historical facts. Much like Sally Hemings before her, Harriet Tubman has been subjected to more fictional treatments than serious historical examinations, a reflection not of her place in the American past but of a failing on the part of the academy. This absence of scholarship must be recognized as a form of "disremembering." While Tubman was alive in the imaginations of schoolchildren and within popular and underground culture, she was a mystery to professional historians, who consistently mentioned her but failed even to set the record straight about her role and contributions.

Over the past half century there has been a renewed interest in the life experience of slaves as well as a flood of literature concerning the way in which slavery shaped our American past. Concurrently, scholarship in women's history has blossomed. Within these twin literary revivals the lives of women slaves have emerged, and the experiences of fugitive and runaway slaves have been tentatively and creatively mapped. Scholarship on the worlds within slave cabins and those behind the scenes of the Underground Railroad has always been handicapped by the lack of traditional documentation.

But scholars in the twenty-first century have persisted, re-creating with ingenuity and imagination the lives of those denied literacy and of those forced to carry on clandestine struggles. Major historical prizes have been awarded to scholars who have created histories of those who did not leave behind diaries and letters. Underground history is gaining ground, as oral history and other methods of recovering lost experiences have proved fruitful. Scholars within and outside the academy are by necessity becoming more adventurous, recognizing there is a world outside the archives which requires our attention as well.

During the research for this book, I found twenty-first-century scholarship and family lore from descendants as useful as the conflicting published accounts of the nineteenth century. I have tried not to privilege one set of sources over another, and to weigh competing accounts, rival agendas. Tubman's character and accomplishments dwarf efforts to try to capture her between two covers. But she remains a figure whose determination can push those of us who work on her to probe even harder to try to tap into the core.

Harriet Tubman maintained an unblemished record of vigilance, creating a legacy of sacrifice and struggle that carried into the twentieth century. She never grandstanded on any particular issue and made all her public pleas for the benefit of others. Tubman inspired those who took up similar causes during the civil rights movement and feminist revivals of the 1960s, but had a broad humanitarian bent — which is perhaps why she has become a figure with such universal appeal.

Yet she cannot remain a "Mammy" figure, a warm, nurturing historical caricature. As with Pocahontas before her, Tubman's life demands more than pop culture projections and forces us to seek the underlying causes that make her legacy so powerful today.

Though Harriet Tubman became an icon during the last years of the twentieth century, with this book I hope she might become human as well. We may never fully recapture the past, but we can take on some of the struggles of those who came before, in the name of those who will come after, and in this way truly remember Harriet Tubman.

# HARRIET
# TUBMAN

# Chapter One

# Born into Bondage

―――――◄◊►―――――

A T THE TURN of the nineteenth century, the Eastern Shore of Maryland was in many ways a world apart — the rich, rolling fields semicircling Chesapeake Bay, abutting Delaware to the east and grazing Pennsylvania to the north. Fields dappled with sun and lush with grain were crisscrossed by dozens of waterways throughout the peninsula, joining rivers flowing from marshes out to the beckoning salt water. Waterfowl and wildlife were abundant, offering hunters as rich a harvest as that gathered by those who cultivated the land. The Eastern Shore was separated from its sister slave counties by the oyster beds that spread underneath the water to Maryland's other, western, shore, where the bustling ports of Annapolis and Baltimore dominated the regional economy.

Beaver traders originally populated the Eastern Shore, but by the 1660s the pelt trade was depleted and planters began to settle the region. Commercial rather than domestic agriculture flourished, as tobacco farms dominated at first. By the 1750s, fields of tobacco were replaced by fields of corn, as planters found it less labor intensive and more profitable to plant food for export to the West Indies. Philadelphia merchants moved south along Indian trails, scouting for grain, finding eager suppliers along the Choptank River.

In early America, the planters who settled the marshes of the Eastern Shore, the African Americans who struggled within the bonds of slavery there, and the clusters of emancipated blacks who formed pockets of liberty within the countryside created a complex tangle of competing agendas. Black and white, slave and free, acquisitive and hardscrabble crowded together within this narrow strip of Maryland.

This was the world into which Harriet Tubman was born and came of age, a time and place gnarled by slavery's contradictions. She was born near Bucktown in Dorchester County, Maryland, to parents who named her Araminta and cared for her deeply. Yet because she was born a slave, the exact year of her birth remains unknown, unrecorded in an owner's ledger — lost even to the parents and child themselves.

Most accounts offer her birth year as 1820, 1822, or circa 1820, roughly two hundred years after the first boatload of Africans was sold off a Dutch slave ship in 1619 at Jamestown, Virginia. "Circa" affixed before a birth year is one of the most common legacies of slavery. "Like sources of the Nile," the antebellum black leader Samuel R. Ward confessed, "my ancestry, I am free to admit, is rather difficult of tracing."[1] Harriet believed that she was born in 1825, and testified to this fact on more than one occasion.[2] When she died, her death certificate indicated her birth year was 1815. Her gravestone listed her year of birth at 1820. Whatever the year affixed, details of the earliest years of Araminta Ross are equally obscure.

And so is her place of birth. Educated guesses place her mother at several different locations during the period 1815–1825, but the Brodess plantation near Bucktown, Maryland, is most likely her place of birth and is certainly where she spent her earliest years, with her mother. Family lore claimed she was one of eleven children, but no family Bible with names inscribed survived, and family records present conflicting accounts about the names and the number of Tubman's brothers and sisters.

There is no firm evidence of Araminta's place in the birth order. However, she later recalled that she was left in charge of both a baby and another younger brother while her mother went to cook up in "the Big House."[3] Tubman also indicated that she had older siblings, so clearly she was born somewhere in the middle of a string of children, perhaps nearly a dozen. She might have arrived near the end, as her mother was in her forties when she was born.

Araminta was born to Harriet Green[4] and Benjamin Ross, a slave couple who spent a good deal of their married life in close proximity to one another. They struggled, like most enslaved spouses, to create conditions that would allow them to live together, or at least near each other. They negotiated with their owners — and they had different owners throughout their time in slavery — to create a more stable family life.

With each new child, hope might spring anew for slave parents, and Tubman was no exception. She recalled that her cradle was carved from a gum tree — most likely by her father, who was a skilled woodsman. She remembered being the center of attention when young white women from the Big House visited the slave cabins. They playfully tossed her in the air when she was just a toddler.[5] These two hazy memories — the cradle and being tossed in the air — are Tubman's only recorded recollections from her youngest years.

Harriet confessed that during her youth she was described as being "one of those Ashantis."[6] While she may have had ancestors from Ghana who were of Asante lineage, there is no evidence for this. Perhaps it was the Asante proverbs that Harriet picked up as a young girl ("Don't test the depth of a river with both feet") that led her to these claims. All her grandparents might have been African born, but we know the origins of only one.

Tubman's mother's mother arrived on a slave ship from Africa, was bought by an Eastern Shore family named Pattison, and was given the name Modesty.[7] She gave birth to a daughter named Harriet, who was called Rit (by her family) and Rittia (in Pattison records) sometime before 1790.[8]

In one biographical article published the year before Tubman died, the author alleged that her mother, Rit, was the daughter of a "white man," but there is no mention of this in any other records or in family lore.[9] In 1791 Harriet Green was listed as property in the will of Atthow Pattison: "I give and bequeath to my granddaughter Mary Pattison, one Negro girl named Rittia and her increase until she and they arrive to forty-five years of age."[10] This language was standard in nineteenth-century wills and indicated that Rittia was to be given her freedom at forty-five, as would any of her issue born while she was a slave.

If Harriet Green had been the daughter of a white man — even of Pattison himself — this would explain why she was given this special dispensation. It was not an uncommon practice among Chesapeake planters to make a provision for the emancipation of illegitimate, mixed-race offspring.

Mary Pattison inherited Rittia in 1797 and three years later she married planter Joseph Brodess. It was also not uncommon for the father of an illegitimate, mixed-race daughter to "give" the slave daughter to his legitimate white daughter — much as Sally Hemings was brought to the Thomas Jefferson household by his new wife, Martha, as part of her dowry. Half sisters commonly lived under the same roof as mistress and slave.

Whatever their relationship, Rit accompanied her mistress to a new household after Mary wed Joseph Brodess, on March 19, 1800. Brodess and his brothers inherited a 400-acre plot of land only six miles east of Chesapeake Bay, known as "Eccleston's Regulation Rectified." This land had come to their father to settle a debt in 1792. The nearest settlement was Bucktown.[11]

Even less is known about Tubman's father, Benjamin Ross. Nearly all accounts suggest he was a "full-blooded Negro," which may have been to contrast his bloodline with that of his wife. His owner indicated he was born in 1795, which would have made him years younger than his wife. However, this was Ben's age as calculated by a master who inherited him. As Ben was also entitled to his freedom at the age of forty-five, his master may not have been scrupulous about Ben's year of birth. Postponing emancipation meant maintaining added income from the labor of a skilled slave.

As slaves, Tubman's mother and father were forced to do a master's bidding, their child's fate determined by their chattel status. Araminta was doubtless provided little more than the bare necessities of life. Planters doled out a minimum of food to keep slave offspring alive.[12] Clothing for these children was scanty and inadequate. One former slave recalled:

> The clothes that I wore did not amount to much, just a one-piece dress or gown. In shape this was more like a gunnysack, with a hole cut in the bottom for me to stick my head thru, and the corners cut out for armholes. We never wore underclothes, not even in the winter. . . . We never had more than one at a time, and when they had to be washed, we went naked until they had dried.[13]

To an owner a slave child was purely a commodity, one whose labor could be bartered, whose sole purpose was his own gain. The clarity of this fact overwhelms any effort to give Araminta a childhood.

Slavery's ferocious foothold in British North America began in the Chesapeake region, where Araminta spent her entire youth. By the first decades of the seventeenth century, when attempts at permanent settlement of European colonies commenced, land was bounteous but labor was scarce. The English in North America welcomed and eventually institutionalized human bondage, fueling a boom in the African slave trade.

By the time of the American Revolution, slavery was as much a part of Maryland as the tobacco planted in its soil and the oysters harvested from its muddy shores. Although they were shifting into grain agriculture by 1800, slaveholders on the Eastern Shore owned, on average, eleven slaves apiece.[14]

The children of the earliest Africans in the North American colonies were not always born into bondage. Some blacks came as sailors and explorers. Others came as indentured laborers later granted their freedom. A few of these went on to own slaves themselves. But free blacks continued in the minority, and over time, racial boundaries became more rather than less rigid. Even after the prolonged battle for independence, when cries for liberty rang throughout the countryside, opportunities for both emancipation and free blacks diminished. Whites assumed the innate inferiority of those with darker skin and imposed their prejudices through custom and law.

For example, Maryland slave law took a dramatic turn in 1712, when the colonial legislators adopted a new measure: the status of a child would follow the status of its mother, *partus sequitur ventrem*. This statute overturned centuries of patriarchal tradition and law. This radical shift was in response to sex across the color line, most especially white males coupling with slave women.

As the number of persons of color with white ancestry began to grow, the exponential growth of a mixed-race population presented a threat to the white hierarchy. The 1712 law allowed white men to pursue their appetites and maintain the status quo, while white women were hemmed in by increasingly rigid prohibitions and restrictions on their behavior. A white man who fathered a slave child could mask his illicit sexual connection. A white woman risked not just ostracism, but exile or worse if she was discovered in any sexual connection with a black. By law, any child born to her would be born free. Abolitionist Frederick Douglass, who was born in 1818 on a plantation on Maryland's Eastern Shore, near present-day Easton — less than thirty miles from Harriet Tubman's own place of birth — never knew the name of his father. Speculation points to a white slaveholder, perhaps his mother's master, but the details of his lineage remain unconfirmed.

By the close of the eighteenth century, the invention of the cotton gin (1793) fueled a stampede of slaveholders further south and west. Fortunes could be made planting cotton once an easier, inexpensive way of processing the crop was developed. Settlers began pouring into the new states of Kentucky and Tennessee, where Revolutionary War veterans cashed in on land grants. Georgia, Alabama, Mississippi, and eventually Louisiana lured thousands onto their rich soils with a promise of extravagant fortunes, all to be made in the wake of slavery's widening sphere.

By 1808 the external slave trade was prohibited due to constitutional mandate. After almost two hundred years of imports, cutting off the supply of slaves from Africa and the Caribbean had a profound impact on slavery in the United States — with especially drastic results for slaves in the upper South, where Tubman and her family lived.

The domestic slave trade became crucial to slaveholders eager to settle the southwestern frontier. Suddenly, enslaved African American women, already expected to perform harsh and exacting physical labor, became the sole legal source of slave labor. Deep South politicians were in a frenzy to see their plantation economy thrive and to keep slavery booming. Cotton was not a cash crop in Maryland, but its plantations produced one of the most invaluable crops for the southern antebellum market: slaves. The children of slaves quickly became a vital commodity and source of income for cash-poor planters of the Chesapeake, and of increasing significance to the prosperity of the lower South.

When the international slave trade ended, the enslaved population in America was not quite 2 million. Less than fifty years later, with the outbreak of the Civil War, slaves in the American South numbered nearly 3.5 million. This was an astonishing growth rate, given the high mortality among slaves, especially infant mortality. Slave babies commonly succumbed to any number of childhood diseases that plagued all newborns in the South but that visited the slave cabins with depressing regularity. The mortality rate for black children in the Chesapeake during the first half of the nineteenth century was double that of white infants. While enslaved mothers were in the plantation fields picking throughout September and October, infant mortality spiked. Further, many slave mothers had to contend with their own ill health during the winter season, when congestive diseases might fell both mother and child. These illnesses proved more often fatal for infants and young children.

The southern climate also meant that blacks, and especially slave children, endured exposure to malaria, cholera, smallpox, and a range of fevers, including the deadly "yellow jacket" (yellow fever). In the antebellum South any outbreak or epidemic (with the exception of malaria) hit African Americans in much higher numbers than whites. Despite these health and medical statistics, the increase in the slave population was explosive. By comparison, while the black female birth rate skyrocketed during the half century leading up to the Civil War, the white female birth rate in the country was declining, and reduced by half by century's end. During this same period approximately 10 percent of adolescent slaves in the upper South were sold by owners; another 10 percent were sold off in their twenties. Slave parents lived in abject terror of separation from their children. This fear, perhaps more than any other aspect of the institution, revealed the deeply dehumanizing horror of slavery.

All over Maryland, slaves dreaded the "Georgia traders," the appellation given to any slave buyers who appeared. By the 1820s Maryland newspapers were filled with advertisements seeking slaves for sale; sometimes as many as two hundred were sought at a time.[15] The Eastern Shore was a prime place to seek slaves to funnel into the Deep South, and there were approximately 5,000 slaves in Dorchester County (between 1810 and 1830).

Tubman was deeply aggrieved by the disappearance of siblings, carried off by the slave coffle: "She had watched two of her sisters carried off weeping and lamenting."[16] Tubman was permanently affected by this episode, as she witnessed the "agonized expression on their faces."[17]

No record of her sisters' fate has ever been uncovered, and even their names are a source of confusion.[18] White records suggest these daughters were called Linah and Soph.[19] A family tree constructed by one of Ben and Rit's descendants identifies them as Harriet and Mary Lou, while a later version by another descendant called them Katherine and Marie.[20] Whatever the names of these lost sisters, these women were sold away, stolen from their families and never reunited with parents, siblings, or children.

Those left behind suffered more than just mourning. Family members lost to slave sales were worse than dead, as there was no peace or closure.

Fugitive slave Lewis Hayden painfully recalled: "I have one child buried in Kentucky and that grave is pleasant to think of. I have got another that is sold nobody knows where, and that I never can bear to think of."[21]

Slaveholders treated slave children as commodities, and as a means of anchoring adult slaves on the plantation. Owners believed parenthood reduced the rate of runaways. Thus southern masters actively promoted pair bonding and childbearing, even though the integrity of these families was constantly threatened by sales. The rates of miscarriage were much higher for African American women than for white women, and better care and feeding during pregnancy was the exception rather than the rule for enslaved women. These were the "family values" shaped by slavery in the decades leading up to the Civil War.

Nonetheless, the pregnancies of slave women interfered with women's productive roles as slaves. Indeed, one Maryland slaveholder advertised one of his chattels as "young NEGRO WENCH, with a Male Child two years old. She can wash and iron." But, he added with some disdain, she "is sold for no fault but for being pregnant."[22]

Planter records indicate that supervisors of female slaves were often suspicious of their claims of impending childbirth. Owners, physicians, and overseers regularly accused female laborers of pretending to be pregnant. The charge of "shamming" was a self-serving lament as much as a legitimate concern, as it was rare for pregnant women to be given any dispensation. Some supervisors did lighten the workload of expectant women in the advanced stages of pregnancy to reduce the chances of miscarriage. Thus slave childbearing provoked a host of contradictions for plantation society.

During the crucial first months of a slave child's life, little was done by owners to combat infant mortality.[23] Few slaveholders reduced the hours for nursing mothers. Fanny Kemble, married to one of the largest slaveowners in Georgia, indignantly reported in 1838 that her husband sent women back into the fields only three weeks after their confinements. While Kemble condemned his regimens as brutal, his Sea Island neighbors viewed her husband as a model and indulgent slaveholder. She described the plight of a mother who lost a newborn to snakebite: her nursing infant was bitten while lying in a field where the mother toiled nearby — but not near enough to save her child.[24]

In 1801 Tubman's mother's master, Joseph Brodess, died. He left behind his widow, Mary, and their infant son, Edward, who presumably would inherit the five slaves in the household. In 1803 Mary remarried widower Anthony Thompson, and Harriet Green, once again, came with the marriage. Mary Brodess's new husband owned Ben Ross, which is presumably how Harriet Green met her husband.

Upon Mary's premature death in 1810, the nine-year-old Edward's legal guardian and stepfather, Anthony Thompson, looked after the boy's interests. During this period, Harriet and Ben were able to live together as man and wife and start a family. By 1820 Thompson owned nearly forty slaves.

But Edward Brodess broke up the Ross family by starting his own. In 1824, now twenty-three years old, Edward Brodess married Elizabeth Anne Keene, and the couple moved into the home his stepfather had helped him build on his late father's land near Bucktown, less than ten miles away. Harriet Ross and her children went with them, while Ben most likely was forced to remain behind. By 1840 Brodess headed a household that consisted of his wife and two sons. His slaves included Rit and eight children: one boy under five, two boys between ten and twenty-four, one older male, two girls under ten, and two girls ten to twenty-four. Harriet was one of these females.

Brodess expanded his holdings by buying thirteen acres, a part of "Taylor's Delight" on the road from Bucktown to Little Blackwater Bridge, in September 1834. Except for census data, a marriage license, and abstracts from land records, Edward Brodess left very little to offer us clues to his life as a Maryland planter. In 1852 his will was burned in a fire that destroyed the Dorchester County courthouse, and its provisions were reconstructed in 1854. Ironically, more information about his role as a slaveowner comes from black sources.

According to Harriet Tubman's brother, their mother, Rit, was able to keep her family together when a slave sale threatened to rob her of a child. Rit became alarmed after seeing her master take money from a Georgia man named Scott. Hearing the master then summon one of her sons, Rit appeared unexpectedly in the room. Brodess attempted to distract her by ordering her to bring him a pitcher of water. After returning to her work, she overheard Brodess call for the boy again, this time to harness a horse. She immediately returned to Brodess's side. Tubman's brother Henry witnessed Brodess's exasperation with his mother and his complaint, "What did you come for? I hollered for the boy."

Harriet's mother then accused Brodess of wanting her son for "that (ripping out an oath) Georgia man." Unwilling to resort to force, Brodess was stymied when Rit kept her son hidden in the woods and with friends for over a month. This prolonged period of subterfuge testifies to the complex strategies and networks of slave resistance, which extended throughout the Eastern Shore. It also suggests that relations between master and slave might have been less rigid, more negotiable, than they were in the Deep South.

Seemingly more annoyed than infuriated, Brodess finally found a servant who knew where the boy was hidden and tried to enlist him to set a trap. When this ploy failed, Brodess went to Rit's cabin to demand the boy, but she threatened, "The first man that comes into my house, I will split his head open." Harriet Ross must have been both a valuable and a formidable woman, to stand up to her master and protect her child with such ferocity. In this case, her tactics succeeded. Such family lore, too, would have provided Tubman with a powerful example of the possibilities for resistance.

Tubman's brother Henry reported that finally Scott gave up and returned to Georgia. At the end of the standoff, when Rit's son returned home, Brodess "said he was exceedingly glad she hid the boy, so that he couldn't sell him."[25]

Henry's account raises many questions about the complex negotiations between owners and slaves. Was Brodess himself torn up over the prospect of sale, and sincere in his expression of gratitude over Rit's measures to prevent it? Or was he trying to placate her? The cat-and-mouse game lasted for over a month, suggesting the persistence of either the Georgia buyer or the ambivalence of the Maryland seller. When Rit stood up to Brodess in this case, was it because she had already lost children to sales and would not allow another to be taken?

This and other family lore make it clear that Harriet's parents fought to keep their family together. Henry grimly confided that Brodess pledged that if Rit would remain "faithful" (presumably meaning obedient), "he would leave us all to be free."

Despite such promises, Harriet's brother recalled, "at his death, he left us all to be slaves."[26]

## Chapter Two

# Coming of Age
# in the Land of Egypt

————◇————

A T WHAT POINT would any child born into bondage "come of age" and be made aware of her status? Four? Five? How quickly would she discover that the larger world designated some people free and some slaves? What about the color line? When would the difference become crystalline and its consequences devastating?

Most slave children in the antebellum era learned the twin maxims of slavery by harsh experience: their labor was not their own, and they could be deprived of kin. Although African Americans toiling in the field might be seen as the quintessential image of slavery, the more potent symbol of the system was the auction block. Josiah Henson, a fugitive slave who published his memoir, bitterly recalled, "My brothers and sisters were bid off one by one, while my mother, holding my hand, looked on in agony and grief." Henson was also sold apart from his mother.[1] In this way slaves were forced to confront their utter powerlessness, "soul by soul," as one scholar has characterized it.[2]

Children were particularly vulnerable to the devastation wrought by the selling off of siblings. More than any other insult, this would have sharpened their sense of the fragility of their existence. Tubman experienced the loss of at least two siblings to the slave coffle. One older sister was forced to leave her own two children behind. How could grieving parents explain this loss? Ben and Rit withstood these tragedies by maintaining their faith in God, by seeking comfort in biblical wisdom. While enduring such sorrows they could only hope for a better world beyond the "land of Egypt," where all their brethren suffered the scourge of slavery.

Slave children had every stage of childhood cut short, from nursing onward. They were propelled into adulthood by slaveholders' impatience. Many were sent to the fields as human scarecrows as soon as they were able to walk.[3]

In an account of Tubman's life written by her later patron and friend Sarah Bradford, her childhood is presented as a series of tough seasonings. From the earliest age, her sense of the world was defined by the displacement whites imposed as much as by any loving circle forged by parents and siblings. In interviews she gave in later life, Tubman indicted the treatment she experienced during her formative years: "I grew up like a neglected weed, — ignorant of liberty, having no experience of it."[4]

Araminta's birthplace was one county over from the headquarters of a notorious crime ring, the Cannon gang.[5] The Cannons had been accused of kidnapping free blacks and selling them in Virginia as early as 1815. A decade later, by the time Harriet was born, the gang had become so notorious that Mayor Watson of Philadelphia targeted them as public enemies. Investigators were sent to find the route along which abducted blacks were shipped south (a mirror image of the later Underground Railroad lines). Authorities discovered that men and women had been chained up at several Cannon properties prior to transportation to the auction block.[6]

The gang's activities might have continued unabated had it not been for a tenant farmer on Cannon land who, in the first week of April 1829, stumbled upon a buried box of human bones. After the discovery, a circus atmosphere prevailed, as people came from miles around to watch as authorities excavated Cannon land — searching for more bodies. The only gang member who didn't flee, sixty-year-old Patty Cannon, was indicted on three counts of murder, including the strangling of a black child.[7] Cannon died in her jail cell before going to trial.[8]

Many children grow up with fears of bogeymen. But young Araminta lived only a short distance from the Cannons' real-life house of horrors, where children disappeared, skeletons were dug up, and slavery's evils were confirmed in the headlines — after years of gruesome rumors on the grapevine. Tubman came of age at the heart of a crossroad, where abolitionists, kidnappers, slavecatchers, and fugitives hid out from one another.

No matter how hard they tried, Araminta's parents were unable to protect her from the harsh realities of bondage. When Araminta was only five years old, a woman in the neighborhood, a "Miss Susan," drove up to her master's plantation and requested "a young girl to take care of a baby."[9] Araminta was sent off without a moment's hesitation — an all too common fate for young enslaved females.

Tubman recalled in later years that this new home was the first place where she had seen white people eat, and that she was "ashamed" to eat before them. She was plagued by the strange, uncomfortable newness of a white household. She also was bitterly homesick, "like the boy on the Suwanee River [sic], 'no place like my ole cabin home.'" In her new surroundings, she slept on the floor and would cry herself to sleep. Araminta longed to be back in her own cabin, where she might crawl into her mother's bed at night.[10]

She was far too young to take on the responsibilities she was assigned. She remembered being so small that she had to sit on the floor to safely hold the white baby in her lap. Once installed in a new master's household, she was given a full load of domestic tasks, as well as caring for the infant. After a long day of doing her mistress's bidding, the five-year-old Araminta remained on duty at night, instructed to rock the cradle constantly to prevent the baby from disturbing the master or mistress. If the baby wailed, this mistress did not go to comfort her child but instead lifted her hand to grab a small whip from its shelf — to punish her slave attendant for negligence.

One day, Tubman recalled, she was whipped five times before breakfast — and her neck bore the scars from this incident for the rest of her life. When her wails awoke the mistress's sister, a Miss Emily, she was given a brief reprieve as Emily tried to offer assistance rather than punishment, tutoring rather than harshness. Even though this kind woman interceded on her behalf, Araminta remained unable to please her mistress and was run ragged in the process. The young girl was returned to her family severely debilitated, weak and undernourished.

Rit nursed her daughter back to health, only to have her sent away again as soon as she recovered. This became part of a pattern. During childhood Araminta was hired out year after year, serving a variety of masters as a household worker.

Tubman recalled an episode that provoked her to run away when she was only seven years old:

> My mistress got into a great quarrel with her husband; she had an awful temper, and she would scold and storm and call him all kinds of names. Now you know, I never had anything good, no sweet, no sugar; and that sugar, right by me, did look so nice and my mistress' back was turned to me while she was fighting with her husband, so I just put my fingers in the sugar bowl to take one lump and maybe she heard me for she turned and saw me. The next minute she had the rawhide down. I gave one jump out of the door.

The young Araminta knew what the consequences would be for swiping sugar and fled from the yard. She stopped only when she was too tired to go on. Exhausted and frightened, she tumbled inside the fence of a large pigpen, and "there I stayed from Friday until the next Tuesday, fighting with those little pigs for the potato peelings and other scraps that came down in the trough." It became more and more difficult to fight off the mother sow. Finally Araminta was so starved that she went back to her mistress, regardless of what awaited.[11]

During one of the times when she was a slave for hire ("put out again for vittles and clothes," as she called it),[12] she was required to break flax.

Scutching flax was heavy, onerous work, hardly suitable for an adolescent, much less a child.

Once when sent to work in the home of James Cook, she was forced to wade in water up to her waist, fetching muskrats from traps. On one of these wading expeditions, she was ill with the measles and, upon returning to the house, collapsed. Incapacitated by illness, again Araminta was sent home — too sick to work and worthless to the master who had hired her. She described herself during this period of severe neglect: "My hair had nebber been combed an' it stood out like a bushel basket."[13]

There are few descriptions of Araminta when she was a girl, except for white observations that she was "sickly."[14] Was she bright and talkative? Was she shy and introspective? Curious? Stubborn? Was she scrawny as a child? Or sturdy? Did she enjoy playing with whittled dolls, or was she happier wandering in the woods? Or would she ever have had the luxury of time to herself? Slavery may or may not have robbed this child of traits and preferences, but the absence of historical accounts offers little on which to speculate.

In one account of her childhood Tubman confessed that one of her mistresses would whip her almost every day, first thing in the morning. So when she was in this woman's household, Araminta got into the habit of putting on "all the thick clothes she could" to protect herself. When the punishment was administered, she would wail, as if the "blows had full effect." In the afternoon, when she was out from under her mistress's watchful eyes, she would "take off her wrappings." Another account described an occasion when Tubman was being punished for an infraction; she bit her master's knee, and her show of temper meant she was left alone in future by this master. From an early age, Tubman was clever and resourceful, able to provide herself some protection from slaveholder's wrath.[15]

By the age of twelve, Araminta had graduated from domestic labor. By then she so resented the close company and smothering supervision of white women that she was considered unsuitable as a domestic servant. She became more valuable in fields, where she could hoe and harvest, more contented alongside her fellow African Americans. The once-weak young girl grew into a strong adolescent, of whom much was expected — and much was delivered.

As an adolescent, Araminta was farmed out to a man who subjected her to backbreaking drudgery, hoisting barrels of flour into carts. Because it was outdoor work and she was often in the company of a brother, she learned to prefer if not enjoy physical exertion. In the wide-open spaces of the woods and fields, she came into her own. She developed awesome stamina. By this time she always wore her hair pulled back tightly, or wrapped in a bandana or headcovering.

She learned to love the land, where flora and wildlife reflected seasonal change. The skunk cabbage would bloom in early spring, sometimes as early as February. Whippoorwills would serenade on summer evenings, and during autumn Canada geese might squawk overhead while migrating south. Winter would slow down outdoor activities on farms, as a general hibernation set in, but the seasonal buzz of activities would begin anew each year.[16]

Growing from a girl into a young woman, Araminta experienced an intensification of her Christian faith, a deep and abiding spiritual foundation that remained with her throughout her life. Perhaps because she had been so gravely ill during her youth, her mother must have spent as much time as possible by her daughter's sickbed, and naturally filled her head full of Bible stories. Araminta was never taught to read or write. All of this religious lore would have been absorbed from chapters and verses spoken to her by her parents, who were also illiterate.

Tubman would later complain of her owner's lack of Christianity, which suggests that he was not a churchgoing man.[17] His lapse in faith or lack of faith meant he likely did not provide for the religious instruction of his slaves, nor allow preachers to attend to their spiritual needs. Dorchester County supported a variety of churches, but there are no indications that Araminta attended any of these local houses of worship. If she had, as a slave she would have been segregated into a Negro's pew.

She would not have been permitted to attend an independent black congregation. By early adolescence, she would have learned that slaves' religious practices were a preoccupation for slaveowners. Masters demanded complete control of every aspect of slaves' lives.

Worship for blacks in the region, especially slaves, was strictly supervised. Slaves could congregate for religious services only with white approval and under white surveillance. In this way, religious instruction emphasized a doctrine of obedience. Slaveholders restricted expressions of faith and maintained an iron rule, especially in rural settings.

The Ross family was well acquainted with Samuel Green, a local free black Methodist preacher. Green had the same last name as Araminta's mother, but no family connection has been established. Green may nevertheless have had a strong influence on Araminta as she was growing up. She maintained such a strong and abiding Christian faith that her early years may have been marked by contact with local black preachers and deacons. Their example, if not their tutelage, shaped her during these formative years. The black church in the plantation South was not characterized by buildings; indeed any slave congregations felt themselves secret and subversive. Regardless of slaveholders' repressive regime, slaves' religion was key to black culture in the first half of the nineteenth century, so much so that one scholar has labeled it "the invisible institution."[18]

On a deserted road in Dorchester County, a small wooden structure, once a store, can still be found. The building has a porch and ceilings too low for anyone over six feet to stand upright. At the small crossroads of Bucktown, Maryland, only the asphalt and telegraph lines, plus an occasional passing car, suggest it is a later century than Tubman's. A sense of the past haunts this secluded spot. Even on a bright day, the place has an air of melancholy.

When Araminta was an adolescent, she was hired out to work on the harvest for a man named Barrett. When another slave, a male coworker, left the fields and headed toward Bucktown, the overseer followed.

Araminta raced ahead to warn her fellow field hand, knowing there would be trouble. The confrontation between white and black took place at this crossroads, in a small village store.[19]

The overseer was determined to punish the field hand who had deserted his post with a whipping. In the confusion of the confrontation, the frightened slave bolted from the store. As the slave made haste, Araminta reportedly blocked the angry overseer's path of pursuit by standing in the doorway — just as he picked up a lead weight from the counter and threw it at the escapee. The weight hit Araminta in the head and delivered "a stunning blow."[20] The overseer was accountable for neither his temper nor his bad aim. Araminta's wound was deep and severe.

She later recalled that she had been wearing a covering on her head, and when the weight struck her it

> broke my skull and cut a piece of that shawl clean off and drove it into my head. They carried me to the house all bleeding and fainting. I had no bed, no place to lie down on at all, and they lay me on the seat of the loom, and I stayed there all that day and the next.[21]

Araminta's condition was so grave that she was sent back to her owner, Brodess, with the report that she was "not worth a sixpence." Her parents feared she might never recover. In the following weeks, she would slip into "a lethargic sleep from which it was almost impossible to awaken her."[22] These "spells" would come over her without warning. Her family could do little for her but pray, as she lay in her sickbed for months on end. Brodess tried to sell her. Luckily for the Ross family, he could find no takers.

When Araminta was recovered she was hired out to a local entrepreneur named John Stewart, who had employed others of her family, including her father, for many years. Stewart had only one free black working on his lands in 1820, suggesting his involvement in agriculture was minimal. But over the decades he built up a thriving lumber business, clearing tracts along the Eastern Shore and selling his product to cities nearby. A canal connecting prime sites was dug sometime during the 1830s; "Stewart's canal" enabled him to transport his vast lumber shipments by water.[23] By 1840, in addition to his five sons and four daughters, his household supported four slaves and two free blacks.

Stewart invited both Araminta and her brothers to join their father in working on his burgeoning lumber operation. She regained her strength and became even stronger during her time working under Stewart's supervision. Soon after she arrived on Stewart lands, she began to chop logs and tote timber. Her daily haul was roughly half a cord of wood, a sturdy amount that few men could match. She seemed to flourish, unbowed by the reversals she had been dealt. By this time she had grown to her full adult height of five feet.

Araminta's father managed the shipping of Stewart's timber to the Baltimore market. The relationship between Ben Ross and John Stewart was a relatively enlightened one, considering the constraints of slavery and race relations in the region. Ben's daughter was extremely industrious and earned more than what she was required to hand over to her owner. During one year while working for Stewart, Araminta was able to save enough money to buy a pair of steers. This liberal arrangement between a slave for hire and her employer demonstrated that Stewart used incentive to motivate his workforce.

Frederick Douglass wrote in his autobiography that his mother was hired out to a slavemaster named Stewart. Douglass reported he was not a bad master.[24] Though neither Douglass nor Tubman subscribed to the myth of the kindly slaveholder, a man named Stewart was singled out by both as a master better than most — strengthening the possibility that they were talking about the same Eastern Shore man.

Ben Ross was owned by Anthony Thompson, who promised to emancipate him at the age of forty-five. Anthony Thompson finally died in 1836. The old man's son and heir, Dr. Anthony Thompson, honored his father's promise when he determined Ben had reached the age of forty-five. Ben Ross was granted his freedom in 1840.

Manumission did not outwardly transform his daily life: Ross continued to work for Dr. Thompson, the man he had previously served as a slave. He continued to reside along the Eastern Shore, to remain near his wife and children still held in bondage. But he had won his freedom, a precious commodity in a slave state.

As a free laborer, Ben Ross became a key player in Anthony Thompson's financial operations. In 1846 Thompson bought 2,100 acres in Caroline County in an area known as Poplar Neck. There were roughly twenty-six sawmills in Caroline County, including Thompson Mill, on Marsh Creek. Thompson needed to clear as much of the valuable hardwoods on his newly acquired spread as possible, depending on the rich forests of oak and hickory to help him pay off his steep mortgage.[25] When Thompson moved from his home in Cambridge to the remote riverside estate at Poplar Neck, Ben and Rit most likely accompanied him, so Ben could serve as Thompson's timber estimator and foreman.[26] Araminta may have joined her parents at this Caroline County location sometime in 1846 or 1847.[27]

Little is known about the other most important aspect of Araminta's coming of age: her relationship with the man who would become her husband, John Tubman. He was born near White Marsh, in northern Dorchester County. By the time he and Araminta married, in 1844, he was a free black, though whether he was born in freedom is unknown.

Tubman was the family name of wealthy Dorchester County planters who owned Lockerman's Manor, a 265-acre spread on the western edge of Cambridge, Maryland, overlooking the Choptank River, an estate established in the seventeenth century.[28] These Eastern Shore Tubmans were Catholic slaveholders. In 1769 a Richard Tubman II of Meekins Neck built St. Giles Church, the first Catholic church in Dorchester County.[29]

Many blacks in the area were known by the name Tubman, suggesting the planter family's vast slave holdings. In 1840 there were eight Tubman households in Dorchester County, Maryland — three black and five white. John Tubman may have been among the African Americans residing there, but within which household is impossible to tell.

The free black community, especially in the border states, steadily increased at the turn of the nineteenth century. No black population grew more dramatically during the early years of the republic than Maryland's. Its free people of color made up the second largest free black population in 1790 — and became the largest free black population of any state by 1810. It remained the largest throughout the antebellum period.[30] As a result, Baltimore passed a city ordinance that "all free persons of color" were required to register with the mayor, who created a "Negro Entry Book."[31]

The post-Revolutionary generation of free blacks, men who as soldiers had fought hard for their rights, were forced to watch opportunities shrink. For example, artisans closed ranks and commenced discrimination on the basis of color. Some sons of free blacks, who a generation earlier would have been welcomed as apprentices, now encountered doors shut tight.[32] African Americans in Maryland felt under siege.

Where free blacks and slaves had easy access to one another, whites feared that fraternization would lead to resistance, or worse, to rebellion. Yet these relationships managed to flourish throughout the slaveholding states, particularly in the southern cities of the upper South during the fifty years following the American Revolution.

Intermarriages between slave and free were statistically significant in Maryland. In the wake of Nat Turner's rebellion in 1831 in Southampton County, Virginia, and in response to fears of slave insurrections, in 1832 the Maryland legislature proposed a statute to remove all free blacks from the state. The bill required manumitted slaves to renounce their freedom if they wished to stay behind with their families.[33]

Free blacks were faced with the prospect of choosing liberty in exile or a return to enslavement by remaining with their families. The legislation did not pass, as the fear of an exodus of valuable black labor from the state outweighed other concerns.

Any union between a slave and a free black was not a legal marriage but an informal arrangement. A slave's master could choose to honor or ignore the couple's commitment, rendering such unions inherently unstable. The sale of the slave spouse might throw the entire relationship into limbo. Thus slaves who chose a life partner, whether a free black or another slave, constantly confronted fears not only that their marriage might be shattered through sale, but that they might lose contact with their children as well.

Intermarriage between free and slave was not the general rule. But in Maryland, especially along the Eastern Shore, marriages between free blacks and slaves were increasingly common. Women outnumbered men within the free black community, and with this kind of gender imbalance, often a free woman of color would attach herself to a slave husband.

After the 1712 Maryland law providing that a child's status would follow that of its mother, a liaison with a free woman of color was the only way a slave father could insure freedom for his children. For this reason, it was an even more rare intermarriage when a free black man married a slave woman. By marrying Araminta Ross, John Tubman was consigning to slavery any children their union might produce.

Slaveholders often tried to coerce their human chattel into what they deemed were suitable liaisons, and often tried to break up couplings of which they disapproved. Along with slave sales, white matchmaking was one of the bitterest indignities slaves endured. Civil rights activist Ella Baker recalled family lore that when her light-skinned grandmother, a house slave, refused the partner her mistress had picked out for her, wanting instead to marry the man she loved, she was banished to work in the fields.[34]

Further, if a slave wife did not become pregnant within a year or two, a new husband might be chosen, or she might be replaced by another woman. Masters demanded that slave unions produce offspring to supply more workers. Disgruntlement might result in a spouse's banishment to another plantation or outright sale. Nothing was sacred.

The majority of slaves struggled against this tide of indifference to their desires. They engineered love matches and cemented unions with ceremonies. Marriages among slaves could be grand and festive. A mistress might donate castaway clothing to the slave bride for the ceremony, or the master might authorize a celebration meal. Weddings for slaves were generally held on slaves' only day off, Sunday. (Whites generally married any day of the week, but rarely on Sundays, as ministers were busy with regular duties.)

Even if a preacher presided over a slave wedding, most newlyweds on plantations performed a folk ritual called "jumping the broom," in lieu of or in addition to the exchange of vows. The bride and groom would each jump backwards over a broom handle held a few inches above the floor, and raised slightly with each leap. Whoever stumbled first was, according to lore, forced to heed the wishes of the other.

There are no surviving descriptions of Araminta and John's courtship, nor even any hints about how they first met. It is likely that the two became acquainted while she was working for John Stewart. John Tubman was perhaps working nearby, or perhaps even for Stewart as well. But how and when they met or any notion of what attracted them to each other remains a mystery.

Nor are there descriptions of their wedding, record of a date, nor any oral history about the event. Of course, the Tubmans' marriage would not be verified by any official county record. But local African American churches have no documentation either. What evidence remains from family lore indicates that Araminta was very deeply in love with John Tubman. Because she considered herself married to him for life, they most likely exchanged religious vows that included the pledge "until death us do part."

That John Tubman chose to marry a slave woman despite a surplus of free black women to choose from suggests that he too was deeply attached to his partner. Surely Araminta's qualities would have been on display by the time they met. Even if she was a slave, she was an enterprising and overachieving worker by all accounts. This and her personal magnetism may have led Tubman to disregard her status.

John Tubman remains an enigma. There is little or no information on his background or his trade. Dorchester County records list a Thomas Tubman as a black sawyer, but we have no idea if he was any relation to John.[35] Where Araminta and John lived once they were married, or if they were allowed to reside together, is also unknown.

In later years, Harriet Tubman confided that from 1847 until 1849 she resided on the property of Dr. Anthony Thompson, most likely on his

Caroline County estate near Poplar Neck. In the case of a slave–free black union, the couple was required to live with the slave's master, so doubtless both Araminta and her husband lived there. Slave women's marriages were not formally acknowledged by owners but indulged to keep the peace. Araminta remained very attached to her parents, as all evidence indicates. Perhaps she chose to remain near them, even in preference to going off to be with her husband.

Again, although there is no literary evidence confirming the date of Araminta's marriage, the couple were wed around 1844, when she was just nineteen. Shortly after her union with Tubman, perhaps prompted by her husband's free status and her father's 1840 emancipation, Araminta Ross Tubman paid a lawyer to investigate her own status by looking into her mother's background. Araminta knew that a slave mother determined a child's status, and she had suspicions that her mother might be legally free. For five dollars, the attorney examined the will of Tubman's mother's first master, Atthow Pattison. Pattison had owned her grandmother, and had given her mother, Rit, to a granddaughter by the terms of his will.

The attorney discovered that when Rit was bequeathed to Mary Pattison, it was with the provision that she would be Mary's slave until the age of forty-five. The will did not specify that she would be emancipated, but it certainly could be inferred from the language included. Rit would have turned forty-five after she and Ben were married and began having a family. The lawyer also advised Araminta that any of Rit's children would, by the terms of this will, no longer be slaves when they reached the age of forty-five. The codicil provided that any of Rit's children born after her forty-fifth birthday were freeborn.

But the provision was meaningful only if it was viewed as a promise of emancipation and subsequently honored. White family members neglected or conveniently misinterpreted this stipulation of Pattison's will. Instead, Rit and her children became part and parcel of Edward Brodess's inheritance and designated as the property of his only child. This broken promise was tragically brought home when Mary Pattison Brodess died in

1810 and Rit's emancipation and her children's freedom were lost in the slaveholders' shuffle.[36]

With the closing of the slave trade in 1808 and the increasing value of slaves, no doubt Mary Brodess's white heirs refused to face the consequences of losing property and income. Rit and her children were worth thousands of dollars, in addition to the valuable labor they provided any master. What was the likelihood that Rit knew the precise terms of her first owner's will? Even if she did, how could an illiterate slave woman secure evidence to obtain her freedom? How could she confront any of the chain of owners who had held her in bondage after her forty-fifth birthday? Whether it was mere indifference or intentional fraud, Araminta's mother and her progeny were cheated out of their freedom.

The lawyer's findings were devastating to Araminta Ross Tubman. She now believed, on the advice of a white authority, that her mother had been kept a slave for well over a decade past the point when she should have been legally emancipated. Even more damning, perhaps some of Araminta's siblings had been born free. It was the discovery of this betrayal that fueled her resolve to liberate herself.

Araminta's plans for liberty optimistically included her husband's support. Naturally she wanted to be free, and if it took journeying north to escape slavery, then that would be her path. It was not a journey she wanted to make alone. Removing to the North would be a dangerous and dramatic adventure.

In the years before learning the truth about her mother's legal status, Tubman had been visited by powerful visions, waking dreams that she felt were sending her messages. Ever since her skull injury, she suffered from episodes that were likened to narcoleptic spells. She would fall into a "stupor," which might come upon her "in the midst of conversation, or whatever she may be doing, and throwing her into a deep slumber, from which she will presently rouse herself, and go on with her conversation or work."[37] She might have several of these episodes a day.

Regardless of their source, the images that haunted Tubman were graphic and terrifying. While still in bondage in Maryland, she complained of a recurring nightmare of horsemen riding in to kidnap slaves — hearing the clatter of hooves and the shrieks of women having their children torn from them. Araminta herself did not yet have any children, but her marriage to John Tubman surely introduced fears for any child she might bear while still enslaved. Perhaps the fate of this child was too much for either Araminta or John Tubman to contemplate: any life they brought into the world could be snatched away by the slave power.

Even without the terrible fears slavery imposed, childbearing could be a very stressful and sensitive subject for any couple making a life together. The absence of a child, which was still the case five years into their marriage, might have introduced a wrinkle in the relationship.

Family was of utmost importance to Tubman, and yet if she failed to become pregnant, she must have been frustrated about the effect this had on her marriage. She had no concerns about fulfilling her reproductive responsibilities to her master, but what if she and John could not have children? Did her illness interfere with her reproductive capacity? Was she barren? Could there be something wrong with her husband?

Fears must have plagued Araminta, longing for a child, yet frightened of the consequences. And again, yearning for a child and dreading infertility. John Tubman, as later evidence would show, clearly wanted children. His wife's failure to become pregnant during their first years together must have been a stumbling block, and might have lessened his commitment to the marriage.

As the couple felt themselves pulled in different directions, Araminta described a palpable longing for a place — the promised land of the North.[38] While she was increasingly drawn to this vision, John Tubman may have become equally withdrawn — from her and from the marriage. He certainly did not share his wife's vision; perhaps as a free man, he did not feel the same urgency to relocate. Whenever rumor of sales swept through the slave cabins, she felt especially desperate, and turned to prayer for solace.

At one point in 1849 Araminta began a lengthy prayer vigil, pleading for the soul of her master, whom she believed was immoral and un-Christian. By this time she blamed him for holding her and other family members in bondage illegally. First she begged for Brodess's conversion to Christianity, so that he would see the error of his ways and perhaps repent. In 1849 she heard a rumor that he was planning to "sell her down the river," and might trade a couple of her brothers for cash as well. So she switched strategies: "[I] changed my prayer, and I said 'Lord, if you ain't never going to change that man's heart, *kill him,* Lord, and take him out of the way, so he won't do no more mischief.'"[39] She expressed guilt when, shortly thereafter, Brodess did die. She regretted her entreaties for her master's death and proclaimed that she would happily trade places with him. But this was really just a fog into which she disappeared before she faced her future with clarity and flinty determination.

At this juncture her faith and her fate become powerfully entwined. The year 1849 became a turning point. To best fulfill her destiny, Tubman realized, she must actively seek a role in God's plan, rather than letting others dictate her path. For Araminta, this was an important step forward, a significant leap of faith, especially faith in herself.

More than a decade before, another young woman in her twenties, Isabella Baumfree, born a Dutch-speaking slave in rural New York, resolved her spiritual crises by running away from her master and eventually changing her name to Sojourner Truth. She seized the opportunity for emancipation in 1826, and dedicated herself to securing and protecting freedom for her children. Challenges within her own life and the cultural chaos of her times convinced Truth to embark on a career of antislavery radicalism and feminist persuasion. Not unlike the former slave Isabella, Araminta knew by 1849 that she could no longer be a supplicant and trust in prayer for deliverance. She needed to combine faith with action. By escaping to the North, she felt, she would be doing God's will.

With her owner's death, Araminta faced a series of perplexing questions. What would become of her mother and siblings once they all became the inheritance of the Brodess children? Would her family be sold and scattered to the four corners of the South? Where would Araminta end up? Sold away from her family? Sold away from her husband? Tubman, in her early twenties, confronted the possibility of abandoning her parents, her husband, and the Eastern Shore — the only place she had ever called home. Araminta's sisters had disappeared with a slave coffle and she felt an intensifying need to leave before she too was swallowed up by the void.

Years later Tubman likened her decision to an epiphany: "I had reasoned this out in my mind; there was one of two things I had a right to, liberty or death; if I could not have one, I would have the other."[40]

## Chapter Three

# Crossing Over to Freedom

When through the deep waters I cause thee to go,
The rivers of sorrow shall not overflow.
—*Traditional Spiritual*

———————◄o►———————

TO PROTECT THEMSELVES fugitives who settled in the North assumed a new identity — and to assert themselves they took a new name. "Frederick Bailey" was the name Frederick Douglass was known by when he "crossed over." The fugitive kept his first name but adopted a new last name more than once during his first few weeks in the North, before settling on the surname Douglass. His new name was a badge of freedom, and the act of naming himself a powerfully liberating feat.

Once freed, Araminta decided to take a new first name: Harriet. This was the name of her mother and may also have been the name of one of her sisters who disappeared in the South. Perhaps as a sign of her continued devotion to her husband, she kept his last name. When Araminta escaped the hell of slavery for the "heaven" of liberty, she had "crossed the line of which she had so long been dreaming," and was reborn as Harriet.[1]

Her escape was remarkable. For one thing, the overwhelming majority of successful fugitives were men. But here was a girl in her twenties, venturing out of her home counties for the first time, hoping to make it to freedom on her own. That she made this treacherous and unknown journey shows the nerve and resourcefulness that would become her trademark.

That first time out in the open, Tubman must have dreaded the baying of bloodhounds signaling a posse in pursuit. Would she have known to rub asafetida (a foul-smelling herb) on her feet to elude tracking dogs? She knew to follow the North Star, but what if clouds filled the autumn night sky?[2] It must have been a terrifying experience for her, leaving behind loved ones and familiar terrain.

In her later years Tubman shared stories about her escape with Sarah Bradford, the reformer in Geneva, New York, who wrote an authorized biography in 1869. Bradford's account suggests that Tubman had wanted to run away for several years. But when she confronted the practicalities of an escape, with few resources and no guide, she was rightly hesitant. Also as a married woman, Tubman was reluctant to leave her husband behind. However, she felt being sold south was far worse than the open road and determined to head north in the fall of 1849.

The impending sale of Brodess slaves to cover debts may have catapulted Tubman along her road to freedom. Details vary in the accounts of her departure, but sometime during September 1849, Harriet took off. A notice in the October 3, 1849, *Cambridge Democrat* promised a reward for the recovery of "MINTY, aged about 27 years, is of a chestnut color, fine looking, and bout 5 feet high." Readers were told she had run away on September 17 and would fetch $50 if located in Maryland, $100 if found "out of the State." This notice, signed by "Eliza Ann Brodess," also sought "Harry" and "Ben," presumably Tubman's brothers.[3]

During the 1930s, when Jacob Lawrence was researching his magnificent series of paintings depicting the life of Harriet Tubman, the artist included a runaway notice as text for one of his thirty-one images.[4] The caption spoke of a "negro girl, Harriet, sometimes called Minty. Is dark chestnut color, rather stout build, but bright and handsome. Speaks rather deep and has a scar over the left temple." She had run away on September 24 and was being sought by a George Carter of Cambridge, Maryland, who was offering a $500 reward.[5] A search of all available Eastern Shore and Baltimore papers from the period has not yielded this notice, but then again, the Brodess notice only surfaced in 2003.

Whether Tubman left with her brothers or ventured out on her own, whether recapture would fetch $100 or $500, and regardless of who sought her return, she struck a blow by liberating herself. Tubman and Tubman alone fled Maryland and made her way through the treacherous byways of Delaware and into Pennsylvania.

Also in her favor, Tubman knew antislavery pockets dotted the countryside and perhaps she could take advantage. The Choptank Abolition Society had been founded in the 1790s and promoted antislavery in nearby Greensboro (Caroline County). The local marshes had been abundantly hospitable to runaways, if newspaper advertisements were to be believed. Many Quakers in the region, charitable toward antislavery, offered shelter and guidance to slaves on the run.

Tubman confirmed that a white woman assisted her on the first leg of her journey:

> Harriet had a bed quilt which she highly prized, a quilt she had
> pieced together. She gave this bed quilt to the white woman. . . .
> The white woman gave her a paper with two names upon it, and
> directions how she might get to the first house.[6]

This story offers considerable ambiguity. Was the white woman a sympathetic friend? In which case Tubman could have offered the prized quilt as a gift, knowing she couldn't take it with her. Or was the quilt a bribe in exchange for information?

The assistance Tubman was granted was punishable by law. The penalties were quite stiff. The story reveals that Harriet had skills besides her talents as a field-worker. Also, she had contacts with white women as well as blacks within the region. When she set her mind to something, she was resourceful and utilitarian.

Since Harriet Tubman was illiterate, the names supplied in writing by the white woman would mean something only to the person to whom she presented the slip of paper. It was intended to verify that the bearer was a genuine fugitive. The pass, delivered into the right hands, elicited further assistance along the route north. When she showed the paper to a woman at the house to which she had been directed, the woman brusquely instructed her to take a broom and sweep the yard. Perplexed at first, she decided this was meant to make her appear innocuous, just a servant, to arouse no suspicion in anyone riding by.

When the woman's husband, a farmer, came home in the evening, he loaded Tubman into his wagon. After dark, the man transported her to another town, where she was given her directions to a second "station." Arthur Leverton's farmhouse might have been the one in which Tubman first took refuge.[7] The Levertons were known abolitionist sympathizers who lived less than a day's walk from Anthony Thompson's Poplar Neck estate, where Tubman resided.[8] By the time of Harriet's escape, Jacob Leverton had already died of natural causes, while being prosecuted for aiding and abetting the flight of a young slave girl.[9] His son Arthur, who lived in an adjacent farmhouse, and Jacob's widow, Hannah, continued to serve the antislavery cause.[10] Whether the Levertons provided this initial assistance or not, Tubman was aided along the way by members of the Society of Friends.

Scholars debate how and when the web of assistance for fugitive slaves, conveying them from hiding place to hiding place along clandestine routes, began to emerge. By the 1840s, informal networks were well established, as was the reigning metaphor of the Underground Railroad (UGRR).

The system required a series of safeguards for fugitives bound for freedom, and catchphrases and secret rappings were abundant. The use of the call of a hoot owl was a popular sign in the west of Virginia.[11] The members of this secret network used code words and spoke of themselves as "agents" of the UGRR. Some were "stationmasters" at "stations" or "depots" (safe houses) where "conductors" (UGRR escorts) and their "cargo" (fugitives) might rest before resuming their journey on "the liberty lines" (paths where escorted fugitives were smuggled north). When they corresponded with one another, they might use other kinds of subterfuge, as when Delaware stationmaster Thomas Garrett wrote: "I sent you three bales of black wool" (three fugitives).[12]

Most likely Tubman took what had become the most common route for fugitives from the region: northeast along the Choptank River, which reaches far inland, cutting a swath across the verdant Delmarva peninsula (shared by western Delaware, eastern Maryland, and a small offshore slice of Virginia at the southernmost point). She later confided that she had observed that all the streams she knew ran north to south. So Tubman might have used the direction of flowing water as a guide during her first foray.[13]

There are several creative and credible scenarios attached to this historic journey. For Tubman, the particulars of her own escape were secret matters. Clandestine operations were safeguarded by her silence and the silence of other conspirators, and to this day remain obscure.

Fugitives kept on the move at night, then rested and hid during the day. If Harriet took refuge in the woods, they were a retreat that she knew well. She might have sought her daily rest near a hollowed-out tree, looking for a nest of brown bats, as they would gobble up the pesky mosquitoes that plagued her. She would try to fade into the landscape during sunlight, perhaps refreshing herself with provisions such as dried muskrat (called marsh rabbit by the locals). After dusk Harriet would resume her journey northward.

There is every reason to believe that by 1849 she would have been given both shelter and guidance by members of the UGRR, who maintained safe harbors for fugitives throughout Delmarva. Except for the wagon ride mentioned at the outset, her entire journey was most likely by foot until she was out of the peninsula.

Although Delaware was a free state, both Dover and Smyrna were hospitable to slavecatchers, private posses or professional bounty hunters hired by owners to recover their runaway property. These slavecatchers were a considerable threat to fugitives on the open road. Tubman might have heard rumors about the dangers these two towns presented fugitives and avoided highways leading into and out of them whenever possible. It was roughly eighty miles from Tubman's Maryland home to Wilmington, and a few more miles to the Pennsylvania state line. This nearly ninety-mile journey would have taken Tubman anywhere from ten days to three weeks on foot. Fugitive slaves escorted by UGRR conductors would travel approximately ten miles a night, but the particulars of Tubman's stealth and speed remain unknown.

Crossing the state line and leaving Delaware behind, Tubman might have stopped off at the estate of UGRR stationmasters Isaac and Rachel Mendinhall, who lived near Longwood, Pennsylvania. Their homestead featured imposing stone gates that framed the path to their mansion. These gates came to symbolize freedom for hundreds who passed through en route to Philadelphia, nearly thirty miles farther on.

For years before her escape, Harriet was visited by a recurring vision of a "flight" to freedom. In this dream, she was

> flying over fields and towns, and rivers and mountains, looking down upon them "like a bird," and reaching at last a great fence, or sometimes a river, over which she would try to fly. . . . It "'peared like I wouldn't have the strength, and just as I was sinkin' down, there would be ladies all drest in white over there, and they would put out their arms and pull me 'cross."[14]

Tubman left no account of who actually reached out during her escape to freedom. She luckily arrived in Philadelphia unharmed and had high hopes for her new status — a status which, unfortunately for most American slaves of Tubman's era, remained but a dream.

Since the earliest days of bondage, those captured and enslaved spent enormous reservoirs of energy trying to unchain themselves. The vast majority of slaves hoped in vain. They prayed for freedom but resorted to seeking salvation in the afterlife. This was an immutable refrain, as sixth-century Greek philosopher and poet Damascius wrote in an epitaph for a slave girl:

*Zosima, sometime a slave,*
*though a slave in her body only*
*Even for her body now*
*has won to freedom at last.*

This theme of being a slave "in body only" proved a constant refrain for Christianized African Americans. Those who embraced redemptive faith believed they would "ascend" up to heaven, while many others cherished the image of crossing a river, moving beyond Jordan to a better place. African American spirituals were filled with such sentiments:

*Dark and thorny is the pathway,*
*Where the pilgrim makes his way;*
*But beyond this vale of sorrow,*
*Lie the fields of endless days.*[15]

In this promised land, "slavery and prejudice, sin and sorrow in every form, are unfelt and unknown."[16]

The states north of the Mason-Dixon Line that had passed emancipation statutes were revered as a kind of Canaan — a place where blacks could work and worship, marry and raise children, freely pursuing life and liberties. Once they crossed over, fugitives would be unfettered by bondage. Most southern bondspeople had little or no contact with this free northern black world, but idealized what might await them once they fled.

From the very founding of the nation, slaveholders had to deal with the thorny issue of fugitive slaves. On May 12, 1786, George Washington complained about a slave of his who escaped to Philadelphia toward "a society of Quakers in the city formed for such purposes."[17] Not only were slaves fleeing, they also found accomplices to assist them in crossing to freedom.

The problem was so widespread that in 1793 Congress passed the first Fugitive Slave Act. This law provided substantial fines and prison time for those aiding or abetting slaves in flight. In keeping with the sanitized language of the Constitution, the text of the statute ironically included no explicit reference to slavery. Rather than use the term "slave," the Constitution makes reference to "three-fifths of all other persons," in a clause on proportional representation. With similar linguistic reluctance, the 1793 law read:

> No person held to service or labor in one state, under the laws thereof, escaping into another, shall, in consequence of any law or regulation therein, be discharged from such service or labor, but shall be delivered up on claim of the party to whom such service or labor may be due.[18]

Any slave found "abroad" (off the plantation) without a white escort required legal proof that he or she was not a runaway. For the rural slave, a pass was an absolute necessity to prevent detainment, whipping, or both. A pass was dated and signed by an owner, giving a slave explicit permission to do his bidding. This is partly why literacy was such a forbidden fruit in the antebellum South: if slaves learned to write, they might forge their own passes.

Southern local authorities often took matters into their own hands, raising "slave patrols" to prevent escape across county or state lines. These security forces were essentially private enterprise. Sheriffs might deputize a group upon occasion, but they were generally unofficial posses.

When slaves sneaked a visit with a spouse living abroad, or with a child sold away, or some other missing relative, patrollers (called paddyrollers by slaves) might sweep them into their net, trying to keep African American mobility in check. Upon occasion, the absentee slave was attempting to make a permanent break for freedom, but more often than not, he or she was simply taking time off to be with kin.

Whatever the excuse, the planter regime exerted an iron grip. Through the enforcement of capture and punishment, the white man enhanced his status at blacks' expense. Both whiteness and maleness became exalted through this strategy, a legacy that remains to this day.

Despite slaveholders' repressive rule, three major slave rebel conspiracies leapt into the national headlines during the first third of the nineteenth century. These widely publicized insurrections sent quakes throughout the slave South. Whether successful or foiled, plots to overthrow slavery, both by their example and by their impact, demonstrated slaveholders' vulnerabilities.

In Richmond, Virginia, in 1800 a conspiracy was thwarted by bad weather. The night of the planned uprising, rains caused creeks to overflow and made clandestine travel impossible. The dozens who had participated in secret meetings, led by a blacksmith named Gabriel, were unable to get to their caches of homemade weapons or to coordinate their attack on the city of Richmond and the surrounding countryside. Gabriel's role as a rebel leader was betrayed by a "loyal servant," who was rewarded with freedom, while Gabriel and other conspirators were executed.[19]

Within a few years of Tubman's birth, a former slave who had bought his freedom with lottery money became the focus of a controversy. In the bustling South Carolina seaport of Charleston, Denmark Vesey was part of a circle of free blacks who fraternized with slaves in local African American houses of worship. Vesey was accused of being at the center of a ring of conspirators bent on overthrowing slavery by violent means. Vesey's 1822 conspiracy remains a contested historical episode, with free and slave, black and white, all caught in the web of slaveholders' justice. Dozens of men were put on trial for their alleged role in an insurrectionary plot, which may or may not have been real. Whatever the details, the events had a wide impact in antebellum South Carolina and throughout the American South.[20]

The most famous uprising of the era was Nat Turner's revolt, which erupted spontaneously in the summer of 1831, in Southampton County, Virginia, less than a hundred miles from where the young Araminta was living. Turner's band of more than fifty slave followers decided to liberate themselves, killing nearly sixty whites in the process.[21] Turner himself escaped following the uprising and eluded his captors for weeks. Every plantation owner in the region was on alert, and slaves were well aware of the high stakes involved.

The hunt for Nat Turner, his capture, trial, and subsequent execution held the South hostage to sensational headlines and a potent rumor mill. Shortly after Turner's death, lawyer Thomas Gray published *The Confessions of Nat Turner* (1831), which only increased the local and national interest in this slave rebel and his motives.[22]

The slave grapevine and Virginia's proximity to the Eastern Shore meant Tubman's family was familiar with the Turner uprising, despite masters' efforts to suppress the news. Both black and white households within the upper South were aware of Turner's actions and the ripple effect the uprising created.

Southern whites demonized Nat Turner, portraying him as a bloodthirsty savage bent on raping white women and murdering children. At the same time, African Americans rejected this racist caricature and he became a heroic figure within black folklore.[23]

Slaves in the Chesapeake and Maryland were deeply affected by Turner's rebellion and its aftermath, more than any previous insurrection. Virginia held legislative debates to abolish slavery, while Maryland tried to expel free blacks from the state. Although neither law passed, it demonstrated how directly Turner's example influenced race relations in the Chesapeake.

Although Harriet Tubman was just a young girl when this slave rebel's reputation blistered across the southern countryside, there is every reason to believe he became a towering figure for her. Perhaps she saw him as a Joshua, a fierce warrior for his people, or even a benighted Moses, who tried to lead his people from slavery. Over the years, many within the black community took Turner at his word, and believed he was a latter-day prophet:

> I heard a loud voice in the heavens, and the Spirit instantly appeared to me and said . . . I should arise and prepare myself, and slay my enemies with their own weapons . . . for the time was fast approaching when the first should be last and the last should be first.[24]

Turner's passionate explanations bespoke his evangelical fervor. Following his execution, slaves turned him into a martyr.

The symbolism blacks attached to Turner's death allowed him to emerge as a messianic figure. When he was finally apprehended by authorities in the Virginia countryside, this rebel leader was dragged into the town of Jerusalem, where he was reviled by an angry mob. After his trial and conviction, so reminiscent of Jesus's treatment at the hands of the Romans, Turner was sentenced to die. He mounted the gallows and was hanged in the middle of a trio — strikingly emblematic for African Americans. Even more stirring to black imagination, the weather chimed in: "The sun was hidden behind angry clouds, the thunder rolled, the lightning flashed, and the most terrible storm visited that country ever known."[25]

Harriet would come to feel that freedom was something worth dying for, a creed by which Turner had lived and finally died.[26] His uprising to defeat the slave power may have failed, but he succeeded in stirring generation after generation to contemplate slavery's evils.

Rebels and fugitives were far less common than runaways at the turn of the nineteenth century. Slaves might run off temporarily to escape harsh routines, seizing autonomy by straying off the plantation, but the majority of those who left without permission returned within weeks, or even days, and most often voluntarily. An item in a Maryland newspaper demonstrated the kinds of negotiations these absences might produce: In 1794 slaveholder James Gunn advertised for the return of his twenty-four-year-old slave John Scott. He promised that if Scott "returns before my departure for Georgia I will give him his freedom at age 31."[27]

Absenteeism and running away were part of day-to-day resistance within the slave community. Such was the case of the hapless slave Tubman was trying to warn at the Bucktown store when she received her head injury. Harriet's mother, Rit, sent her son to the woods in protest when her master planned to sell him away to Georgia. It was a tactic that worked in this case, but it was a stratagem rather than a solution for those caught in slavery's thrall.

Harriet Tubman is doubtless the most famous fugitive slave in American history, yet we have no evidence that she was prone to running away. These two phenomena — being a runaway and being a fugitive — tend to be blurred in historical literature and are indistinguishable in the popular imagination. Only those who sought permanent escape, those willing to risk all for exile, were considered fugitives.

Tubman had ample opportunity to run off as an adolescent and young adult. From an early age, she was hired out, frequently at distances from her home. That she had not taken available opportunities until 1849 suggests that escape was not a step taken lightly.

If a slave was recaptured, some masters branded them as punishment. Branding held folkloric horror for whites, and provided detailed identification for runaway advertisements: "Adam, 36 years old has several marks of the switch on his back. He had been branded on the right cheek with the letter R for his former villainy."[28] One master in Columbus, Mississippi, burned his own initials into his slaves, to discourage them from trying to escape.[29]

If a slave made repeated attempts to flee, a master might cut the slave's Achilles tendon to hobble her and prevent her from escaping. Although whites inflicted most of these injuries, there were equally grim stories of self-mutilation. The following is excerpted from an antislavery pamphlet:

> One woman was told by a slave dealer who lived near her, that he had bought her; she said, "Have you bought my husband?" "No." "Have you bought my children?" "No." She said no more, but went into the court-yard, took an axe, and with her right hand chopped off her left. She then returned into the house as if nothing had happened, and told her purchaser she was ready to go; but a one-handed slave being of little value, she was left with her children.[30]

"Runaway ads" began appearing in colonial broadsheets and dominated the back pages of southern newspapers on through the Civil War. Of course, as most slaves were headed north, slaveholders used Yankee papers as well to try to locate absent slaves.[31]

For fugitives like Harriet who settled in the North, the dread of recapture remained acute and constant. This further circumscribed their ideal of freedom. Almost every black northern family was touched by these tragedies. One free black leader reported:

> Two of my father's nephews, who had escaped to New York, were taken back in the most summary manner, in 1828. I never saw a family thrown into such deep distress by the death of any two of its members, as were our family by the re-enslavement of these two young men.[32]

Sometimes slavecatchers would guess where a slave might go to church, then send a note to the pastor requesting that this member of his congregation, asking for the person by name, should pay a call to a "dear friend." At the designated place and appointed hour, slavecatchers would be lying in wait.[33] Even worse, on Sundays a gang might hover near departing worshippers at a black church, then seize a fugitive in broad daylight.[34]

Runaway ads, slavecatchers, and other devices for recapture plagued fugitives trying to blend into free black communities. Yet a steady stream of slaves continued their flow out of the South, crossing over to freedom despite the dangers. For even if they were constantly forced to look over their shoulders, they knew the land of Egypt would remain behind them, whatever might lie ahead.

# Chapter Four

# In a Free State

Philadelphia was the natural gateway between
the North and the South, and for a long time there passed
through it a stream of free Negroes and fugitive slaves
toward the North, and of recaptured Negroes and
kidnapped colored persons toward the South.

— *W.E.B. DuBois,* The Philadelphia Negro

F OR INCOMING FUGITIVES, black Philadelphia was an impressive community. The streets bustled with black vendors peddling matches and flowers, roasting oysters, chestnuts, and corn (boiled in husks). Steaming peppery pot was served right on the street — a dish of vegetables, meat, and cassava, imported by West Indians.[1] Black milliners and seamstresses, barbers and caterers abounded. Carters and haulers, longshoremen and sail makers also crowded the alleys near the water. The seaport filled with black sailors and mariners, a large and thriving subset within the colored population.

During the years leading up to Harriet's escape into the North, the triangulated region covering southeastern Pennsylvania, most of Delaware, and northeastern Maryland contained the largest concentration of free blacks in the nation. By 1850 more free blacks resided in these three states than the number of free blacks in all other states combined.[2] Wilmington, Baltimore, and especially Philadelphia supported large communities of people of color. Philadelphia maintained the largest, with a city and county population of 20,000 blacks by 1847.

Only a small portion of Philadelphia's blacks were native born; nearly one-third were from Delaware or Maryland.[3] For those who wished to journey north, Philadelphia was the first stop on the road to freedom during the antebellum era. In just one year, between June 1849 and June 1850, two hundred seventy-nine slaves fled Maryland (Harriet Tubman among them) — the highest number of fugitives to leave a slave state.

This migrant population was grateful for the gifts of freedom Philadelphia bestowed, and many gave back to the community. Some former fugitives specialized in helping those who came after, such as ex-slave James Walker, who operated an Underground Railroad depot on South Union Street.[4] There were sophisticated clandestine networks for funneling runaway slaves in and out of the city, often in creative ways. Fugitives might be transported in an "UGRR car," a box made of "light boards, to fit into a gardener's market wagon: the forepart formed a seat, and the back part was so high that a person could sit on the bottom, extending the feet forward under the driver's seat."[5] This modified vehicle would accommodate two hidden passengers. An enterprising black Philadelphia mortician was known to "fake" a funeral cortege, to hide one or more fugitives in a coffin, and then transport them far outside the city, as if traveling for burial at a distant cemetery.

Tubman and other fugitives who sought asylum in Philadelphia were elated to reach their destination. The Pennsylvania Society for the Promotion of the Abolition of Slavery, headquartered in Philadelphia, was one of the oldest and most ardent abolition societies. Benjamin Franklin was its first president, and from 1845 to 1850 black Philadelphian Robert Purvis headed the society. During the nation's first census, in 1790, Philadelphia's slave population had shrunk to a mere 300 (down from 6,000 in 1750), which by 1830 was reduced to less than a dozen. Yet also by 1830, one in twelve Philadelphians was black.

This port city became not only a beacon for fugitive slaves but also an important mecca for black reformers in nineteenth-century America. When Philadelphia hosted the first black national convention, in 1831, sixteen delegates gathered from five states. The city's growing black middle class welcomed sophisticated political activism. Free black leader James Forten wrote with some pride of his birthplace: "Pennsylvania has always been a refuge from slavery, and to this state the Southern black, when freed, has flown for safety."[6]

Tubman stood in awe of the liberties black Philadelphians enjoyed and promoted. As early as 1688, members of the Society of Friends had protested against the "traffick of men-body."[7] By 1776 Philadelphia Quakers expelled from meeting any members who continued to hold slaves. Black evangelicals may well have adopted forms of address — calling one another "brother" and "sister" — from this sect. The influence of Quakers, with an integrated vision of Zion and a commitment to radical abolitionism, shaped the city's cultural landscape.[8]

Mobility and economic opportunity were also striking to a young woman fresh from the Eastern Shore, where her movements were strictly controlled. During her first weeks in the city, Tubman might have kept to herself and lain low, fearing an encounter with someone from the Eastern Shore or, if her owner had put out the word, a slavecatcher seeking a woman of her description. But she would have quickly learned that the large black population guaranteed anonymity. The city was awash with fugitives such as herself, and the city's black network would have alerted her to the antislavery grapevines and helping hands available.

Shortly after her arrival Tubman found employment and became self-supporting, though little is known about what work she took on. She and other newcomers would have discovered the flourishing demand for black domestics, especially nursemaids, kitchen labor, and laundresses — many households required live-in help. In addition, most employers were willing to take on casual day labor, extremely helpful to those without references.

Harriet would have been overwhelmed by the contrast of her new home in Philadelphia with her former Maryland home. In Cambridge, the nearest town, grain brokers and visiting slave traders dominated the local economy. In the unpaved roads of Cambridge, slaveholders swaggered while custom and law hemmed in blacks, free and slave.

Philadelphia was more than twenty times larger, with a population in the city of 122,000 by 1850. Tubman might freely wander the sidewalks and find public gardens as well as private cultural institutions open to her. There were lectures and debates hosted by African Americans at the Rush Library and Debating Society, the Demosthean Institute, and, for women, at the Edgeworth Literary Society. Clarkson Hall, the headquarters of the Pennsylvania Antislavery Society, on Cherry Street, doubtless impressed her. There, blacks and whites mixed freely to promote the cause of abolitionism. It was a matter of great pride to blacks in Philadelphia that the Free African Society, founded in April 1787, still flourished.

Harriet arrived just as Philadelphia was expanding dramatically. During the 1850s, the city annexed adjoining suburbs to expand the city lines; by 1860 the city included over half a million people and claimed to be the fourth largest metropolis in the world — after London, Paris, and New York. This bustling seaport boasted flourishing marine industries, manufacturing, and mercantile interests, which tied the city to a global market. Blacks as well as whites played a role in augmenting the economy. By 1850 African Americans in Philadelphia owned real estate totaling over $530,000 and supported such institutions as the Library Company of Colored Persons.[9]

When faced with discrimination, the free black community persisted in building its own institutions: insurance societies, cemetery societies, building and loan societies, and separate branches of the Odd Fellows and Masons.[10] The establishment of an upwardly mobile black working class could be seen in the more than one hundred mutual benefit societies.[11] Nearly half of Philadelphia's black population were members of one of these organizations. Not long after Harriet arrived, two thousand black schoolchildren could be found enrolled in eight segregated public schools and more than twenty charity and private institutions.

The emergence of black churches and charities also fostered the perception of opportunity, especially to those newly arrived from slave states.

Religion was the principal institutional means for black self-improvement in the antebellum North. Philadelphia flourished as a center for black Christianity and supported a variety of independent black churches, including the Mother Bethel African Methodist Episcopal Church at Sixth and Lombard, established in 1794. For the first time in her life, Harriet was able to visit a house of worship founded by independent African Americans over half a century earlier.

The most powerful early black church in America, the African Methodist Episcopal had appointed Richard Allen its first bishop in 1816. By the late 1850s, Philadelphia supported nearly twenty African American churches — AME, Baptist, Methodist, and other prominent denominations. Within these sacred walls, black congregations were not only allowed to worship freely but to speak to the needs for expanding freedoms. Having an open forum to discuss black rights and freedom, to openly challenge slavery, even to plan assistance for runaways and fugitives — all this was revolutionary to Harriet Tubman, and may have partly accounted for the swiftness of her transformation from enslaved to free black woman.

While the opportunities and liberties her new home afforded may have initially exhilarated her, slavery's dark side quickly intruded. Free black communities were plagued by terrors reminiscent of the slavecatcher fears of Harriet's childhood. The Cannon gang had been replaced by a new generation of slave stealers, people who made a business of kidnapping free blacks to sell on the auction block.[12] Harriet, as a fugitive slave, was even more vulnerable.

Fear of kidnapping was a constant within free black communities in early America, especially for parents of free black children. The narratives of antebellum African Americans are replete with tales of stolen children.[13] Jermain Loguen's mother remembered being just a girl of seven in Ohio when she was dragged against her will into a wagon by a strange man. She recalled "several other little colored children in the wagon with her," all destined to be sold off as slaves in Kentucky.[14]

Hundreds of free black adults were annually deprived of liberty as well. The Virginia Abolition Society reported to the American Convention in 1800 that it was involved in lawsuits for more than one hundred individuals stolen away — and could not keep up with rising caseloads. The Protection Society of Maryland was founded in 1816 to prevent these kidnappings and within two years had rescued sixty free blacks from slave stealers. White abolitionist James G. Birney complained that such crimes were carried on "without the necessity of secrecy or concealment. Scores of unsuspecting colored persons, born free, are annually spirited away from the free States and sold into slavery."[15]

By the 1830s, too, the prominence and proliferation of African Americans in Philadelphia posed a growing psychological threat to white residents suffering from status anxiety during the antebellum era. "Self-improvement" within the black community was viewed by many as suspect. Thus demographic shifts stimulated an increase in race prejudice and mob violence, especially among working-class whites and European immigrants also pouring into the city.[16] The race riot became an irregular eruption within the urban landscape.

Philadelphia's reputation as a city plagued by racial strife emerged during the 1830s. One city father bemoaned: "Whoever shall write a history of Philadelphia from the Thirties to the era of the Fifties will record a popular period of turbulence and outrages so extensive as to now appear almost incredible."[17]

A pub fight in August 1834 turned into several days of looting and arson in the black neighborhood of Moyamensing (an old Indian term that rather unromantically translates into "pigeon excrement"). Gangs of white youth roamed the streets of Philadelphia — the Blood Tubs, the Rats, the Bouncers — fueling the flames. They described themselves as "hunting the nigs." The mayor had to swear in three hundred extra constables to try to take back the streets.[18] A year later, in a conscious nod to the Boston Tea Party, angry protestors seized hundreds of abolitionist pamphlets, ripped them to shreds, and dumped their remains into the Delaware River.

But Philadelphia's infamy leapt into the national spotlight with the burning of Pennsylvania Hall. On May 14, 1838, in a ceremony highlighted by John Greenleaf Whittier's dedication poem, Pennsylvania Hall officially opened to welcome the second Anti-Slavery Convention of American Women, where white and black delegates mingled. Overnight fifteen thousand protestors gathered outside the hall. As a matter of public safety, the mayor ordered the building closed on May 16. That night arsonists set Pennsylvania Hall afire. The mob cheered as the empty hall burned to the ground, and then rioters moved on to pillage the Mother Bethel AME Church and a colored orphanage.[19]

Blacks in Philadelphia became the target of angry whites who blamed crime and other urban ills on them. African Americans were thrown in jail on petty or trumped-up charges, locked up over "foul language" and bad conduct. When local justices of the peace were allowed to pocket the fines they imposed, arrests and convictions multiplied. Black abolitionist William Wells Brown complained that "colorphobia is more rampant here than in the pro-slavery, negro-hating city of New York."[20] And black leader Robert Purvis echoed: "Press, Church, Magistrates, Clergymen and Devils — are against us. The measure of our sufferings full."[21] Doubtless Harriet Tubman's awareness of the subtleties of race prejudice dawned slowly, after the initial rush of enthusiasm for her adopted home.

To counter white prejudice, Philadelphia abolitionists commissioned an impressive statistical study, *Present State and Condition of the Free People of Color of the City of Philadelphia* (1838). This survey showed that, contrary to unflattering stereotypes, blacks were increasingly upstanding citizens. African Americans contributed to the city's economy: to the market, to the service sector, to booming consumerism. The documentary evidence proved too little too late. That year the legislature in Harrisburg drew up a new state constitution, which included prohibition of black male suffrage. Whites charged "the whole of the free colored people unworthy of any favor," and claimed they were "nuisances in the community fit only to fill alms houses and jails."[22] This prejudice carried over and prevailed, as racist rants in the popular press became all too common.

Who, in fine, is the most *protected,* the most *insolent,* the most *assuming,* the most *depraved,* the most *dangerous* of our population? We answer the *Negro*; THE NEGRO; THE NEGRO! — the Thick-Lipped, Wooley-Headed, Skunk-Smelling, combination of the MONKEY AND THE DEVIL.[23]

By the time Harriet arrived in the city, racial vitriol had taken its toll. The overwhelming majority of Philadelphia's African Americans were crowded into poor neighborhoods, with the black per capita value of personal property decreasing 10 percent in the 1840s.[24] Less than half of one percent of the adult black males in the city were able to find factory jobs. Skilled black labor, which had prospered in Philadelphia the generation after the Revolution, faltered. White artisans and journeymen refused black apprentices in favor of newly arrived Europeans.[25]

The rising number of fugitives fleeing from the slave states encouraged southern congressmen to demand federal protection. Slaveholders complained that the inroads of the Underground Railroad meant a loss of slave property valued in the neighborhood of $200,000 per year by the late 1840s. Finally, less than a year after she arrived to start a new life in Philadelphia, Harriet was confronted by a piece of legislation that seriously jeopardized her own future and that of thousands of other slaves who had liberated themselves and settled in the North. More than race prejudice, this law would seriously redefine what it meant to be free. On September 18, 1850, Congress approved the Fugitive Slave Law as part of the Compromise of 1850, an omnibus bill designed to settle differences between North and South over the issue of slavery. Blacks and abolitionists nicknamed it the Bloodhound Law.

The incendiary issue of fugitive slaves had been debated within the national political arena for more than half a century. The 1793 Fugitive Slave Law had not been particularly effective. Several northern legislatures even passed statutes against kidnapping, aimed at preventing slavecatchers from seeking slaves within their states.

In 1826 Pennsylvania legislators passed a law that provided for harsh penalties for slavecatchers, defined as anyone "who should take or carry away from the State any negro with the intention of selling him as a slave, or of detaining or causing to be detained such negro as a slave for life."[26] This was overturned in a landmark decision, *Prigg v. Pennsylvania* (1842), when the U.S. Supreme Court ruled that Pennsylvania's law was unconstitutional because "the owner of a slave is clothed with entire authority in every State in the Union, to seize and recapture his slave, whenever he can do it without any breach of the peace, or any illegal violence."[27]

In 1842 George Latimer, a fugitive from Norfolk, was arrested in Boston and threatened with return to Virginia. Bostonians demanded that the city jailer be fired when they discovered he was the slaveholder's agent. Abolitionists prevented Latimer's return to slavery until his owner agreed to sell him; once the $400 price was paid, Latimer was a free man again.

After all the publicity generated by the *Prigg v. Pennsylvania* decision and the Latimer case, northern legislators decided to tackle the issue with another strategy. Massachusetts prohibited state officials from aiding in the arrest or detention of fugitive slaves, and further declared state jails could not be used for fugitives' confinement. This was nicknamed the Latimer Law.[28] In 1843 Vermont and Ohio adopted similar legislation, followed by Connecticut in 1844, Pennsylvania in 1847, and Rhode Island in 1848. These acts became known as "personal liberty laws."

After the Fugitive Slave Law of 1850 these laws were effectively voided. Local federal commissioners were given sweeping authority in fugitive slave cases. They could deputize, preside over summary hearings, remand captives back south from the furthest reaches of northern cities — and most galling of all, render a verdict without trial by jury. Any resistance to enforcement would result in exorbitant fines. This law may have protected slaveholders' rights to property but, critics howled, it was unconstitutional.

Commissioners in the North were given financial inducements to get into the slavecatching business. If a black was caught in a dragnet and evidence indicated he or she was indeed an escaped slave, the detaining authorities were paid a fee of ten dollars. If the kidnapper was wrong, the fee was halved. But promising five dollars for even a mistaken identity made it open season on northern blacks. Many northern whites, previously on the fence, despised the prospect of upholding slaveowning in the flesh rather than endorsing it in the abstract. They resented being dragooned into defending the rights of slaveholders in their own backyards.

In Syracuse on October 4, 1850, a vocal band of citizens argued the new law was "utterly null and void." An October 5 meeting at the African Meeting House in Boston called for the establishment of a "League of Freedom . . . to rescue and protect the slave, at every hazard."[29] On October 21, Chicago's city council passed resolutions to nullify the law within city limits.[30] Underground Railroad activist Thomas Garrett buoyantly predicted to Boston abolitionist leader William Lloyd Garrison, "I very much doubt, whether on the whole there will be more arrested under the new Law."[31] But this was wishful thinking on his part.

In New York City, only ten days after the law was enacted, James Hamlet became one of the first African Americans seized under new federal guidelines. On September 28, 1850, local authorities plucked him out of a community of 10,000 Manhattan blacks. Alarm spread quickly throughout the city: thirty fugitives decamped to Boston by week's end, and more than one hundred relocated to Massachusetts by November 1. But the Bloodhound Law also threatened blacks in Massachusetts. The *Boston Daily Evening Traveller* reported "quite a number of families, where either the father or mother are fugitives, have been broken up, and the furniture sold off, with a view of leaving for safer quarters in Nova Scotia or Canada."[32] By October 1850 over three hundred African Americans within the relatively small black community of Pittsburgh decided to migrate to Canada.[33] The prospect of the new Fugitive Slave Law's enforcement propelled as many as 3,000 ex-slaves out of their northern homes and into Canada within ninety days.[34]

Those who elected to remain in the North decided to take precautions. The *Rochester Advertiser* reported, "Negroes were pricing and buying fire arms . . . with the avowed intention of using them against the ministers of the law, and our orderly citizens, should they be called upon to aid in executing the fugitive law in our city."[35] In Chicago's small black community, where a little over 500 resided, African American guards patrolled the streets, to provide some warning for residents should slavecatchers arrive.

Frederick Douglass, a former fugitive who eventually bought his own freedom, became the black spokesperson who led the charge against this law. He ticked off a list of seven other African American leaders who had faltered in the face of this calamity:

> We have lost some of our strong men — Ward has been driven into exile; Loguen has been hunted from our shores, Brown, Garnet and Crummell, men who were our pride and hope, we have heard signified their unwillingness to return again to their National field of labor in this country. Bibb has chosen Canada . . . and the eloquent Remond is . . . silent.[36]

Douglass became part of a growing cadre of male ex-slaves drafted by the abolitionist establishment to publicly "testify" to the horrors of slavery. These first-person accounts were intended to stir up sympathy and to stimulate donations. In 1845 Douglass published his *Narrative of the Life of Frederick Douglass, an American Slave.* After a tour in England and the purchase of his freedom, he moved to Rochester, New York, in 1847. Douglass broke with his former patron, William Lloyd Garrison, and gave voice to his independent abolitionist views with his own newspaper, the *North Star.*

On the matter of the Bloodhound Law, as well as all other matters affecting race relations, Douglass had strong views. His outspoken role in this national debate catapulted him into greater prominence. He argued, "The only way to make the Fugitive Slave Law a dead letter [is] to make a half dozen or more dead kidnappers."[37] William Lloyd Garrison concurred: "Every fugitive slave is justified in arming himself for protection and defense — in taking the life of every marshal, commissioner, or other person who attempts to reduce him to bondage."[38] An abolitionist editorial declared, "The state motto of Virginia, 'Death to Tyrants,' is as well the black man's as the white man's motto."[39]

By March 1851 more than sixty attempts to recapture fugitives were recorded, with over one hundred African Americans involved in these roundups.[40] In the autumn of 1851, two spectacular cases burst into the headlines. The first, in rural Pennsylvania, showed ordinary people taking a stand to protect slaves from recapture, and fugitives themselves willing to risk death rather than return to slavery. The second, in Syracuse, featured organized and armed resistance to defy the law. Both were ominous to slaveholders, as well as to federal authorities. Both demonstrated the iron resolve of abolitionists, black and white, to resist injustice and appeal to a higher law.

In the first case, two slaves ran away from their master in Maryland. On September 11, 1851, the runaways' owner, Edward Gorsuch, led a posse to the home of William T. Parker, a local black farmer in Christiana, Pennsylvania, where the fugitives were allegedly hiding. When the marshal and Gorsuch's posse approached Parker's home, bugles blared — as horns regularly warned that slavecatchers were in the neighborhood.

Gorsuch's slaves were at Parker's but refused to come forward, even after the marshal read out his warrant. A white Quaker neighbor named Castner Hanaway appeared on the scene, as a growing crowd responded to the alarm. Hanaway was asked to intercede but refused. Shortly thereafter shots were fired. In the ensuing melee, Gorsuch was killed — as were three blacks who participated in the standoff — but the fugitives escaped unharmed. A grand jury in Philadelphia indicted forty-five of the Christiana resistors, charging them with treason. But when the test case against Castner Hanaway failed to result in conviction, charges against all others were dropped. For radicals, this case ushered in a new era of resistance.

With this incident fresh in mind, national delegates from the Liberty Party, the breakaway coalition of Whig and Democratic politicians dedicated to promoting "Free Soil and Free Labor," gathered for a convention in Syracuse the last week of September 1851. The Fugitive Slave Law was on the agenda. But just as the meeting opened, local federal marshals took a fugitive slave, William "Jerry" Henry, into custody. If the timing was an accident, it was a very fortuitous accident, both for the fugitive slave and for opponents of the 1850 law.

Jerry Henry (as he was known in Syracuse) was far from an ideal candidate for rescue.[41] He was a cooper at a local carpentry shop who had worked in Syracuse for two years since his 1849 escape from his Missouri master. But he was also a convicted felon who had tangled with the law and racked up four arrests.[42] Frequent police contact may have led to his recapture, as often the local constable, Russell Lowell, wrote to owners and told them where to claim their former slaves.[43]

As Jerry Henry was taken into custody on October 1, church bells rang throughout the city to signal members of the local vigilance committee. When the crowd arrived at the commissioner's office, Henry was being held in handcuffs. In the middle of the hearing, a group of black and white men attempted to free Henry. He was hustled out onto the street, where the sympathetic throng parted to let the ex-slave flee but blocked the lawmen in pursuit. However, he was finally apprehended and placed in leg irons as well as handcuffs.

Under heavy guard, Jerry's hearing resumed at the police station, but it adjourned when a menacing crowd surrounded the building. By evening local abolitionists were in high gear. Gerrit Smith, who would later become a friend and patron of Tubman's, advocated: "A forcible rescue will demonstrate the strength of public opinion. . . . It will honor Syracuse and be a powerful example everywhere."[44]

A rescue party, armed with clubs, axes, and a battering ram, consisted overwhelmingly of black faces — largely because most white participants decided to use burnt cork as disguise. When the mob rushed the building, shots were fired. But the attackers refused to back down. They shattered the prison's wooden door, and Jerry's guards fled. The rescued fugitive was bundled into a carriage and given safe passage to Canada.

Falling on the heels of the disaster at Christiana, this setback made federal authorities howl. Eventually twenty-six men were indicted for their roles in the riot. But when these cases finally went to trial, one man was convicted, another was acquitted — and then, mirroring the outcome at Christiana, the charges against the others were dropped. As one of the participants crowed:

The fugitive, Jerry, is safe in Canada. His honor the President, Millard Fillmore, has received a nice box, by express, containing Jerry's shackles. . . . Judge Lawrence, who was so officious in kidnapping Jerry . . . has been presented by the *ladies of Syracuse,* with 30 pieces of silver, — (3 cent pieces) — the price of betraying innocent blood.[45]

Tubman would have been particularly impressed both by the strength this coalition of free blacks and fugitive slaves manifested and by the assistance white Quakers offered. The failure of the prosecution to obtain a conviction in Pennsylvania would also have raised Tubman's expectations about her new home state. The resistance at Christiana and the legal outcome signaled growing resolve on the part of blacks and whites together to resist the slave power, and the publicity given to the "Jerry Rescue" in Syracuse signaled bolder resistance to come.

Yet despite these isolated cases of defiance, the Bloodhound Law also unleashed waves of fear within the African American community. Free blacks and fugitives alike dreaded the consequences of slavecatchers given federal empowerment and the "arrest first, ask questions later" attitude of white authorities.

An abolitionist periodical in Delaware (colorfully named the *Blue Hen's Chicken*) reported an incident that highlighted black terror. A trio of free blacks traveling with a child were on a southbound train, planning to get off in Newark, Delaware. When they discovered that they had missed their stop and were headed to Maryland, a slave state, they panicked:

> The young woman was so frightened that sooner than run the risk of going to Maryland, she jumped from the platform; and next followed the man with his child and were safe. His wife's turn came next; but observing her great danger, we seized her by the arm and prevented her, assuring her that we would get her a pass to return when we arrived at Elkton. She implored us to let her go, that she would be arrested and sold into slavery. She fell on her knees and wrung her hands — a more painful or affecting sight we never beheld.[46]

Although the black woman made it back safely to Delaware, all who witnessed her abject terror were moved.

In the wake of the Fugitive Slave Act, so soon after her arrival in Philadelphia, Harriet Tubman saw this climate of fear mushroom. She had just begun to enjoy the fruits of freedom when the realities of a country divided over slavery became clear. Tubman's growing realization that all people of color — slave, fugitive, or free, in both North and South — were imperiled by the very existence of racial bondage made 1850 a critical turning point in her life, as her own personal journey to freedom expanded to include the aspirations of all slaves.

Despite the concrete daily benefits of her new environment, within a year of her arrival Tubman experienced an increasing sense of deprivation. She suffered the constant ache of loneliness during her time in the North. The line she had once celebrated crossing had become a daunting divide, even as the real border of freedom had moved north to Canada. Harriet would never have traded her new status for her old, but she keenly mourned the separation from her family.

Harriet Tubman left little of her emotions or personal details in recorded accounts. Yet she once told the poignant story of a man sent to prison for twenty-five years, a man who spent his time inside his cell dreaming of home. But upon his release,

> he leaves the prison gates, he makes his way to his old home, but his old home is not there. The house in which he had dwelt in his childhood had been torn down, and a new one had been put up in its place; his family were gone, their very name was forgotten, there was no one to take him by the hand to welcome him back to life.[47]

About her exile from Maryland, Harriet added: "So it was with me."

## Chapter Five

# The Liberty Lines

Thou shalt not deliver unto his master the servant
which is escaped from his master unto thee.
—*Deuteronomy 23:15*

————◄○►————

IN THE YEAR 1831, the legend goes, a Kentucky slave named
Tice Davids escaped his home and headed for freedom in Ohio. During
his flight, Davids was being tracked by his master. When he reached the
Ohio River, with his master close on his heels, the slave jumped in and
swam across. His master, trying to keep his slave in sight, was delayed by
seeking a boat. He found one and began to row across, but he watched as
Tice Davids scrambled up on shore and vanished. When the master abandoned his search in a nearby town, he told someone that the slave had disappeared so quickly that he "must have gone on an underground road."
Allegedly this was the origin of the nickname Underground Railroad.[1]

In 1839 a Washington newspaper reported that a young black boy
named Jim had been arrested while lurking near the Capitol and "would
disclose nothing until he was subjected to torture by screwing his fingers in
a blacksmithing vice." After a prolonged bout of torture, the frightened

young man revealed that he was supposed to go north on a railroad and "the railroad went underground all the way to Boston." This was perhaps the first time that a fugitive network was identified in print both as a "railroad" and as underground.[2] Within years, such references would become commonplace.

Scholars may dispute the role and scope of the UGRR, yet debates over who risked what, when, and how remain an intriguing set of historical questions. First, because of the clandestine nature of the UGRR movement, determining its true scope and extent is hard. There is a dearth of traditional evidence. As a descendant of a Pennsylvania UGRR agent argued: "Men and women who did their work in daily peril of their fortunes and perhaps their lives, of course, kept no regular records."[3]

Some scholars want to see this fugitive movement as a feud between black rebels and white racists, a battle waged before the war. Others believe the Underground Railroad reflected vanguard elements of a cooperative interracial movement, akin to the civil rights struggle in the mid-twentieth century. African Americans boldly pioneered, but eventually blacks and whites attacked racial injustice side by side.

Of course, in these racial passion plays, though the "good guys" might have been either black or white, the villains were nearly always white. It was tricky for the majority of blacks during the antebellum era to separate friend from foe. As one African American confided: "They [whites] was all . . . devils and good people walking in the road at the same time, and nobody could tell one from t'other."[4]

Daniel Gibbons, a white abolitionist whose house near Bird-in-Hand, Pennsylvania, frequently sheltered fugitives, was seventy-five when the Fugitive Slave Law was passed in 1850. Gibbons first became active in helping runaways to freedom in 1824. By 1850 Gibbons had assisted more than a thousand slaves, recording carefully both the fugitive slave's name and his or her new identity in a journal. But with the Bloodhound Law, Gibbons destroyed forty pages of lists. These records were not just self-incriminating, but would have revealed the identities of hundreds of fugitives "living underground" as free blacks in the North.[5]

Thomas Garrett was another legendary UGRR stationmaster. Living in Wilmington, Delaware, he doubtless helped Harriet when she escaped Maryland and became her introduction to the machinery of the liberty lines, as the routes north on the UGRR were called. Garrett too began his rescue work before Tubman was born.

One day in 1803 a young free black woman was kidnapped from the rural Pennsylvania Quaker household in which she worked. This girl was wrenched away by two kidnappers who found her easy prey. She was the household servant of a middle-class white family headed by Thomas Garrett Sr., of Upper Darby, Pennsylvania, who supported his eleven children with his mill and toolmaking operations. When twenty-four-year-old Thomas Garrett Jr. returned home to find his mother and sisters weeping over the servant girl's fate, he set out to recover her. He found the stolen servant in the kitchen of a tavern in nearby Kensington, and brought her back without violence.

This was the first of many rescues Garrett would assist. Like many involved in vigilance, he moved from protecting free blacks from kidnappers to helping fugitives on the run to freedom. Again and again Garrett insisted that he never coerced slaves into running off.[6] Yet he believed it was his duty to help any fugitives sent his way.

Garrett joined the Pennsylvania Society for the Promotion of the Abolition of Slavery in 1818. In 1822 he moved with his wife and three young children to Wilmington, Delaware, a thriving crossroads. On Shipley Street he established a blacksmith shop and a hardware store and ran a cobbling operation. By day his Wilmington businesses thrived, while slave smuggling absorbed his energies at night.

Garrett became the linchpin of a core group of Delaware abolitionists, primarily Quakers, who assisted fugitive slaves northward. Rescues from the Eastern Shore were promoted by this extensive Wilmington network. Not only Garrett, but also Isaac Flint, John Hunn, Joseph Walker, and a trio of brothers, Benjamin, Thomas, and William Webb, were committed to this new enterprise. They sent most of their "cargo" (as slaves were called) north to Philadelphia.

When a local slaveholder vowed to shoot him on sight, Garrett made a point of going to visit the man and exclaimed: "How does thee do, friend? Here I am, thee can shoot me if thee likes." Once a gang of white southerners beat Garrett up and threw him off a train he had boarded to rescue a black woman. Garrett dismissed his injuries, commenting he was only "slightly bruised by the railing of the cars, but well in a few days."[7] In 1848 he was tried for aiding and abetting slaves and fined $5,000, a sum that wiped him out financially. Despite such setbacks, his devotion to the cause did not waver.[8]

Beginning in the mid-1840s, Garrett kept meticulous count of the slaves who passed through his capable hands in Wilmington, Delaware. By the time of the Civil War, this Quaker merchant had lists of more than 2,500 fugitives to whom he had rendered assistance. Clearly Daniel Gibbons and Thomas Garrett were two of many stationmasters who aided the passage of hundreds and even thousands to safety. This pair was unusual only in that each had at one time kept careful records.

Robert Purvis, an African American leader of the Philadelphia UGRR, also kept a logbook of slaves passing through his headquarters, until his family persuaded him to destroy the records after passage of the Fugitive Slave Law.[9] Blacks working for the UGRR were much more vulnerable than whites in the slavery wars, and took greater risk in keeping and hiding secret records.[10] Even if blacks contributed more significantly to the UGRR, a lack of documentation is not surprising, even understandable.

One black UGRR participant did keep count. Frederick Douglass made his Rochester home available to fugitives on the run. Nearly four hundred Canada-bound slaves found temporary refuge with Douglass during the decade leading up to the Civil War. The Reverend Jermain Loguen, another former fugitive who became an important spokesperson for his black community, played a similar role in his hometown of Syracuse, sheltering more than 1,500 slaves in his home or at his church.

Democratic and radical impulses defined the Revolutionary generation that founded America. The egalitarian ideals of abolitionist activists, especially UGRR agents, were perceived as a tribute to the country's founding generation.[11] Promoters of the liberty lines echoed the sentiments of American's founders: impassioned opposition to tyranny and oppression. A participant characterized his involvement in the UGRR on the dedication page of his memoir:

> To the millions of happy grand-children of a generation fast leaving the stage of action, and who must get their knowledge of the Rebellion [the Civil War] and its causes from the lips of those who saw and participated or from the pages of history, as we, the grand-parents, got ours of the Revolution from those long since passed away, and from the written records of that thrilling period, this little volume of unique but wonderful history is sincerely and most affectionately dedicated by one of the Grandfathers.[12]

Blacks embraced these patriotic themes. James Pennington, a fugitive slave who became a minister, argued in 1831 that "our fathers were among the first that peopled this country. Their sweat and their tears have been the means in a measure of raising our country to its present standing. Many of them fought and bled and died for the gaining of her liberties."[13] Pennington and other firebrand black abolitionists demanded that they become part of the *pluribus* of *E pluribus unum* (Out of many, one), the motto on the Great Seal of the United States. They desired America to become in reality a "land of the free." To that end, radicals advocated civil disobedience, especially in regard to fugitive slaves. Thus the UGRR was a full-fledged grassroots resistance movement, representing the true national goals of democracy and liberty.

It is hard to date the birth of this movement, but fugitives themselves made telling observations. William Wells Brown, an ex-slave who fled from St. Louis in 1834, suggested that when he made his escape "there was no Underground Railroad." African Americans believed that before the 1840s "the North Star was, in many instances, the only friend that the weary and footsore fugitive found."[14]

When southern bounty hunters began aggressive campaigns in the

North, seizing free blacks as well as fugitive slaves, ordinary citizens — not just Quaker radicals or Methodist zealots — joined in to protest kidnappings. They created vigilance committees to prevent these startling and random abductions. In November 1835 one hundred citizens formed the Vigilance Committee of New York City. In 1838 an equally dynamic group, spearheaded by its black officers, Robert Purvis and Jacob White, organized in Philadelphia. These groups pledged to protect free blacks from slavery's net, in the streets and in the courts.

They soon shifted focus, and vigilance committees became not just shields against proslavery kidnappers but groups willing to offer assistance to fugitives in transit. As time went by, these groups broadened again — to support and even enlist the flight of slaves to freedom — and evolved into the backbone of a loosely organized UGRR.

The UGRR became a vast tangle of interconnected networks dedicated to rescuing African Americans from slavery and shepherding them to freedom. Naturally there was no national organization, election of officers, or advertisement of activities. The group carried out dangerous and clandestine operations, using code words to protect their identities.

Eventually UGRR stationmasters, conductors, and elaborate transportation schemes for "cargo" supplemented the North Star during the years leading up to the Civil War. An intrepid volunteer army of underground agents blossomed. Their commitment to deliver slaves from bondage proved a remarkable crusade. Very few took a public stand, especially because of the clandestine nature of their work. Some emerged as heroes by fighting battles in the courts, but most carried on their activities anonymously and undetected. Agents of the UGRR not only strengthened the antislavery movement, but the radical threat they posed hastened the coming of the Civil War.

The vast majority of these UGRR agents never visited the South. Indeed, most conductors conveyed slaves from one specific depot only to the next depot on a liberty line, not all the way to freedom. The very few who ventured into the South to extract slaves were often called "abductors" by their contemporaries; this was to distinguish them from the vast majority of conductors, who guided fugitives on very limited segments of their journey. Abductors were a highly skilled and rare breed of UGRR conductor.[15]

Only a handful gained any notoriety before Harriet Tubman came onto the UGRR scene, all of them white men.[16] Their activities became known because they were caught abducting in flagrante, which in all but one case curtailed their UGRR careers.

In 1844 a Massachusetts sea captain, Jonathan Walker, was detained offshore in Florida with a boatload of fugitives. Walker was caught in the act of assisting runaway slaves as he used the open seas as an escape route. Convicted by a Pensacola jury, Walker was first locked into a pillory, where he was pelted with rotten eggs. Then he was given excessive fines and forced to serve nearly a year in jail — until antislavery friends could raise enough cash to secure his release. But the punishment for which he became infamous was what was branded on his right hand by a U.S. marshal: the mark "S.S." — for Slave Stealer, a term white southerners used as an epithet to identify those who assisted fugitives. John Greenleaf Whittier composed a poem in tribute to Walker's heroic scarification, which ended with the verse

> *Then lift that manly right hand, bold*
> *plowman of the wave*
> *Its branded palm shall prophesy*
> *"Salvation to the Slave."*[17]

The three other most prominent abductor-conductors of the era were also white: John Fairfield, Charles Torrey, and Calvin Fairbank.

John Fairfield was the most unusual of the three. The son of a slaveholder, he renounced his birthright to spend his time and energy liberating slaves, assisting them to Canada. He operated very independently, mainly moving through Cincinnati on his trips north. His activities were well known to the famed Indiana UGRR leader Levi Coffin, although Coffin disapproved of Fairfield's daredevil techniques.

Fairfield was arrested several times during his UGRR activities, and twice broke out of jail. He "was always ready to take money for his services from the slaves if they had it to offer, but if they did not, he helped them all the same."[18] As his reputation grew, blacks in Canada would proffer their savings and beg him to undertake a specific rescue on their behalf — something that proved increasingly dangerous, but a vocation at which he excelled.

Charles Torrey, a Yale-educated Congregational minister, resigned his post at a church in Providence in 1838 to become committed full-time to abolitionism. He became an antislavery editor in Albany but eventually shifted his operations to the Washington, D.C., area, where he actively pursued the rescue of slaves. He was caught transporting a slave family out of Virginia in 1843 and sentenced to six years hard labor in a Maryland penitentiary. He wrote to an abolitionist friend: "If I am a guilty man, I am a very guilty one; for I have aided nearly four hundred slaves to escape to freedom, the greater part of whom would probably, but for my exertions have died in prison."[19] Torrey himself died after only two years in jail and became a martyr to the cause.[20]

Equally infamous, the Reverend Calvin Fairbank learned to hate slavery while a student at Oberlin College in Ohio. By 1837 he began making trips into Kentucky to transport slaves to freedom, helping them cross the Ohio River. He enlisted an assistant, Delia Webster, a white schoolteacher from Vermont. In 1844 the two were arrested for helping a woman and child escape. Webster went free but Fairbank was sentenced to fifteen years in jail for his role in "slave stealing." He was pardoned in 1849 but arrested again for UGRR activities, and sent to prison again, serving twelve of his fifteen years. Fairbank confided that he was whipped repeatedly during his prison terms.[21] He too became a symbol of resistance and sacrifice to the UGRR faithful.

Over his years with the UGRR, Fairbank had smuggled nearly fifty slaves to freedom, beginning with a fifteen-year-old girl who was adopted into the family of the esteemed UGRR leader Levi Coffin. Fairbank spirited the girl away from her eighty-year-old master in Montgomery County,

Kentucky. "[She] was the fifth in direct descent from her master," he later wrote, "being the great-great-great granddaughter of a slave whom he took as his mistress at the age of fourteen. . . . And now he was expecting to make this girl his mistress."[22] This kind of sensational revelation became standard abolitionist fare.[23]

While all these men gained notoriety with their abductions during the 1830s and 1840s, their careers could not match the fame that Tubman accrued with her string of rescues during the 1850s, especially because she was operating after the passage of the Fugitive Slave Law. Not only was she one of the most intrepid abductors, her status as a fugitive guaranteed her more acclaim than any of her rivals.[24] Also the fact that she was never caught enhanced her reputation.

Levi Coffin became the most famous stationmaster within the UGRR. He had learned the ropes of assisting fugitives as a young man by working with his cousins Vestal and Addison Coffin, who operated out of North Carolina. He explained: "These outlying slaves knew where I lived, and, when reduced to extremity of want or danger, often came to my room, in the silence and darkness of the night, to obtain food or assistance."[25]

By 1826 Levi and his wife, Catherine, moved to Indiana, settling near the town of Newport. The Coffins' two-story brick home became a major depot for three liberty lines. They used their basement to conceal fugitives, and their horse and wagon were nearly always hitched and ready to go. Coffin recalled in his 1876 memoir:

> We knew not what night or what hour of the night we would be roused from slumber by a gentle rap at the door. . . . When they [fugitives] were all safely inside and the door fastened, I would cover the windows, strike a light and build a good fire. By this time my wife would be up and preparing victuals for them, and in a short time the cold and hungry fugitives would be made comfortable. . . . The fugitives would rest on pallets before the fire the rest of the night. Frequently wagon-loads of passengers from the different lines have met at our house, having no previous knowledge of each other. The companies varied in number, from two or three fugitives to seventeen.[26]

The lit lamp at John Rankin's hilltop home in Ripley, Ohio, equally symbolized the impressive constellation of clandestine operations fanning out from this UGRR hub.[27]

Many "stations" or "depots" employed the usual hiding places: potato cellars, attics, barns. Some stationmasters created hidden rooms, secret tunnels, and fake closets. Scores of brave and committed UGRR agents, from the border states of Kentucky and Indiana to the far reaches of Illinois, Ohio, Pennsylvania, and even Vermont, risked their lives to safeguard refugee slaves. Nearly every northern state from Michigan to Maine can boast some remnants of the liberty lines connecting abolitionists from one outpost to the next.

Over the 1850s, Harriet Tubman would become familiar with scores of UGRR depots, scattered across the upper South and the North. She recalled visiting stations in the following Delaware towns: Blackbird, Camden, Dover, Laurel, Middleton, New Castle, and, of course, Wilmington.[28] When she began ferrying fugitives to Canada, she became more familiar with depots in upstate New York, such as Quaker James Canning Fuller's home, Evergreen, near the town of Skaneateles.[29]

By the 1850s, hundreds and eventually thousands of whites who were morally opposed to slavery began to contemplate active resistance. In the North, religious and secular associations organized boycotts against slave products — "free produce" stores sprang up in New England towns and cities. Agricultural societies, for example, promoted raising beets for sugar to decrease dependence on cane crops harvested by slaves. Volunteers solicited funds to underwrite vigilance committees, and women's groups gathered food and clothing for refugees in need. All of this was standard charitable practice.

But a new breed of antislavery leader, notably philanthropist Gerrit Smith, did more. Smith began as a reform-minded businessman but converted into a radical abolitionist firebrand and Liberty Party politician. He became a defiant and outspoken critic of the slave power when elected to Congress.

Smith's father, a Utica storeowner, was a partner with John Jacob Astor. When his father retired in 1818, the twenty-one-year-old Gerrit inherited an impressive financial empire worth nearly $400,000. He took over not just the family store but thousands of acres of land in Oneida County, as well as vast acreage around Oswego and throughout the Adirondacks. He was a man of great wealth and influence in his upstate home of Peterboro.

During the Panic of 1837, Smith lost nearly all his money, and facing a mountain of debt, he moved from his ancestral mansion into a more modest home, "The Grove." He hoped "that when [my debts] are paid, I shall have a heart to reduce myself, if not to a poor man — by purchasing the liberty of the enslaved poor."[30]

In 1841 Smith purchased a slave family of seven from Kentucky, settling them into freedom. This practice was frowned upon by many abolitionists, who felt payment for slaves — even to emancipate them — acknowledged the legitimacy of human bondage. But Smith defended his actions as humanitarian.

During financial reversals Smith had shrewdly held on to most of his real estate, thousands of acres of land, which later made him a multimillionaire. Over his long philanthropic career, Smith gave away the equivalent of $600 million in contemporary sums.[31] Between 1846 and 1850 Smith donated 200,000 acres of land to black and poor farmers. John Brown was among those who settled on one of Smith's charity tracts. Black abolitionist Henry Highland Garnet took refuge in Smith's Peterboro home, which had become a magnet for those seeking support. Harriet Tubman was a frequent guest and consulted with him about her antislavery activities and UGRR career.

Smith received a letter from an antislavery friend in Tennessee who wanted him to buy a slave maimed by whipping and "carried indelible evidence of severe punishment on his person."[32] This abolitionist thought Smith might want to have this "living exhibit" to put on display at abolitionist meetings in the North, a scarred body to win converts to the cause.

Smith turned this proposition down, but was part of a growing cadre of abolitionists who were not afraid to use sensationalist publicity to advance an abolitionist agenda.

Yankee propagandists mounted public campaigns to champion both the cause of emancipation and the plight of the fugitive. The very symbol of the American Antislavery Society was a black male, shackled, arms upraised, pleading: "Am I not a Man and a Brother?" The idea of putting a maimed slave on display was rejected by Smith — but at the same time, abolitionists were eager to have ex-slaves parade before sympathetic audiences.

Boston was the home base of the most radical clique of white abolitionists, led by William Lloyd Garrison, whose newspaper, *The Liberator* (founded in 1831), took the most uncompromising antislavery stance. It was Garrison who tapped Frederick Douglass as a public speaker, calculating that his eyewitness testimony and personal appeal might drum up greater sympathy for slaves and more generous donations for abolitionist coffers.

Although the antislavery campaign was spearheaded by men, women sustained the movement, and even assumed positions in local and national leadership. This was not true of the Underground Railroad. The active agents identified on lists compiled after the fact were overwhelmingly male, with few women identified with this clandestine movement.[33]

If a woman did appear in the UGRR records, she was almost always cast in the role of helpmeet, as the wife or sister of a prominent male leader. This was the case for Leah Smith, the sister of Chester County, Pennsylvania, stationmaster Thomas Whitson, and Catherine Coffin, Levi's wife. Graceanna Lewis kept a home opened to fugitives with her sisters near Philadelphia. UGRR stationmasters Elizabeth Buffam Chace and her husband operated out of Valley Falls, Rhode Island. She described in riveting detail the risks her family faced on one occasion:

> In hourly fear and expectation of the arrival of the slave-catchers; our doors and windows fastened by day as well as by night, not daring to let our neighbors know who were our guests, lest some one should betray them. We told our children, all at that time un-

der fourteen years of age, of the fine of one thousand dollars and the imprisonment of six months that awaited us, in case the officer should come, and we should refuse to give these poor people up; and they heroically planned how, in such an event, they would take care of everything.[34]

Thus for most women involved in the UGRR, their participation was a family affair.

One exception to this rule was white UGRR agent Laura Haviland, who began as an educator in 1837 in her native Michigan. During her long reform career, she kept several safehouses and is credited with helping many fugitives to freedom.[35] She was a teacher in Canada West during 1852–53, where she devoted energies to the care and comfort of black refugees in Windsor.*

This is what makes Harriet Tubman's accomplishments so remarkable, as she was certainly the lone woman to achieve such a prominent role within the UGRR.[36] Also she was one of only a handful of blacks publicly associated with these extensive clandestine operations to shepherd slaves to freedom. Again, she was the lone fugitive to gain such widespread fame. Her unique vantage point — being black, fugitive, and female, yet willing to risk the role of UGRR abductor — is what allowed her to become such a powerful voice against slavery during the years leading up to the Civil War.

When she spoke out against slavery, she was not attacking it in the abstract but had personally known its evils. She risked the horror of re-enslavement with every trip, repeatedly defying the slave power with her rescues and abductions. These risks elevated the significance of her contributions to the UGRR movement.

The idea that the Underground Railroad originated along the Atlantic Seaboard directly contradicts popular lore indicating that Levi Coffin's operations made him either the "father" or the "president" of the Under-

---

*Canada West was the name used from 1841 to 1867 to describe the region now known as Ontario.

ground Railroad. The establishment of an Underground Railroad Freedom Center in Cincinnati, Ohio (2004), may enhance the idea of the midwestern interior's geographic and organizational primacy, as critics have suggested. Although with so many records of this nineteenth-century movement lost, destroyed, or never maintained (due to secrecy), there is insufficient evidence to provide satisfactory explanations.

By the time Harriet Tubman began leading slaves to freedom in the early 1850s, there were three liberty lines into Pennsylvania. The one generally used by Tubman during her years on the UGRR was the main line, a route from Maryland, through Delaware via Wilmington. This usually meant passing through the hands of Thomas Garrett, who was at the center of a reliable network of agents, with spurs radiating outward from his home base in Wilmington.

This may have been part of the first established line of the UGRR. Some contemporaries claimed this particular liberty line was active from the late 1830s, with "its southern terminus in Washington, D.C., and extended in a pretty direct route to Albany, New York, thence radiating in all directions to all the New England States and to many parts of this [New York] state."[37]

Regardless, Levi Coffin has had more and better press over the years. His ascendancy began with a painting by Charles Webber, *The Underground Railroad,* exhibited at the Columbian Exposition held in Chicago in 1893, which depicted Coffin taking in a band of fugitives.[38] After Webber's heroic portrayal of Coffin, viewed by millions at the exhibit, his name and face became permanently linked with the Underground Railroad.

There is no evidence Tubman ever met Levi Coffin. For her, the father of this movement was surely Thomas Garrett, who was so central to operations along the eastern liberty lines where Tubman expended most of her energies. Second only to Garrett was William Still, a prominent free black in Philadelphia, who became a great comrade and benefactor of Tubman's.

William Still was, like Tubman, born into a family deeply wounded by slavery. Long before Still was born in 1821, his mother escaped her master, taking her daughters with her. She was forced to leave two sons behind when she joined her husband, who had settled in New Jersey. Still's mother hid her fugitive slave status from her children until they were fully grown. She only confided the news that she had been living underground when she felt they were old enough to help locate their older brothers, long since sold south.[39] Thus William Still was born into a free black community in New Jersey but felt the scars of slavery inflicted by his mother's fugitive status and his brothers' disappearance.

In 1844, at the age of twenty-three, Still migrated to Philadelphia, where he quickly blended into radical abolitionist circles. He was employed by the Pennsylvania Antislavery Society as a clerk from 1847. The original Philadelphia Vigilance Committee, founded in 1838, had funneled three hundred fugitives a year northward from Philadelphia, until it disbanded in 1844. But a General Vigilance Committee reestablished itself in 1852; with William Still on the acting committee, the group was once again revived.

He became the primary mover and shaker, spending much of his career risking jail and sheltering fugitives. He also kept a remarkable record of the stories of those who passed through his station from 1852 onward. His notes were hidden away in a cemetery until after the Civil War. Finally, in 1872, the publication of Still's manuscript provided the most detailed record of the inner workings of the Underground Railroad. This volume offers a black eyewitness to these extensive operations and amazing tales.

The black community within Philadelphia was galvanized by William Still's leadership. His enterprise proved exemplary to Philadelphia colleagues. He was at the center of a core of vigilant Philadelphia UGRR agents; one can imagine Tubman crossing paths with Still soon after her arrival in Philadelphia.

She would have become intimately acquainted with the safe harbors provided for fugitives, including the home of Dr. James Bias, a black physician, who "gave his bed freely" to slaves on the run.[40] Black abolitionist Robert Purvis's house in the Philadelphia suburbs was equipped with a room hidden behind a trapdoor. William Whipper's home in

Columbia, Pennsylvania, was frequently crowded with fugitives, who after a night's rest might travel hidden in Whipper's own boxcar — which made frequent runs to both Philadelphia and Pittsburgh.[41] Whipper was never jailed for his activities, but his prosperous lumberyard was set on fire more than once in retaliation for suspected antislavery activities.

Together whites and blacks built up an extensive network of trails and safeguards, lines and way stations. Reconstructed maps trace elaborate routes out of slavery, stretching from Alabama to Canada, from Florida to Mexico. But clearly a very large percentage of fugitives made their way northward along the Eastern Seaboard, and many crossed over to freedom via Philadelphia.

The majority of fugitives who embarked on journeys to freedom, like Tubman, escaped alone. It would attract attention and was riskier to move in groups. Mass escapes cropped up most frequently in the 1850s — and became a specialty of Harriet Tubman's. Few slaves were willing to travel as a large party unless accompanied by a guide, preferably a UGRR abductor who had made the trip before.

Once fugitives landed beyond their owner's reach, many got word back to their families. Since most had taken off without any hint of their plans, they were anxious to send back reassurances to those left behind. Fugitive James Masey made his way from Maryland to Canada. Once north of the border, he wrote to his abandoned spouse:

Dear Wife — I take this opertunity to inform you that I have Arive in St. Catharines this Eving. After Jorney of too weeks, and no find mysilf on free ground and wish that you was here with me. but you are not here, when we parted I did not know that I should come away so soon as I did. But for that of causin you pain I left as I did, I hope that you will try to come. . . .[42]

Tubman was deeply concerned about getting word back to her family on the Eastern Shore. She may have dictated a letter to be sent to a free black in the community who could convey news of her safety to her loved ones, but this would have been in code, as southern postmasters frequently examined the mail to blacks before delivery.

Alternately, and more likely, she may have sent a message back along the slave-UGRR grapevine. She could perhaps have offered some address in the North — which would probably have been care of an antislavery organization, such as Still's operation. Regardless, contact was established within a year of her escape.

Slave runaways spent enormous time and effort trying to keep in touch with family members still in slavery. Laura Haviland, while living in Windsor, Canada, knew fugitives who made secret arrangements with whites to smuggle letters back to family. They might come from as far as six miles to beg her to take down dictation so they could forward their messages home.[43]

An escaped slave writing from his new home in Auburn, New York, in 1858 wanted to get word back to his mother, to tell her, "I am well and doing well . . . and I feal intersted about my Brothers I have never heard from them since I left home you will Please Be Kind annough to attend to this Letter."[44] He sent this missive along to William Still, to get the message back south, showing that Still was informally the postmaster of the UGRR as well.

The clandestine channels by which letters and information were smuggled from the North back south (and from the South to the North), the varied and multiplying routes for fugitives up and down the coast and interior, all demonstrate a web of conspirators, literally of enormous dimensions. Surviving family letters smuggled back down to slavery produce a chain of evidence confirming these secret networks.

In a movement dominated by white northern males, how did a black southern female, once a former slave, become both an abductor for the Underground Railroad and a champion of the radical wing of the abolitionist crusade? Tubman was described by a black colleague as "one of the most ordinary looking of her race, unlettered, no idea of geography, asleep half of the time [in a reference to her illness]."[45] Yet she used underestimation to her advantage, again and again. She transformed herself from a follower of the North Star to a leader among her people.

Given its clandestine nature, the UGRR has left historians with few ways to re-create its activities or measure its extent. Yet this unique woman's career offers efficacious insight. Through sheer power of will and fierce determination, Harriet Tubman pursued her own road to freedom, and in doing so, she led the way for others.

## Chapter Six

# The Moses of Her People

> If you come to us and are hungry, we will
> feed you, if thirsty, we will give you drink, if naked,
> we will clothe you; if sick, we will minister to your
> necessities, if in prison, we will visit you; if you need a
> hiding place from the face of pursuers, we will provide
> one that even bloodhounds will not scent out.
> — *American Antislavery Society*

————◄◊►————

WHEN HARRIET'S MASTER DIED in 1849, his wife was left all his slave property in trust, to help her provide for several minor children. Brodess's wife petitioned the court to sell the slave woman Keziah.[1] Keziah, known as Kizzy, was the daughter of one of Harriet's sisters sold south, and had been especially close to her aunt Harriet, whom she called Sister. Kizzy, along with two children, was slated for sale in December 1850. Her husband, John Bowley, a free black, was determined to rescue them, and got word to Harriet in Philadelphia about the impending sale.

This message was conveyed only weeks after passage of the infamous Bloodhound Law. The free states were in turmoil over the invasion of slavecatchers, now sanctioned by federal authority. Thousands of fugitives settled in the North were relocating to Canada. In the midst of it all, Harriet was confronted by this severe personal crisis. Would history be repeating itself? Would Kizzy be lost to the Deep South, as her mother was? Would her children be sent elsewhere, left motherless, as Kizzy had been? What could Harriet do to interrupt this tragic cycle? She had tried to put her recurring nightmares of women's screams and hoofbeats behind her, but with this message from home, she would be haunted once again.

Her family knew she had made it safely through to freedom and calculated that she might have contacts and advice to offer Bowley. It was a tribute to Tubman that she, a fugitive slave, would be sought out for advice — and by a free black at that. It is doubtful that Bowley would have asked his wife's beloved aunt Harriet to take any risks, but by being the first to seize her freedom, she was clearly looked up to by the extended family and local community.

This dire news from home created the opportunity for Harriet to explore the antislavery and UGRR networks within Philadelphia. She was at the very hub of UGRR activity along the Eastern Seaboard liberty lines, and it was not difficult for a resourceful fugitive to secure such contacts. With limited capital, she was in no position to finance a rescue, but she felt compelled to use her own resources to save Kizzy. It is extremely doubtful that Harriet's communication back home could have been extensive or detailed. Rather Bowley would as soon as possible have let Harriet know about the slated sale, and Harriet would have sent back brief messages, perhaps only a contact name or location.

There is no way of knowing what convinced Tubman that she herself must go back into Maryland, a slave state, to help with the rescue. It was one of the first signs of her extraordinary personal courage. Harriet was determined to find a way to bring this favorite niece and her children out to freedom before they were put on the auction block. She perhaps could not countenance any return to the Eastern Shore, where a reward for her recapture remained fresh. She sent word that she would be waiting to assist Bowley when he made his way across the bay from Dorchester County.

It was remarkable that Tubman was willing to travel back into Maryland, and even to Baltimore, a notoriously dangerous city for fugitives. Any black traveling by boat, train, or any public transportation was required to present free papers for inspection. Whether she had obtained forged papers or not, Baltimore remained a risk — and an unknown environment for Harriet. Perhaps her months in Philadelphia imbued her with confidence about her abilities. It was still a great leap of faith for Tubman to venture into a new city, the first of many on her road to freedom.

Again, little is known about the particulars of this escape, except that by the time Kizzy and her offspring were taken to the slave trader in Cambridge, Maryland, a plan to rescue her was in place.[2] Family lore suggests that when the auctioneer went to dinner, John Bowley took the opportunity to smuggle Kizzy and her two children aboard a boat. He rowed them across the bay to Bodkin's Point on the Chesapeake's western shore.[3] Bowley delivered them safely to Tubman, who hid the family in Baltimore until she could find a way to transport them out to freedom. It is known that John Bowley later joined his family, but there is no record that he remained in Baltimore on this occasion.

This first rescue demonstrates Tubman's powers of adaptability. Within a year of her own escape, she was able to head into the new and strange streets of Baltimore, locate assistance, find a safe house, and navigate the shoals to freedom. Although it is entirely possible that Tubman did this on her own, it is equally likely that her contacts with black brethren and white abolitionists in Philadelphia provided inroads into Baltimore. UGRR contacts would naturally have smoothed the operation.

Perhaps she sought help from a conductor named Coleman, who drove his merchandise on the turnpike from Baltimore to Pennsylvania, hiding slaves in his wagon.[4] Maybe she was able to tap Jacob Gibbs, a black UGRR agent operating in Baltimore. All that mattered was that she safely guided Kizzy and her children from slavery to freedom. When she crossed over, like her aunt before her, Kizzy took a new name: she became known as Mary Anne.[5]

Surely her success with this first operation whetted Tubman's appetite, particularly with her parents, several siblings, nephews, nieces, and especially her husband all left behind on the Eastern Shore. And so she made her second trip back into Maryland in the spring of 1851. Perhaps she sent word along the grapevine that she would be coming, or perhaps she simply ventured south and improvised.

On this, her second expedition, Tubman not only rescued one of her brothers, perhaps James Isaac, but also two other men. Her brother was often hired out and might have been living outside Dorchester County, perhaps farther north in Talbot County.[6] The two other men may have been coworkers who demanded to be taken along once they learned of her brother's plan to escape.

By now Tubman would have been connected with both Thomas Garrett's Wilmington, Delaware, operation, and the networks established in and out of Philadelphia.[7] Abductors were often advanced expenses associated with rescues, but this was barely adequate funding. There is no evidence that Tubman received any financial help at this time; however, she did secure UGRR funds for later operations and may have been using donations to help with these earliest excursions.

In the autumn of 1851, on her third trip south, Harriet undertook her most desperate gamble. She wanted to persuade her husband, John Tubman, to come away with her. So she returned once again to the Eastern Shore. But on this trip she ventured back even closer to home, flirting with detection by going to Dorchester County, where she was still well known. Her first two rescues were successful and important, but this third raid was far more significant for a variety of reasons.

Harriet was on an even more personal mission than she had been during her first two returns, which had been in response to pleas from her family. This trip was taken on her own initiative and the outcome was much less certain. She approached Cambridge and sent a message to John, asking him to meet her and to accompany her on the journey back north.

While she was in hiding, Tubman discovered that her husband had taken another wife, a woman named Caroline. As he had in 1849, John

Tubman again refused to leave. While she risked everything for a chance that they might be together, he turned her down. Worse yet, he allegedly would not even go to see her.

Her friends reported that Harriet took this turn of events very hard. Harriet considered that she and John were still married, and assumed they both longed to be together. Not only were her feelings not reciprocated — she had been replaced.

Throughout their separation of less than two years, Harriet held out hope that she and her husband would be reunited and free together. John Tubman's liaison with another woman (a woman who would bear his children) dashed all dreams of reunion. At first she "thought she would go right in and make all the trouble she could," but she realized "if he could do without her, she could do without him."[8]

She was holed up in a dangerous place, worried with each daybreak that she might be betrayed and recaptured. One can only imagine what a difficult time this must have been. She knew that she had to reimagine another future for herself — one that did not include John Tubman. This moment in 1851 may have proved as much of a watershed as her initial escape two years before.

Her previous successful rescues had built up her confidence. Over the weeks and months in the North she had come in contact with an expanding network of reliable antislavery contacts. For months she had been trying to reconstitute her own family circle, but she realized that so many other slave families were in similarly desperate straits. She had ridden the liberty lines to freedom more than once, more than twice — indeed three times, including her own escape.

Fate must have led her to this juncture. She had great fears about her future course, and confided, "The Lord told me to do this. I said, 'Oh Lord, I can't — don't ask me — take somebody else.'" But Tubman also reported that God spoke directly to her: "It's you I want, Harriet Tubman."[9]

To that end, in December 1851 she made her first commitment to the UGRR. It would not be a wasted journey. Boston abolitionist Franklin Sanborn described with admiration: "She did not give away to rage or grief, but collected a party of fugitives and brought them safely to Philadelphia."[10] Members of her fugitive band included not only family members and their acquaintances; for the first time, Harriet guided out strangers as well.

This group of eleven included her brother William Henry and his sweetheart, Catherine. Back in Maryland, William Henry had long wanted to marry Catherine, but her master refused permission. So the couple decided to take matters into their own hands and run off together. In order to facilitate Catherine's escape, William Henry bought her a suit of men's clothing to use as a disguise. She found the male attire at their secret hiding place and dressed like a man to make her getaway from the neighborhood.[11] She connected with her husband-to-be, and they joined Harriet's caravan — which continued all the way to Canada.

By this time Tubman had decided, "I wouldn't trust Uncle Sam with my people no longer, but I brought 'em clear off to Canada."[12] When she took on the role of abductor she took an even more proprietary interest in her flock. Even though she had never been so far north before, she decided that Canada was the new Canaan, and Niagara her new River Jordan. Harriet made her first border crossing in December 1851.

On this journey Tubman may have used Frederick Douglass's home in Rochester as a safe house. He recalled in his autobiography: "On one occasion I had eleven fugitives at the same time under my roof, and it was necessary for them to remain with me until I could collect sufficient money to get them to Canada."[13] He does not indicate if this was Tubman's group, but because of the timing, and the rarity of such a large party, it is likely that it was.

These were significant firsts for Tubman: she would solicit and encourage fugitives to make their escape, and escort them all the way to Canada. She would dedicate herself to this new and important work, becoming a UGRR abductor. Except for her husband's demurral, her missions thus far had been entirely successful. At this juncture, she confessed, "he dropped out of [my] heart."[14] She left John Tubman behind, keeping only the memories and his last name.

This transformation would become as significant as Tubman's self-emancipation. Just as she had crossed over to freedom, now she would begin a new chapter of her life. She would take on a mission that would lead her to be called Moses by her abolitionist colleagues. With this new vocation, she would become the most famous conductor on the UGRR.

Antislavery activists wasted no opportunity to champion the dramatic symbolic significance of Tubman's role: a fugitive slave willing to venture behind enemy lines to liberate other slaves. When she decided to focus all of her energies on rescue missions, to serve as an abductor for the UGRR, her decision was groundbreaking. Her role took incredible nerve and stamina. Harriet doubtless saw her faith, rather than her own personal courage, as her only armor.

She would return again and again to the South, cheered on by former fugitives, but never *joined* by them on her expeditions. She alone took these risks, eventually bringing hundreds out along liberty lines to freedom. Even with a concealed identity and clandestine partnerships, her aboveground fame grew. With her spectacular achievements, she was likened to the biblical hero of her code name, Moses.

From 1852, Tubman regularly made at least one trip a year, often two, deep into slave territory. She usually moved her cargo through Wilmington or Philadelphia, where she had dependable contacts. She also made connections in New York City, and became well known to UGRR agents from the Mason-Dixon Line to the Canadian border. Nearly all of her "abductions" were in Maryland and Virginia, and she kept no record of her raids.

She developed a pattern that allowed her to successfully ferry at least ten fugitives at a time at least once a year. She kept to the backroads and never traveled by day while in the "land of Egypt." One admirer noted, "She always came in the winter, when the nights are long and dark, and people who have homes stay in them."[15]

After depositing her brother William Henry, Catherine, and the others in Canada in the winter of 1851, Tubman remained for several weeks north of the border before returning to the States in the spring of 1852. She was eager to plan more and larger operations. At this time, funds for rescues came primarily from her own labors as a cook and domestic. She moved from place to place during the summer and into the fall of 1852, heading as far afield as Cape May, New Jersey.

Cape May, at the southernmost tip of New Jersey, was a resort community, boasting sea bathing and luxury accommodations. Both coaches and boats ferried summer visitors from Philadelphia to the town's seaside inns, as advertisements promised: "It is the most delightful spot that the citizens may retire to in the hot season."[16] It was in this pleasure cove that Tubman cooked for families and hotel kitchens to build up her war chest.

In the late fall of 1853, we know Tubman returned again to Maryland, where she engineered another exodus. Following this raid, she headed to upstate New York and past Niagara Falls with nine refugees in tow. During this period, Tubman was learning the ropes of safe routes and stations available in upstate New York. By the winter of 1853–54, she had made at least five trips, transporting nearly thirty slaves to freedom.

Thus began a seasonal pattern of migration for Tubman: rescuing a large party in the fall, then back to Canada in the winter. After a brief hibernation, she would head for northern haunts to spend time earning money during the spring and summer, and then, during autumn, plan and execute additional raids in the South. She made an occasional rescue in the spring, but much less frequently than in fall. There is evidence that she would make brief and isolated trips across the Mason-Dixon Line to rescue immediate family members of those for whom she had already secured freedom, almost always missions to reunite families.

Harriet Tubman was one of the pioneers of using the actual railway as part of her "underground" railroad. She herself frequently took trains south, reasoning it was less suspicious to have a black woman travel by public transportation into slave states rather than vice versa. During her upper South rescues, escapees traveled by boat or on foot. She only used the hire of private carriages or wagons during an emergency, as the expense was prohibitive. After fugitives arrived in Wilmington, Philadelphia, or

New York, Tubman tried to obtain enough funds to pay for rail fares to Canada — although there would be frequent stops along the way, as circumstances might dictate getting on and off to evade detection.

As she continued to rack up an impressive total of rescues, slaveholders and slavecatchers fumed. Black abolitionist William Wells Brown exulted that "fugitives in Moses's care were never captured."[17] White southern authorities were desperate to end her reign. One Pennsylvania man recalled that during his youth, his abolitionist father introduced him to the "big guns," the "secret officers of the Underground Railway," which is how Tubman was introduced to him.[18] The exploits of this latter-day Moses became known well beyond UGRR circles.

When introduced as the legendary UGRR conductor, Tubman stirred excitement wherever she went. She was treated like a celebrity when invited to Boston, welcomed into the best parlors in Concord and breaking bread with the Bay State's most sympathetic literati. The pocketbooks of abolitionist aristocrats opened when Tubman recounted her amazing tales. William Wells Brown wrote, "The most refined person would listen for hours while she related the intensely interesting incidents of her life, told in the simplest manner, but always seasoned with good sense."[19]

Her self-effacing recollections of rescues held audiences, white and black, enthralled. She told the story of a dark night when three companions moved soundlessly along the deserted turnpike. The two male fugitive slaves had never been on this road before — the pathway to freedom. Blacks abroad, without passes, feared that mounted patrols could come charging along at any moment and sweep them back into slavery's net. They knew that irate masters, pursuing with bloodhounds, might suddenly appear. More than the autumn chill in the air caused them to shiver as they moved as quickly and silently as possible, hoping to reach their next stop before dawn. If cloudy skies obscured the moon, their guide was able to feel the moss on a tree trunk to tell them which direction they must take. Despite dangers and risks, the men were glad for their good fortune, following Moses into the promised land.

During this moonlit trek, Tubman decided to move off the highway and to cross an open field. After a long spell, the field ran out and Tubman faced an unfamiliar river. She walked along the banks to see if there might be a bridge or even a boat to get them across. After a fruitless search, fearing sunrise might overtake them before they made it to cover safely, Tubman insisted that they cross on foot.

The two men absolutely refused, fearing drowning more than the slaveholder's lash. Rather than draw her pistol or waste her breath, Harriet waded across alone. After she made it to the other side, the two men meekly followed.

Soaked and weary, they found they had to ford yet another wide stream before they came upon an isolated cabin. Tubman determined that a black family lived within, and used her powers of persuasion to obtain food and shelter.

There were severe penalties imposed on any who assisted fugitives, and those offering a hiding place needed reassurance. Suspects were thrown in jail with the flimsiest of evidence. The three soaked and weary pilgrims gratefully dried out, and slept all day to rest up for what lay ahead. Once they were restored enough to continue, they humbly thanked their hosts and resumed their journey northward under cover of night. Because Tubman had no money to offer them, she peeled off her undergarments to have something to give to this poor family — showing the depths of her gratitude.[20] Such accounts, rich with exotic detail, kept her listeners rapt.

Harriet's fame before and during the Civil War coincided with the emergence of the daguerreotype and the popularity of the small visiting card portraits known as *cartes-de-visite*. This was a lucky stroke for the UGRR leader, as photographic images became instrumental to the protection of her clandestine activities. Because she was illiterate, letters of introduction were not appropriate. It could be a costly mistake if Tubman were to reveal her UGRR agenda to anyone but a fellow traveler. Her collection of photos of UGRR agents and comrades helped to prevent such mishaps.

When she made contact with persons she had never met before, Tubman's treasured pack of cartes-de-visite became her insurance policy. She showed these persons her images and asked them to name the people in the pictures to test their credentials. If they could identify the images of her antislavery friends, she felt secure, knowing she was dealing with someone who had a personal relationship with her comrades.[21]

Once when she had to pass through a town near her former Maryland home during daylight, she walked the streets incognito, equipped with a large sunbonnet pulled down over her face and, as an extra measure of precaution, two live fowl. When she was approached by one of her former masters (as she frequently had been hired out during her years in bondage), Harriet yanked the strings on the legs of her chickens — and they began to flap and squawk. She tended to the agitated birds, avoiding eye contact with this man, who passed inches away.[22] Harriet was nearly always prepared with a change of costume or some other diversion.

On another occasion, while traveling in a railway coach, she spotted another former master sitting nearby. Instead of panicking, she picked up a newspaper and studied it carefully. Because the former slave known to him was illiterate, he did not take any notice of her, and she made it safely to her destination.[23]

Tubman rarely ventured onto plantations herself during her forays south. Instead she spread the word along the slave grapevine, informing members of plantation communities about the time and place for her rendezvous with candidates for escape. She might provide false information at first, to flush out any betrayals. Once she found local prospects to her satisfaction, Tubman would make a final appeal.

She crafted her expeditions with extreme care. White abolitionist Alice Stone Blackwell reported that Moses would use gospel music and spirituals to signal to fugitives hidden along the road: "She directed them by her songs, as to whether they might show themselves, or must continue to lie low. . . . No one would notice what was sung by an old colored woman as she trudged along the road."[24] Although she might be posing as an "old colored woman," Tubman began her career as "Moses" while still in her twenties and was only thirty-five when Lincoln was elected in 1860.

Saturday evening was the regular gathering time for recruits, as many slaves went to visit family and friends on Sunday, their day off. Any slave who took off with Tubman on a Saturday night would not be discovered missing until Monday morning.[25] Once the absence was confirmed, his or her master could not get a poster printed until Monday, or a notice in the paper until Tuesday at the earliest, giving Harriet at least a full day's lead.[26]

When she was transporting slaves out of Maryland, Tubman usually followed a route north, using the Choptank River as a guide out of the Eastern Shore, perhaps stopping in Odessa, Delaware, where local Quakers used a hidden loft in their meetinghouse as a sanctuary for travelers, or at the Coopers' house in Camden, Delaware, where fugitives could be hidden in a secret room above the kitchen.[27] William Brinkley, a free black UGRR agent in Camden, reported that Harriet would stop at his house when she passed.[28]

On one occasion, Tubman planned to take her party on foot across a bridge through Wilmington, but she was warned by "some secret friend" that police were on the lookout for them. She dispersed the slaves, parking them temporarily in safe houses while she contacted UGRR comrade Thomas Garrett for help. Garrett found a gang of African American bricklayers who regularly traversed the bridge. They rode back and forth daily to their job site in two wagons loaded with tools and bricks. When Garrett called on them for assistance, they volunteered to take on some "extra cargo" for the trip home. During twilight, the Quaker merchant hid Tubman and the fugitives at the bottom of the bricklayers' wagons. The guards were on alert but allowed the singing workmen to pass unmolested as they made the crossing north after a long day's work.[29]

When on a mission behind enemy lines in a slave state, Tubman demanded absolute discipline. She was not afraid to exert her authority and forced everyone to toe the line. Tubman even carried a pistol and was prepared to use it, which earned her a reputation for toughness. There were occasions when circumstances dictated that she use force as well as persuasion.

She recalled a particularly difficult ordeal when she had to shepherd a party of twenty-five fugitives, who were losing heart during a grueling trek. At one point they had to hide in a swamp all day long and well into the night — deprived of food, cold and damp, their resolve crumbling with each passing hour.

One man said he was going to turn around and take his chances back on the plantation. Tubman warned that he could not leave. It would compromise the entire operation. He would have to stay with the group — to which he had agreed at the outset. The other fugitives tried to coax him to keep on going. But when it was time to move forward, he refused. Tubman "stepped up to him and aimed a revolver at his head, saying 'Move or die!' He went on with the rest and in a few days he was in Canada a free man."[30]

Her fearlessness was legendary, and Thomas Garrett confided to a friend: "Harriet seems to have a special angel to guard her on her journey of mercy . . . and confidence [that] God will preserve her from harm in all her perilous journeys."[31]

Divine intervention became a popular rationalization of Tubman's success during her years behind enemy lines. It was certainly her own explanation, as Garrett again observed: "I never met with any person of any color who had more confidence in the voice of God, as spoken direct to her soul."[32] Another contemporary confided:

> She could elude patrols and pursuers with as much ease and unconcern as an eagle would soar through the heavens. She "had faith in God"; always asked Him what to do, and direct her, "which," she said, "He always did." She would talk about "consulting with God," or "asking of Him," just as one would consult a friend upon matters of business; and she said, "He never deceived [me]."[33]

Tubman once visited Garrett's store and told him she was there because "God tells me you have money for me."

Garrett was taken aback and asked, "How much does thee want?" Tubman explained that she needed about twenty-three dollars.

Shortly before, a letter from Eliza Wigham, secretary of the Anti-Slavery Society of Edinburgh, had arrived at Garrett's store. A Scottish gentleman, moved by tales of Moses' heroics, donated the sum of five pounds to her cause and asked that it be conveyed directly to her. Garrett had the five pounds in hand — which worked out to be about twenty-four dollars.[34] This story was recounted as a symbol of Tubman's gift of prophecy, but it also showed her confidence that both the UGRR and the Lord would provide.

Fugitives reported that while in flight Tubman might insist they stop for no reason and then strike out in a new direction; only later would they discover that lawmen had been waiting to ambush them. In many of Harriet's own recollections, her faith provided protective intuition. Perhaps her guidance system was derived from Psalm 32:8: "I will instruct thee and teach thee in the way which thou shalt go: I will guide thee with mine eye."

Tubman herself confessed, "When danger is near, it appears like my heart goes flutter, flutter."[35] She believed her ability was a kind of second sight, something she inherited from her father, who she said could forecast the weather and had predicted the war with Mexico.[36] One of her admirers explained that Tubman was "as firm in the conviction of supernatural help as Mahomet."[37]

Her spiritual mettle was second only to her physical endurance. During a particularly difficult time, out in the wilds while smuggling a group, Tubman was in extreme pain over an infection in her mouth. The inflammation was getting worse and worse, so she simply took her pistol and knocked out her own offending teeth, ending her misery.[38] Losing her top row of teeth, she considered, was a small price to pay for relief.

Further, Tubman still suffered her chronic and deep intermittent "spells" — her narcoleptic episodes — even while on the liberty lines. Her disconcerting habit of "losing time" both horrified those entrusted to her and enhanced her reputation as mystical.

During one trip aboard a boat, a ticket collector asked Harriet and her companion, a fugitive named Tilly, to step aside while he took others' tickets. Tilly was wild with fear, but Tubman kept calm and prayed, "Oh, Lord, you have been with me in six troubles, don't desert me in the seventh." She kept murmuring prayer, and to Tilly's great surprise, the incantation worked: the ticket collector let them proceed, and they made it to their destination without further interference.[39]

Another time, when Tubman was traveling with a large party of fugitives, they were nearing a place where they would be given food and perhaps a hayloft in which to hide and rest during the day. This party was especially exhausted, and the group included two infants, twin girls. Tubman had used opiates to quiet the babies but needed to reach a safe house before the drugs wore off.

She left the group behind while scouting ahead, knocking on the door of a UGRR comrade whose assistance she knew she could count on. Her rapping was a special signal, and when there was no response, she tried the signal knock again.

When a stranger's head appeared in the window, Tubman reluctantly asked for her contact by name. Told he had been taken away "for harboring niggers," Tubman abruptly withdrew.

Light was dawning, and she knew she would quickly need to find a safe alternative. She remembered a swamp outside of town where she could hide her group before sunup. Cold and hungry, the fugitives huddled in the wet grass for hours. Harriet was at a practical loss as to what she might do and resorted to prayer, beseeching the Lord's help during the long day.

During the twilight hour, a man dressed in Quaker clothes passed close by the edge of the swamp. Harriet heard him mutter, "My wagon stands in the barnyard of the next farm along the way. The horse is in the stable; the harness hangs on a nail."[40] She believed her prayers had been answered — and planned to move out after sunset to scout the situation.[41]

Under cover of darkness, Tubman found the farm. She hitched up the wagon (in which provisions for the hungry slaves had been left) and recovered her charges, and they made their way to a distant depot. Tubman deposited the wagon with a Quaker comrade, with instructions for its return to her anonymous benefactor.

Tubman would nearly always spend Christmas in Canada with her family, then settle in for the first two months of the year. Most UGRR caravans made the journey to Canada in the dead of winter — primarily before Christmas, as New Year's Day was the time when masters were most likely to send slaves to the auction block. Winter was a slow season for fieldwork and became the "weeping time" for slaves, when traders came looking for stock to ship south.

During spring thaws Tubman would travel back to the States to earn wages from laundering, cooking, or other domestic service. She would also connect with UGRR contacts and collect more donations. In fall, if she had enough funds, Tubman would head south and infiltrate a slave community. UGRR donations came in handy to cover the cost of bribes and expenses while conducting business within the slave states.

Tubman would take on short-term rescue assignments as well. She might return to a community to extract the remaining relatives of already escaped fugitives. William Wells Brown described: "Men from Canada who had made their escape years before, and whose families were still in the prison-house of slavery, would seek out Moses, and get her to go and bring their dear ones away."[42]

Once a family member had made it safely to freedom ahead of them, many were more willing to risk a trek north. Tubman also made "hit-and-runs" into familiar areas of Virginia, on up through Maryland. She could slip slaves across the Pennsylvania border, into the waiting arms of UGRR contacts. These rapidly executed single or double extractions were often made to prevent sales to the Deep South — similar to Tubman's rescue of her niece Keziah.

Once Tubman went on a dangerous mission of mercy — locating the sweetheart of an escaped slave, stealing her from her master in Maryland, and bringing the woman back to her lover in the North. Her fiancé had been anticipating such a reunion for eight years. He had finally saved enough money to fully finance the rescue. He contacted Tubman and begged her to bring his loved one safely to him.

First Harriet obtained a forged certificate in Philadelphia which identified the bearer as a free woman. Maryland law required all African Americans departing from the state by railway or boat to have free papers. Next

Tubman found a sympathetic steamboat captain willing to issue a travel certificate for her runaway companion. But when the two women were staying at a hotel in Seaford, Delaware, making arrangements for their sea voyage, a slave dealer tried to apprehend them. Their landlord interfered, and Harriet and her companion made a getaway. They fled to the railroad station and purchased tickets to Camden, Delaware. Once in Camden, Tubman located a private vehicle to take them the rest of the way to Philadelphia — and to the woman's sweetheart. Thomas Garrett was alarmed by this close call, but Tubman remained undeterred. "The strangest thing about this woman is, she does not know, or appears not to know, that she has done anything worth notice," Garrett recalled.[43]

After this risky rescue, Tubman bid the reunited couple good-bye. This must have been a poignant mission for Harriet, bringing these lovers back together after eight years. But it also must have been bittersweet in light of her own marital situation, having been forsaken for another. Tubman did not dwell on this but made an immediate turnaround, and headed back south to fetch "a woman and three children."[44]

It is nearly impossible to attach details or particulars, especially dates, to many of Tubman's various escapes. But one of her most famous expeditions involved a return to her former Maryland home in Caroline County. In the winter of 1854, Harriet pulled off a daring raid by liberating three of her siblings: Henry, Benjamin, and Robert Ross.

First Tubman dictated a letter to be sent to a free black in Dorchester County, one Jacob Jackson, whom she trusted to get word to her brothers. She signed the letter "William Henry Jackson," the name of Jacob's adopted son. The letter included coded and biblical phrasing, a Tubman trademark. She may have been illiterate, but she was familiar with chapter and verse of the Bible and, when necessary, used it in her dictated correspondence. Tubman was keenly aware of the significance of characters and incidents from both the Old and New Testament, and she often drew upon this allegorical resonance in her line of work.

She had written that Jackson's brothers should be ready to step aboard when "the good old ship of Zion comes along." White postal authorities intercepted Harriet's letter, and after they read it Jackson was questioned about its contents. When it was read aloud to him, Jackson denied that he had any knowledge of who wrote it or that it was even meant for him. For example, Jackson pointed out that he had no brothers; the letter was a case of mistaken identity. Yet Jacob Jackson clearly understood the letter's intent and eventually got word to the Ross brothers.[45]

Tubman's enslaved brothers were permitted to go abroad (off their own plantation) to spend the December holiday with family, and so Harriet got word to her three male siblings to meet on Christmas Day at the Ross cabin in Caroline County to start their journey north. Henry Ross found it especially difficult to prepare for departure, as he would be leaving behind his pregnant wife.[46]

Family lore recounts that Henry's wife went into labor just as he was set to take off for his rendezvous. Henry delayed his departure so he could fetch a midwife, and remained behind for the birth of his child. Allegedly he still did not tell his wife of his planned departure. But when he left abruptly after their baby arrived, she no doubt guessed his intent.

Most renditions of this rescue leave out the delay caused by Henry's wife's childbirth, focusing instead on a sentimental reunion between Tubman's aged father and his daughter. As the most popular version of the story goes, Tubman knew her father would be cross-examined following his sons' disappearance, and she hoped to make things easy for him by using subterfuge.

Just before the four siblings planned to head north, they had their father blindfolded and brought to an outbuilding by one of the three other slaves that arrived at the Rosses to escape as well.[47] In that way, Harriet could embrace her father and speak with him — after an absence of five years. His eye covering afforded pretense and precaution. If he was interrogated later, Ben Ross could honestly report that he had never "seen" his daughter, not since her disappearance several years before.

Indeed, when Ben Ross was later questioned by authorities, his answer that he hadn't seen his sons over the Christmas holiday sufficed. Even though she chose the Ross home for a rendezvous, Tubman never made contact with her mother and never let her father "see" her or her brothers.

Harriet's mother had a very excitable temperament, and her children agreed to leave her in the dark.[48] Rit was desolate when none of her boys arrived as prearranged — and even more so when she discovered within a few days that they too had fled, like Araminta, Kizzy, William Henry, and James Isaac before them.

A few days later, Thomas Garrett reported: "We made arrangements last night, and sent away Harriet Tubman, with six men [three were her brothers] and one woman to Allen Agnew's, to be forwarded across the country to the city. Harriet and one of the men had worn their shoes off their feet."[49] Garrett supplied them with new footwear.

As with most of Tubman's escapes, we know little about the details. But we do know that the rescue of these three brothers, like that of her niece Kizzy, was extremely timely. Harriet's brother Henry commented that she executed the operation just before the three men were about to be sold, so "she came in good season. She brought us all off together . . . and we rode to Canada, and have been here ever since."[50]

## Chapter Seven
# Canadian Exile

*Farewell, ole Master, don't think hard of me,*
*I'm travelin' on to Canada, where all the slaves are free.*
— *Traditional Spiritual*

◄○►

FROM HER FIRST VISIT to St. Catharines, Ontario, in 1851, Harriet Tubman felt welcome in what was to become her temporary home, a place to which she would return again and again. St. Catharines was the small town where both Tubman and a number of her family members tried to make a fresh start, safe under "the paw of the British Lion," as Harriet called her refuge.[1]

Most did not know what they were coming to, only what they were running from. "Canada was a good country for us, because master was so anxious that we should *not* go there," wrote one former slave.[2] America's northern neighbor boasted roughly 2.5 million people dotting the country's 240 million acres. French speakers were settled in eastern Canada, around Montreal and Quebec City. The larger British population was spread thinly across what was known as Canada West (today's Ontario), with the largest group of English-speaking settlers congregated in Toronto. Most Canadians were settled in rural regions, divided into spartan townships that collected around schools and churches and were anchored on rivers and lakefronts.

Canada had its own long and tangled relationship with slavery. The first slaves in the region were brought into New France as early as 1628. By the 1760s fewer than 1,200 persons of African origin were settled in the French-speaking regions of Canada, with most residing in Montreal and serving in households as domestic slaves.

By 1784 more than 4,000 blacks lived in British colonies north of the Great Lakes. Of these, nearly 40 percent were slaves. Many were recent arrivals, transported to Canada in 1783 by Loyalists escaping north in the wake of the American Revolution, who brought their slaves with them.

British Canada was desperate to encourage immigration, especially of English speakers. At first they were willing to allow settlers to bring in all their worldly goods — including slaves. The government passed the Imperial Act of 1790, which provided for the importation of "negros" duty free (as well as furniture, clothing, and utensils of husbandry).[3]

This policy was dramatically reversed when Lieutenant Governor John Graves Simcoe successfully pushed through "an Act to prevent the further introduction of Slaves, and to limit the terms of contracts for servitude within this Province." Under Simcoe's leadership, the provincial government prohibited any future slaves from being imported while guaranteeing Canadian slaveholders protection for human chattel already in place.

Some were outraged nevertheless. The wife of William Jarvis, provincial secretary of the colony, wrote to her father that Simcoe had "by a piece of chicanery freed all the negroes."[4] This was not true. But Mrs. Jarvis's anger and exaggeration mirrored slaveholders' heightened fears north and south of the U.S.-Canada border. Canada's open-door policy had long been a bane to U.S. slaveholders. In 1827 Kentuckian Henry Clay, then secretary of state, complained that slaves who escaped to Canada were "a growing evil."[5]

In the spring of 1837 Solomon Moseby's Kentucky owner sent him off on horseback with a pass. Moseby's master entrusted him with a message to take to a nearby plantation. The Kentucky slave instead took the opportunity to make his way to the Canadian town of Niagara — arriving without the horse. He was apprehended by authorities when Moseby's owner demanded extradition so that the fugitive might stand trial in the United States.

More than one hundred white citizens signed a petition proclaiming that to return Moseby would set a dangerous precedent, "whereby no runaway slave either now or henceforth will be safe in a British colony."[6] Unfortunately for Moseby, Lieutenant Governor Francis Bond Head remained unmoved. The rule of law required extradition. A prominent local sea captain proclaimed "no vessel commanded by him would be used to convey a man back to slavery."[7] Next, the sheriff was faced with two hundred to three hundred protestors, who kept vigil at the jail round the clock to prevent Moseby's being spirited away.

Finally, in September, the jailer secured a ship and tried to transport his prisoner to the dock. After Moseby was lifted into a wagon, one black protestor grabbed the reins while another lodged a piece of wood into the wheels, locking the vehicle in place. In the ensuing riot, several died, but Moseby escaped to freedom.[8]

When a similar extradition appeal cropped up the next month, Canadian authorities decided that each slave extradition case would have to be judged on its individual merits, but the consensus was that the return of ordinary fugitives would not be considered.[9] As the *Niagara Reporter* suggested, "Only murder, arson, and the rape of a white woman justified the return of a slave."[10]

"North of slavery" was a geographical and ideological designation after the Missouri Compromise of 1820. Congressional legislation admitted Missouri as a slave state after its 1819 application, but balanced the ratio of slave states to free by adding Maine to the Union as a free state. Then Congress drew a line across the millions of acres of the Louisiana Purchase, declaring that only those territories south of the thirty-sixth parallel would be allowed into the Union as slave states. Thus was the country officially divided into half slave and half free.

But even in the free states, more and more, African Americans found their rights disregarded and trampled, their livelihoods imperiled, their safety threatened. Indeed the first organized influx of American blacks into Canada was provoked by restrictive legislation in Ohio. In 1830 more than a thousand blacks fled Cincinnati in response to discriminatory city statutes. When northern states began to circumscribe the lives of free blacks (for example, when Pennsylvania banned African American voting in 1838), many headed north of the border. The governor of Upper Canada extended a generous invitation to African Americans: "We royalists do not know men by their color. Should you come to us you will be entitled to all the privileges of the rest of his Majesty's subjects."[11]

This exodus of U.S. blacks created a host of Afro-Canadian communities dotting the border. Nearly two hundred former Cincinnati citizens of color founded a town on Lake Huron in Canada West, which they called Wilberforce, after the British statesman who spent his career fighting slavery. This settlement symbolized the determination of blacks within the United States to live their lives as free people.

By the 1830s Canada witnessed a steady parade of missionaries, visionaries, and fugitives, making their way across the border to create free settlements for U.S. blacks. The former slaves themselves were the ones most transformed by this migration.

Again and again observers commented on the rapturous response of blacks to arrival in Canada: "The sublimest sight in North America is the leap of a slave from a boat to the Canadian shore. That 'leap' transforms him from a marketable chattel to a free man."[12] The leap may have been fluid for some, but it was a rough transition for others. African Americans who eluded masters and slavecatchers often arrived with little but the ragged clothes on their back. The trickle of refugees with empty pockets created a veritable cottage industry as Ladies' Aid Societies and other charitable groups within the Canadian province took it upon themselves to ease the transition from slavery to freedom. A black pastor, the Reverend W. M. Mitchell, described fugitives as being in "a perfect state of destitution, among strangers."[13]

It was the black community in Canada West as much as white charities that rose to the occasion. For one thing, many were "sympathizing friends" who had made the trek — and leap — themselves. Mitchell further explained: "The coloured population are expected by the white citizens to perform these duties, or at least bear the burden of it, from their identity with the sufferers."[14] So the refugee community took on the care of blacks at the end of their migration.

Most of Canada's black communities were hardly in a position to extend the economic assistance required, as many of them were struggling themselves. Scores of Afro-Canadians lived in isolated, stand-alone outposts dotting the northern U.S. border. Despite dire circumstances, these communities welcomed runaways who turned up on their doorsteps, extending themselves to their fugitive brethren.

Several of these all-black settlements were founded to promote economic self-help and social justice. In 1842 the Reverend Hiram Wilson supervised the purchase of a vast farm north of Chatham in Canada West. Christened Dawn, the farm was sponsored by the American Missionary Association. Rev. Wilson and Josiah Henson, a fugitive slave who later published his memoirs, hoped to create a utopian community in the wilderness.

Within a decade of its founding, Dawn boasted 150 households, including Henson's own. He had moved to Canada at the age of forty, bringing his large family with him. But Rev. Wilson's dream to have a local "manual labor school" create economic independence for the town was not realized; the school was unable to become self-supporting, and the community was faltering by the 1860s.[15]

More successful was Elgin, a settlement that originated when Irish missionary William King freed fifteen slaves and bought roughly 10,000 acres for the use of newly freed blacks. Elgin grew into a town with more than 300 families, an island of black enterprise. These communities filled up with ex-slaves in search of new homes during the 1840s and 1850s.

Former slaves who ended up in larger Canadian communities, where blacks and whites lived in proximity to each other, generally fared better than blacks in separate settlements. In Toronto, as well as in several small towns along the border, former slaves and free black migrants created thriving ghettos within primarily white populations. Despite residential segregation, black immigrants integrated themselves into the larger local economies and made permanent inroads.

By the middle of the century, Chatham, a port of entry into Canada West, was a boomtown, abustle with steamers. Chatham supported two "colored churches," a Baptist and a Methodist congregation, and a black newspaper. The town's population was roughly one-third black.[16] (A brother and a niece of Tubman's would later settle in this prosperous town.)

Chatham streets were dotted with Afro-Canadian shopkeepers, and black builders and blacksmiths flourished. As in the United States, blacks distinguished themselves in the service industries, earning loyal clients as milliners and seamstresses. Rev. Mitchell exclaimed that Chatham was "the headquarters of the Negro race in Canada. . . . [It boasted] the largest, if not the best conducted Sunday School in Canada among the colored people."[17]

The actual number of blacks in Canada during the first half of the nineteenth century is unknown. One chronicler complained that accurate estimates were impossible because census takers did not bother with "designation of colour."[18] Afro-Canadians themselves nearly always suggested population figures that were dramatically higher than official statistics. A black promoter of fugitive slave settlement in Canada argued that by 1860 there were 35,000 to 40,000 American blacks in exile.[19] A professor of divinity at Toronto College during this era suggested a number as high as 60,000 ex-slaves in residence in the 1850s.[20]

In the decade that followed the Fugitive Slave Law of 1850, however, there was a demonstrable spike in the number of blacks found in Canada. The 1850 Canadian census recorded a mere 10,000 blacks in the region. The numbers may have increased as much as fourfold during the following decade. Yet scholars also estimate that the black population declined to only 20,000 by 1861, suggesting that most refugees eventually returned to the United States.

Even with all these competing estimates, throughout the nineteenth century blacks in Canada never exceeded more than 1 percent of the population.[21] The overwhelming majority of these blacks were clustered into Canada West settlements along the border. Nearly half the Afro-Canadians in the 1850s were U.S.-born.

Contact with these early exile communities led Harriet Tubman to settle for part of the year in Canada. Why she chose St. Catharines, a smaller community with Lake Ontario to the north and the Welland Lock on its canal to the southeast, is not known. When Tubman arrived, there were fewer than 300 blacks in the town, with a total population of 2,500. But a decade later the black population had nearly doubled — and half of St. Catharines' blacks were American-born.[22] However, this was slack growth compared with that of other border towns. St. Catharines failed to thrive, one observer suggested, because "the community has been left without competent teachers to instruct the people."[23]

When Tubman, in her late twenties, first arrived in Canada, she might have learned to read during long winters, had there been teachers in St. Catharines. But the business of helping fugitives acclimate to their new surroundings was work enough. After she came across the border each December, Tubman labored long and hard for her family, chopping wood to earn money for food.[24] She had a growing community of southern fugitives looking to her for assistance, and increasing numbers of family who followed her north.

Over the course of her time in Canada, Tubman was able to guide a steady stream of family members — at least five siblings, one grown niece, and eventually her parents — to this safe haven. Whatever its shortcomings, Canada offered her permanent refuge from slavery and allowed a renewed and ongoing relationship with kin, something she had dreamed of from the moment she crossed over to freedom.

Harriet's brother James Isaac (who took the last name Stewart) and his family shared a home in Chatham with the Bowley family, Harriet's niece Kizzy, now known as Mary Anne, and her husband and children.

James Isaac's wife, Kate, gave birth to their son Elijah in March 1853, who joined an older brother, James Henry. A few months later, in Decem-

ber, Mary Anne and John's infant son, Harkless, joined the family —
which included twin brothers, Herbert and Hercules, and a sister, Dorothy. Seeing these nephews born into freedom, having them grow up in a
household spared the fears that haunted children of bondage, must have
been a blessing and a continuing inspiration for Tubman.

While she could not erase the pain of the loss of her sisters or her own
husband, Tubman might take pride in her exertions. One of her lost sister's
grandsons was born into freedom, and lived with his reunited family far
outside slavery's reach.

For Tubman, the winter of 1851–52, her first in Canada West, was
particularly difficult. The weather was bitterly cold. This created hardships
for all refugees from the South, but especially recent arrivals. Poorly
clothed and indigent, exiles earned their keep by chopping wood and finding odd jobs in the community. Many died of respiratory illnesses related
to the harsh weather.[25] Those who survived depended heavily on charity.

A white doctor in St. Catharines who treated many of the refugees reported high rates of bronchitis and other pulmonary infections.[26] But for
every person who claimed the climate was unendurable for African Americans, there were those who countered: "Our people find the climate here
pretty tough for the first winters, but we get used to it after a while."[27] One
fugitive who escaped to St. Catharines confided in a letter to his wife back
in Queen Anne's County, Maryland: "The talk of cold in this place is all
humbug, it is wormer [sic] here than it was there when I left you."[28]

Debate over Canada West's racial climate was much more heated than
over its arctic winters. One St. Catharines woman, ex-slave Susan Boggs,
confessed: "If it was not for the Queen's law, we would be mobbed here. . . .
The prejudice is a great deal worse here than it is in the States." A Mrs.
Brown of St. Catharines reiterated: "I find more prejudice here than I did in
York State [New York]. When I was at home, I could go anywhere; but here,
my goodness! You get an insult on every side. But the colored people have
their rights before the law; that is the only thing that has kept me social."[29]

Despite legal protections, the Reverend L. C. Chambers of St.
Catharines rankled at racist slights:

I went to a church one Sabbath, and the sexton asked me, "What do you want here to-day?" I said, "Is there not to be service here to-day?" He said, "Yes, but we don't want any niggers here." I said, "You are mistaken in the man. I am not a nigger, but a negro."[30]

Black refugees complained that racism created a perpetual battleground. One black homebuilder's house was torn down each night by whites, as he tried to rebuild it by day, in an all-white neighborhood. The Reverend Mr. Proudfoot of London, Ontario, explained that racial bias was a U.S. import, and disingenuously suggested: "It is not a British feeling; it does not spring from our people, but *from your people coming over here.*"[31] It was true that Parliament abolished slavery within all British colonies in 1833 — and by the time Tubman came to call Canada home, most slaveholders knew they would be denied extradition for fugitives. But whether racism was a U.S. import or not, guaranteed legal freedom remained a fantastic advantage, one that Tubman, her family, and her flocks came to cherish.

Harriet's friend and biographer Sarah Bradford recounted the story of a fugitive named Joe, who had first met Tubman at a friend's cabin in Dorchester County and was later to accompany her north. Joe was apparently a very valuable slave to his master, and advertisements for Joe's return offered rewards as high as $2,000, "and all expenses clear and clean for his body in Easton jail."[32]

Joe was among the party of fugitives who hid in the bricklayers' wagons crossing the checkpoint at the bridge near Wilmington. When Joe and the rest of Tubman's party finally reached New York City, posters with Joe's description and notice of the steep reward could be found plastered everywhere. The fugitive fell into a gloomy silence after Harriet and her flock left Manhattan. He had wanted to walk all the way to Canada. Because he was with such a large group, Tubman insisted that they travel by rail, at least for the last leg of the journey.

Tubman would always lead the fugitives in song when they reached the suspension bridge that would take her party across the Niagara into

Canada. All but Joe crowded to the train windows to view the magnificent Niagara Falls, which signaled the passage from danger into safety.

Only when they stepped onto Canadian soil did Joe begin to sing, surrounded by a welcoming crowd as he offered his thanks to God for being delivered. Joe announced he had made his last journey until he ventured into heaven, not an uncommon sentiment.[33]

While Tubman and others plotted raids and escapes, transporting scores of fugitives across the border, the Afro-Canadian community was becoming even more diverse and sophisticated. A trickle of free blacks came as pioneer reformers, such as Mary Ann Shadd Cary, who arrived the very same year as Harriet Tubman. Born the daughter of New Jersey abolitionists, this well-educated young black woman attended an emigrationist convention in Toronto. At the age of twenty-nine, she decided to relocate in Canada.

Cary headed for the wilds across the lake from Detroit. She was welcomed by Henry Bibb, who had fled to Canada in 1850. Bibb hoped the vibrant émigré would help him run his school and his fledgling newspaper, *Voice of the Fugitive*. But she had plans of her own.[34] In 1851 Cary established an interracial school in Windsor. She found herself toting her own firewood and collecting only ten dollars in wages after eight months. As a fallback, she applied to the American Missionary Association for funding. The all-male ministerial board promised her a generous salary of $125 per year, but church sponsorship involved her in bitter sectarian disputes, which eventually forced her to close down her school by 1853.

In the meantime she wrote *A Plea for Emigration, or Notes for Canada West,* which appeared in 1852. Cary urged resettlement where "land is cheap, business increasing . . . and no complexional or other qualification in existence."[35] She offered public lectures, one of fewer than a handful of African American women to earn fame on the speakers' platform. In the United States, Frances Ellen Watkins Harper and Sojourner Truth were the only others who had gained similar notoriety.

Cary launched her own four-page broadsheet, *The Provincial Freeman.*

(Samuel Ward was listed as editor, but Cary, in fact, ran the paper.) On the occasion of the journal's second anniversary, William Still, the dynamic leader of the Philadelphia UGRR, congratulated her: "How you have thus long and well succeeded is to me a matter of wonder."[36]

She lost favor among abolitionist circles in 1855, when she exposed corruption among those who managed funds for the refugees. She accused Hiram Wilson of using charitable donations to build himself a large brick mansion. The abolitionists did not want dirty linen aired, and she became an outcast among the Canadian reform establishment.

Cary and Tubman both spent time in and around St. Catharines; indeed Cary was married there. Yet there is no record of contact between the two women, just the remarkable example of both distinct means of pursuing the fight against slavery. Cary took up her pen to help refugees, concentrating on community building among Afro-Canadians. Harriet Tubman carried a pistol for her work, returning again and again to bring fugitives to the free black communities that Cary, among others, was struggling to improve. Whatever its shortcomings, Canada offered African Americans hopes denied by their homeland. As Samuel Ward confessed: "The freedom of my adopted country works as an antidote to the moral poisons of slavery and the prejudice of my native country."[37]

During her Canadian interlude, Harriet's family stood behind her, and many by her side. In an interview in 1855, she observed: "I have seen hundreds of escaped slaves, but I never saw one who was willing to go back and be a slave. . . . We would rather stay in our native land if we could be as free there as we are here."[38]

## Chapter Eight

# Trouble in Canaan

Awake, awake; millions of voices are calling you!
Your dead fathers speak to you from their graves.
Heaven, as with a voice of thunder, calls on you
to arise from the dust. Let your motto be resistance!
— *Rev. Henry Highland Garnet*

————◄o►————

HARRIET TUBMAN'S DREAM to reunite all her family was blighted by chance, by happenstance — but, most of all, by the impact of an aggressive slave power, gaining influence in the halls of Congress. As blacks and whites worked behind the scenes on the Underground Railroad, a growing band of abolitionists believed that vocal public opposition to slavemongers was necessary to shape national debates.

While Tubman and other UGRR agents toiled to free slaves soul by soul, antislavery propagandists mounted increasingly vehement abolitionist campaigns to try to liberate the entire race. Both of these radical movements raised important issues and expanded consciousness about this moral dilemma. Yet nothing could even come close to captivating the public's imagination as did a work of fiction, first serialized in an antislavery journal but then published as a novel in March 1852: Harriet Beecher Stowe's *Uncle Tom's Cabin.*

The book became an international sensation, selling nearly a million copies in its first twelve months. A contemporary exclaimed, "What truth could not accomplish, fiction did, and Harriet Beecher Stowe has had the satisfaction of throwing a firebrand into the world."[1] Stowe's novel swayed thousands of middle-class whites to sympathize with the plight of slaves. Eliza's flight from the bloodhounds, with her baby in her arms, leaping from ice floe to ice floe, galvanized ordinary Americans into condemning slavery. *Uncle Tom's Cabin* (which prompted a white southerner's literary counterpoint, *Aunt Phillis's Cabin*) stimulated serious intellectual disputes and emotional discussions in parlors and kitchens. Yet the battle over freedom continued to be an abstract principle debated within the well of the Senate.

The country was thrown into renewed political upheaval with congressional deliberations over the Kansas-Nebraska Act. This proposed legislation would ratify "popular sovereignty," so that voters in a territory could determine by ballot a state's free or slave status. Abolitionists were outraged and threatened to ignore the Fugitive Slave Law in retaliation. An Ohio newspaper railed: "We propose to let the southern gentlemen catch their own negroes."[2]

On May 24, 1854, just two days after the Kansas-Nebraska Act's passage, six men in Boston seized fugitive Anthony Burns. The local vigilance committee organized a rescue attempt, forming a mob reminiscent of those who liberated Jerry Henry in Syracuse three years before, but on a much larger scale. Not only did this Boston rescue fail, but a constable named Batchelder was killed in the struggle. Abolitionists aggressively asserted that if the man who struck down Batchelder was guilty of murder, then so was George Washington and so "were all those who wielded swords and bayonets under him, in defence of liberty."[3]

In the wake of this bloody assault, artillery was wheeled in and soldiers surrounded the building where Burns was confined. Poet Henry Wadsworth Longfellow complained of Boston, "The air is pestilential with this fugitive-slave case."[4] On May 30, African American Charlotte Forten wrote in her diary: "His trial is still going on and I can scarcely think of anything else."[5]

Burns's owner wanted to negotiate a price for his slave's freedom, as had happened a dozen years before in the case of George Latimer. But times had changed, and the federal government decided to make an example of Burns, to stage a show trial. Forten reported in despair on June 1: "Our worst fears are realized; the decision was against poor Burns."[6]

Thousands of observers crowded the streets of Boston to watch Burns being marched to the wharf. Businesses were shuttered throughout downtown, and shop windows lining the route were draped in black. A group of antislavery men hoisted an empty black coffin and toted it around to symbolize the death of liberty.

The city became a stage set for antislavery drama, but the government employed elaborate props as well: row upon row of armored police, companies of marines, mounted cavalry. Soldiers with drawn swords formed a phalanx around their lone black prisoner, leading him to walk the plank onto a Virginia-bound ship. Charlotte Forten was indignant that the government would employ troops on behalf of the rights of slaveholders.[7]

Thousands stood mute at the spectacle of Burns being carried back to slavery. Many, like eyewitness Martha Russell, were deeply affected:

> Did you ever feel every drop of blood in you boiling and seething, throbbing and burning, until it seemed you should suffocate? Did you ever set your teeth hard together to keep down the spirit that was urging you to do something to cool your indignation that good and wise people would call violence — treason.[8]

The event would have a powerful ripple effect, as hundreds and then thousands began to rethink their positions after witnessing Burns's disheartening fate.

Poet John Greenleaf Whittier was so roused by his feelings that he wrote to firebrand abolitionist editor William Lloyd Garrison, with whom he had broken years before — but with whom he wished to reconcile. Whittier pleaded, "We must do what has never been done, convert the North. We must use this sad and painful occasion for this purpose. We must forget all past differences, and unite our strength."[9]

Against this backdrop, Tubman persevered. Between 1854 and 1856 she engineered countless missions to rescue fugitives, and mounted campaigns to improve the lives of Canadian refugees. Despite physical disabilities and the dangers her vocation afforded, she remained tireless.

Although he worried about her safety, Thomas Garrett was still collecting money for Tubman's raids. Abolitionists responded generously to stories of her exploits. Even women as far away as England were touched enough by tales of Moses' travails to regularly pass the collection plate for her.

In November 1856 Tubman stopped in Wilmington with a group of four men and one woman, en route to Canada via New York. Garrett commented on the steep reward slaveholders placed on the heads of these fugitives: "2600 dollars offered in the Baltimore *Sun.*" (He also boasted, "My slave list is now 2038.")[10] During this Delaware visit, Tubman told Garrett that she would deliver her charges across the border and return within a matter of weeks.

Nearly four months later, with no word of her, Garrett confessed to William Still:

> I have been very anxious for some time past, to hear what has become of Harriet Tubman. The last I heard of, she was in the State of New York on her way to Canada with some friends, last fall. Has thee seen or heard anything of her lately? It would be a sorrowful fact, if such a hero as she, should be lost from the Underground Rail Road. I have just received a letter from Ireland, making inquiry respecting her.[11]

The continuing silence alarmed Garrett: "Poor Harriet, I fear something has happened to her."[12]

Shortly thereafter, he received assurances from Still in Philadelphia that Tubman was "well, and contemplates making a visit South this week."[13] Once again, Harriet Tubman was restored to the UGRR circuit, keeping fugitives trickling northward.

In the summer of 1857, she undertook perhaps her most dangerous mission: returning to the Eastern Shore of Maryland to assist her elderly parents to abandon their home. Tubman's UGRR colleagues feared she was pushing her luck, returning where she might too easily be spotted and authorities would be on the lookout.

Tubman's parents did not need any rescue from slavery per se, because they were technically free. Ben Ross had been emancipated by his master's will, designated free in 1840. In 1855 he was finally able to purchase his wife's freedom for a token sum of $20.[14]

But the Rosses were separated from most of their children. A half dozen of their children and numbers of grandchildren had taken refuge in Canada. They despaired ever hearing any news of their two daughters sold south decades before. The couple grew lonelier with each passing year. But it was not just loneliness that drove them from their Maryland home in the late spring of 1857.

Ben Ross's house had been a temporary hideout for escaped slaves, an increasingly dangerous proposition. In March of 1857, Henry Predo, of Harriet's own Bucktown, Maryland, was threatened with the auction block by his master. To forestall the sale, Predo organized a group of fugitives, planning to escape with seven others. After the band fled, a reward of $3,000 proved too tempting for a local Delaware man. Pretending to be a UGRR conductor, he handed the fugitives over to Dover authorities.

Locked up in prison, the Dover Eight nevertheless managed a jailbreak. Soon the countryside was filled with posses and bloodhounds.[15] A black UGRR worker described the rescue in a letter to William Still:

> We put them throug, we hav to carry them 19 miles and cum back the sam night wich makes 38 mils. It is tou much for our little horses. We must do the best we can, ther is much Bisness dun on this Road. We hav to go throw dover and smerny, the two wors places this sid of mary land lin. If you have herd or sean them ples let me no. I will Comto Phila be for long and then I will call and se you. There is much to do her. Ples to wright, I Remain your friend.[16]

The Dover fugitives made it to safety, but the Maryland authorities were bent on revenge.

In April 1857 a free black minister in Dorchester County, Samuel Green, was investigated by authorities, suspected of having harbored the Dover Eight. Green had been a local preacher of some repute when Araminta was growing up.

During the excitement over the Dover jailbreak, Green's home was searched by the local constable but yielded no incriminating evidence — except a copy of *Uncle Tom's Cabin.* Under Maryland law, it was a crime for an African American to possess the book. Green was prosecuted and convicted. Because of his high profile within the black community, he was given an unusually harsh sentence: ten years in jail.[17] This punishment was meant to send a message to those who would dare harbor fugitives: they would be prosecuted, with or without evidence, if suspected of such crimes.

Indeed Ben Ross had sheltered the Dover Eight while they were in flight, and feared he might be next. Reportedly, Dr. Anthony Thompson, Ben's employer and former slaveowner, warned him that if he didn't leave the region soon, he risked arrest. Although Ben and Rit were free, they had every reason to fear the dragnet was closing in on them.

Once her father was in custody, there would be nothing Harriet could do. So when Tubman received word through the UGRR grapevine of this imminent threat to her father, she planned a trip south.

Tubman knew her aging parents would be unable to walk by night and sleep by day, the usual escape method into Delaware. She also knew the short nights of summer presented danger. But she ignored her worries as she prepared for a June expedition — the only rescue operation of hers known to have taken place in summer.

She pulled together a rig to transport her parents. Thomas Garrett described their "old horse, fitted out in a primitive style with a straw collar, a pair of old chaise wheels, with a board on the axle to sit on, another board swung with ropes, fastened to the axle to rest their feet on."[18] In this contraption, keeping on the roads only at night, Harriet was able to smuggle Ben and Rit the eighty miles to Wilmington. From there Garrett gave them funds to travel by rail to join the rest of their family in Canada. He also sold the horse and sent the couple the proceeds.

The vigilance committee in Philadelphia reported that although both of the Rosses were elderly, "they seemed delighted at the idea of going to a free country to enjoy freedom, if only for a short time."[19] This "short time" turned into nearly twenty years for Benjamin Ross and even longer for his wife, Rit, who survived him.

Once they arrived in Canada, perhaps fearing an arrest warrant, the couple took the precaution of changing their last name from Ross to Stewart, just as five of their sons in Canada had done before them.

Upon arrival in St. Catharines, they were reunited with their five sons: Robert, James Isaac, William Henry, Henry, and Benjamin. It had been nearly seven years since the Rosses had set eyes on their granddaughter Mary Anne (Kizzy) Bowley. They were thrilled to meet, for the first time, their Canadian-born descendants: three-year-old great-grandson Harkless Bowley, three-year-old grandson Elijah Stewart (born to James Isaac), and Elijah's older cousin, William Henry Stewart Jr. It is hard to imagine how satisfying it must have been for Tubman to witness this family reunion.

With her parents safely ensconced in Canada, Tubman returned to plan another raid back into Maryland. According to family lore, Harriet still had one sister trapped on the Eastern Shore, the mother of three children. Because two of this sister's three children were separated from their mother by a distance of twelve miles, Tubman found it impossible to get all four family members in the same place at the same time. Allegedly, Tubman's enslaved sibling refused to leave unless all three children could accompany her.

This was a period of intense personal struggle for Harriet Tubman. When she made her new life in the North, when she saw what freedom could bring, she was determined to lead every member of her family out of the slave South. As many as three of the Ross children had been "sold south," but she persisted and rescued five siblings from Maryland. Perhaps because she had no prospects of a family of her own, she found it difficult to live without seeing every last one of her extended family shepherded to freedom.

Sometime late in 1858 or 1859, Senator William Seward, who had become an acquaintance and an admirer through the UGRR network, made Harriet a proposition. He would sell her a house in his hometown of Auburn, New York, offering flexible terms that she could afford. This would be a reward for her many nomadic years with the UGRR and give her a base of operation along upstate liberty lines.

Seward was a favorite son of Auburn. Born in 1801 in Orange County, New York, he married into one of the town's most prominent families when he wed Frances Miller in 1824. Her father, Elijah Miller, was a large landholder in Cayuga County, and the newlywed couple moved into the Miller mansion near the town center. Seward's fledgling law practice thrived.

The ambitious young attorney served in the New York state legislature before he was elected governor in 1838. Elevated to the U.S. Senate in 1848, Seward opposed the Compromise of 1850 and became a principled champion of antislavery. When he was reelected in 1855, he became a strong voice for the neophyte Republican Party and one of slavery's leading opponents in the national political arena (which cost him his party's nomination in 1860 and led to Lincoln's election). His home in Auburn, like Gerrit Smith's in Peterboro, was headquarters for antislavery activism.[20] The house and acreage he offered Harriet were part of his wife's vast inheritance from her father.

Auburn was the seat of Cayuga County, in upstate New York. It was the home of the New York State Prison, the town's main employer. During the 1850s Auburn's population never exceeded five thousand, with only a smattering of blacks scattered among the predominantly white farming community. Auburn's climate was quite challenging, as it was a common saying that there were only two seasons upstate, winter and the Fourth of July.[21]

The town had a small but fierce abolitionist circle and was known by the UGRR as a friendly port for slaves on the run. In summer slaves were hidden in the halls of the theological seminary. Seward's own home was also a depot. During the thirty years leading up to the Civil War, nearly five hundred slaves passed through Auburn. Most were sent to North

Weedsport, then to Fair Haven and west toward the Cayuga Bridge. Some slaves in flight might be sent to the nearby village of Sherwood, where Slocum Howland maintained a UGRR station.

Harriet Tubman knew Auburn fairly well, having spent time in Seward's elegant home. She found his offer of her own house on South Street serendipitous, because her parents were finding Canadian winters too long and harsh. They were happy to relocate in upstate New York. Ben and Rit Stewart were both free and, unlike most of their children, did not dread any slaveholder's recapture.

Tubman might have had other reasons for wanting to relocate back in the United States. One account maintained that she came back in defiant response to the 1857 Dred Scott decision, when the U.S. Supreme Court ruled that African Americans were not guaranteed rights as citizens and that slave status could not be outlawed by any state government. But there were perhaps more personal and compelling causes for this move.

Sometime shortly after Harriet secured her new house in Auburn, she made a trip south and brought back with her a young, light-skinned black girl. The then eight-year-old later told a descendant that the two of them traveled on a steamship and that her life began with "Aunt Harriet kidnapping her from her home on Eastern Shore Maryland." This would not be so remarkable but that she claimed she had been living as a free black in relatively comfortable circumstances, and further, Harriet "secretly and without so much as a by-your-leave took the little girl with her to her northern home." This departs radically from almost everything else reported about Harriet's life and actions, and is surrounded with curiosity.

According to her later reminiscences, this little girl was Harriet Tubman's niece, born in Maryland in 1850. She claimed to be the daughter of one of Harriet's brothers, a niece whom Harriet adopted and raised as her own. She is identified variously as Margaret Tubman and as Margaret Stewart. According to Margaret, when she was eight years old, she was removed without permission from the home she shared with her parents and siblings, including a twin brother. It seems unbelievable that Harriet would have kidnapped a child without telling the girl's parents her intentions.

The action is even more incomprehensible if Margaret was the daughter of a "free" brother. Of course, his wife could have been a slave, which would have meant the child's status was "chattel," and it would have made sense for Harriet to rescue her flesh and blood from possible sale. But why just take the girl and not her twin brother? And not her mother as well?

Perhaps as the child was growing into a comely young girl, Harriet feared for her safety, but eight seems a bit young for rescue from sexual predators, even by antebellum slaveholding standards.

In fact, Margaret claimed that neither her mother nor any of her siblings had ever been slaves because her grandfather on her mother's side had bought his wife and children's "time," and they were ostensibly free. Of course, Tubman was wary of such distinctions, as she had seen what might happen in these cases to slaves who thought they were free but found themselves or their children sold away.

Margaret also indicated that her father — supposedly Harriet's brother — was a free man. There is no reference to any of Harriet's siblings in Maryland being emancipated. Further, Margaret's father remains unidentifiable among any list of Tubman's siblings — and her mother's name does not appear in any records either.

Margaret had only a single memory of her early years in Maryland: her family had a pair of chestnut horses and a shiny carriage. She claimed to have begun life in a prosperous black household, even though residing in a slave state. She also claimed that she was so enchanted by accompanying her aunt Harriet on a steamboat "that she forgot to weep over her separation from her twin brother, her mother, and the shiny carriage she liked so much."

What could have possessed Harriet Tubman to make such a move? Margaret's daughter Alice later confided that Harriet knew she was in the wrong, because back in Maryland where the child had been abducted, Tubman's actions caused "sorrow and anger." Alice is one of the few sources for insight into Tubman's personal life. Alice was close to Harriet and wrote a series of letters about her famous relative.[22]

Alice Lucas was born in Auburn in 1900, her mother's final child, and spent her childhood in Harriet's company during her great-aunt's declining years. The young girl enjoyed listening to Harriet reminisce as she sat in her rocker or her wheelchair in later years. Margaret remained her aunt's favorite, and presumably Alice inherited this favored status. (Alice was the grandniece selected to play a part in the unveiling of a marker honoring Harriet at the Cayuga County Courthouse during its dedication in 1914.)

Alice speculated that when Tubman spent time with young Margaret during a visit in Maryland (on one of her clandestine forays perhaps), she "saw the child she herself might have been if slavery had been less cruel." Further, she intimated that Harriet "knew the joys of motherhood would never be hers and she longed for some little creature who would love her for her own self's sake." Both of these might be true, but they do not offer a satisfactory explanation of why Tubman would kidnap a child.

Alice acknowledged that stealing Margaret (her mother) was a selfish, indulgent act. Harriet "knew she had taken the child from a sheltered good home to a place where there was nobody to care for her." After adopting Margaret, Harriet entrusted this little girl to Frances Seward, William Seward's wife, to be raised in her household in Auburn. Alice reported, "This kindly lady brought up Mother not as a servant but as a guest within her home. She taught Mother to speak properly, to read, write, sew, do housework and act as a lady."

This may seem like an unusual arrangement, but it was not remarkable among white abolitionists for someone to open their home to a child of color during this era. When Frederick Douglass went off to England in 1845, his oldest daughter, Rosetta, was left in the care of cousins of abolitionist Lucretia Mott.[23] While Rosetta moved in with a white family in Albany, her younger siblings remained with their mother in Rochester. Perhaps it was part of the antislavery cultural landscape that young black women were imported into abolitionist households for cultivation and refinement. But what were the repercussions?

Alice confided that when Harriet was in town, "Mother was dressed and sent in the Seward carriage to visit her." (And so Margaret was reunited with a fancy carriage, of which she was so fond.) During these intermittent visits, Harriet presumably rejoiced in Margaret's poise, demeanor, and improvement. Margaret remained in residence with the Sewards, even with her grandparents, Ben and Rit, living in the same town.

Margaret was looked after by Lazette Worden, Frances Seward's widowed sister.[24] When Lazette moved back to Auburn in the 1850s following her husband's death, she became her sister Frances's constant comfort and companion.[25]

There is also evidence to suggest that Margaret accompanied members of the family to Washington when Seward was appointed secretary of state by Abraham Lincoln. She may have been in the Seward family's D.C. house when an assassin attempted to murder the secretary of state in his bed on April 14, 1865, the same night that Lincoln was shot.[26]

The mystery of Margaret's identity and status only deepens. Clearly she had a special role within Harriet's extended family, and collateral descendants reported that this was because she was Harriet's favorite niece. Yet some family members offered discordant notes.

In the late 1930s, biographer Earl Conrad wrote to Tubman's niece Katy Stewart Northup, a descendant of Harriet's brother James Isaac Stewart and one of three heirs named in Harriet's will. Conrad asked about the family tree. Northup wrote back that Alice Lucas Brickler was "of no relation neither by blood or through marriage."[27] She warned that no one could rely on any information this "impostor" might supply. Since Alice was clearly Margaret's daughter, Northup's claim must have had something to do with Margaret's complicated place within the family history.

When pressed to respond to this charge, Alice Lucas Brickler was somewhat evasive. She argued that because of the "disappeared" family members in the Deep South (at least two sisters and perhaps one brother) as well as relatives who continued to live in Maryland, many might come forward to claim kinship with Tubman who were completely unknown to those who had resettled in the North. This, of course, was not the case with either Katy Stewart or Margaret's daughter Alice: they were both the offspring of persons rescued from the South by Harriet. They most likely had contact with each other at some time in upstate New York.

But Alice finally confessed that "there is part of the family history that is better never told . . . the family is divided as to color." Alice explained that her mother took pride in her light color "to the point of being snobbish," and that some family members "whenever Aunt Harriet was out of hearing" would taunt her for it. She was called a "pumpkin colored hussey." This seems to suggest that aspersions were being cast about her heritage, perhaps even hinting at illegitimacy. Of course, such a label was rendered largely meaningless by slavery.

Alice more than once explicitly commented that her mother bore a striking resemblance to Harriet Tubman. Considering that Tubman was always referred to as dark-skinned and Margaret was distinctly light-skinned, this might mean that other facial features were remarkably similar. This could suggest a kinship closer than aunt and niece. She further suggested that Margaret's personality was so much like Tubman's that aspects of her character may have been "hereditary."

What can be made of this puzzle, the relationship of this mysterious Margaret to Harriet Tubman? Margaret was said to have been born in 1850 and was the alleged twin of a nephew of Harriet's. But of this twin and of her parents there is no evidence. (And there is no suggestion of any renewed contact after the Civil War, when many black families were reunited.)

Harriet and Margaret shared a lifelong bond, but as a child Margaret was put out with a white family until Harriet settled down in Auburn after the Civil War. Family resentments about Margaret — some even within Harriet's own household labeled her a "hussey" — suggest she had airs. None of this mattered to Harriet, who saw Margaret happily married to Auburn caterer Henry Lucas, mother of seven, living a very full and rich family life.

Is it possible that Margaret was some other relation to Harriet, other than niece? Is it possible that she was a daughter? The child was born around 1850, shortly before or immediately after Harriet left her Maryland home. If Harriet had been pregnant with a child, the child would have been born into slavery if her mother gave birth in a slave state. If the baby had been fathered by John Tubman, surely he would have been more understanding of Harriet's need to flee the Eastern Shore for freedom?

Would he not have accompanied Harriet or helped facilitate her escape for the sake of their child?

If, however, her child was fathered by someone else, perhaps Harriet wanted to conceal her pregnancy. Because Margaret was light-skinned, there is every reason to believe that one of her parents might have been white. Perhaps this also would explain John Tubman's alienation of affection. Even if a slave woman became pregnant by another man because of rape, there is evidence that some black men were unwilling to be understanding of the situation.

There is no reason to believe that Harriet was involved in any consensual affair, especially considering her devastation at her husband's involvement with another woman. Could she have been a victim of rape? Could this have propelled her out of the South, as much as any other motivation?

Could Harriet have had a daughter and kept her hidden? Again, the details of her journey to freedom are unknown. Did she perhaps give birth, then leave this infant behind with a free family while she fled to Canaan, planning to return for her once she found stability in the North? If this was the case, then her removal of the child makes some kind of sense. In such a scenario, taking Margaret would have been a recovery rather than an abduction. Several puzzle pieces might then fit into place, including Harriet's decision to return again and again to Maryland — perhaps on these sojourns she took time to see the child she had left behind.

There is of course no proof to substantiate this scenario, just a circumstantial timeline and some comments handed down in family lore. There is no evidence to suggest anything more than that Margaret was Harriet's niece, as was reported by several descendants.[28] There are too many missing pieces to verify any other claim.

Several collateral descendants did acknowledge that Margaret held a special place in Harriet Tubman's heart, that she was a constant and compelling presence in Harriet's life in upstate New York. Family lore insists it was Harriet's deep need for this particular child that led her to steal the child north, but no reasonable motive has been uncovered. The mystery remains as to why Harriet Tubman would kidnap a child simply because she formed an attachment to her.

By 1858 Harriet Tubman seemed to be building herself a more settled life in freedom — to replace the vagabond and dangerous one she had led for the past decade. Perhaps she wanted to take up residence in her new home in Auburn. With nearly all of her family rescued, with her parents resettled comfortably in upstate New York and her adopted daughter Margaret nearby, perhaps Harriet saw herself as stepping off the UGRR, giving up life as an abductor, perhaps retiring to the role of stationmaster.

At age thirty-three, she could slip comfortably into this new routine, settle in with her parents and little Margaret. Even if this were part of her plan — and even if events conspired to facilitate such a shift — still Tubman would have known the war on slavery was not cooling off, but rather coming to a boil.

Her former home along the Eastern Shore was abuzz over 1857's dramatic events: the Dover jailbreak in the spring, the removal of Tubman's parents in the summer, and then, in the autumn, waves of fugitives heading north. In the month of October nearly sixty slaves from the Dorchester County region alone made it to Philadelphia, nearly forty recruited by Tubman herself. On November 2 local slaveholders met in Cambridge, Maryland, to find a way to stem the tide of escaping blacks northward.[29] Their main target was Tubman herself.

But the waves could not be turned back. Fugitives throughout the South, especially in the border regions, were striking out for liberty and a safe haven beyond slavery's reach. Hundreds if not thousands wanted to follow Tubman. The war against slavery was catching fire. This was especially true when Harriet crossed paths with a man whose determination and valor seemed destined to match her own: John Brown.

## Chapter Nine

# Crossroads at Harpers Ferry

*The first I see is General Tubman . . .*
—*John Brown*

————◄○►————

JUST AS HARRIET TUBMAN had breathtaking dreams about her encounters with freedom, so she had dramatic visions of John Brown before she ever met him. When she was introduced to Brown in 1858, she felt she had known him for a long time. After their first encounter in person, she acknowledged Brown's powerful influence over her. Tubman described the dream that foreshadowed their meeting:

> I was in a wilderness sort of place, all rocks and bushes, when a big snake raised his head from behind a rock, and while I looked, it changed into the head of an old man with a long white beard on his chin, and he looked at me wishful like, just as if he was going to speak to me.

Before he could speak, a crowd of men rushed in and struck him down, while the "old man looked at me so wishful." This dream repeated itself several times. Brown's, she decided, was the "wishful face" of this particular dream.[1]

John Brown and Harriet Tubman first met in Canada in April of 1858. Just as she might have been planning to wind down her own fight against slavery, along came John Brown's elaborate plot to stage an uprising that might lead to a full-scale war. When Brown outlined his ideas to Harriet Tubman, she was deeply supportive. Her encouraging and thoughtful suggestions won him over. He felt buoyed by her faith, as thus far his plans had met with tepid approval, and he had been battered by abolitionists' skepticism.

Brown had a long and colorful career before meeting Tubman, but rather like her, he had undertaken a very personal crusade against slavery. John Brown had spent his entire life seeking a larger role in the world and found an outlet for his boundless passions within radical abolitionism. Born in Torrington, Connecticut, in 1800, Brown spent his early years on the Ohio frontier, before completing his education at schools in Massachusetts and Connecticut. Married at the age of twenty, he worked as a tanner to support his wife and children. In 1832 Brown's first wife, Dianthe, died after giving birth to their seventh child, who also died soon after. In 1835 he moved to Ohio with his children and his new wife, Mary, where he spent the next five years involved in land speculation.

His children grew up impressed by their father's commitment to racial equality. Brown's older daughter, Ruth, recalled her father "[asking] me how I would like to have some poor little black children that were slaves (explaining to me the meaning of slaves) come and live with us; and asked me if I would be willing to divide my food and clothes with them."[2] By attending church services side by side with African Americans, he signaled his commitment to racial equality. Brown railed against prevailing trends: "These ministers who profess to be Christian, and hold slaves or advocate slavery, I cannot abide them. My knees will not bend in prayer with them while their hands are stained with the blood of souls."[3]

In November 1837 Brown's antislavery convictions intensified in the wake of the murder of Elijah Lovejoy, a firebrand antislavery editor murdered by a mob while defending his printing press near Alton, Illinois. John Brown attended a meeting about Lovejoy's murder, and stood up to proclaim, "Here, before God, in the presence of these witnesses, from this time, I consecrate my life to the destruction of slavery!"[4]

Brown became obsessed with the overthrow of slavery — by any means necessary.[5] His views appeared in print in an abolitionist periodical, *The Ram's Horn,* which led to minor fame among antislavery radicals. Frederick Douglass interrupted a speaking tour in 1847 to meet up with Brown in Springfield, Massachusetts. At the time Brown was all fired up with plots, hoping to organize guerrilla bands in the Alleghenies. He believed he could induce slave rebellion by creating a mountain escape route for fugitives. Douglass commented in the *North Star* that although Brown was white, it was "as though his own soul had been pierced with the iron of slavery."[6]

In 1849, the same year that Harriet Tubman escaped to freedom, John Brown made his own move — to North Elba, New York, settling among blacks on Gerrit Smith's donated lands. In 1855, after the Kansas-Nebraska Act stirred up so much trouble, Brown took members of his clan to the Kansas frontier, where passions were running high.

Brown joined in the border wars over slavery. On the night of May 24, 1856, Brown was the instigator of an infamous raid, the Osawatomie Creek Massacre. Leading a band of abolitionists intent on revenge, Brown directed the executions of a handful of proslavery men. These victims were dragged from their homes in the dead of night, despite screams of mercy from wives and children. The offending males were hacked to death with knives — their exposed bodies left for gruesome discovery.

John Brown became even more committed to his violent course: "I have only a short time to live — only one death to die, and I will die fighting for this cause. There will be no more peace in this land until slavery is done for. I will give them something else to do than extend slave territory."[7]

Brown returned east from Kansas with his fame as a man of action preceding him. He sought recruits during a visit to Massachusetts. When he met with William Lloyd Garrison in Boston in 1856, he scorned the abolitionist editor's "milk and water" pacifism.[8] Brown so impressed the Reverend

Thomas Wentworth Higginson, chaplain of the Massachusetts legislature, that Higginson resigned his pastorate and wrote to a friend: "I expect to serve in Capt. John Brown's company in the next Kansas war, which I hope is inevitable and near at hand."[9]

In the early months of 1858, Brown revealed a dramatic and elaborate plot to Gerrit Smith and five others. Brown intended to recruit an abolitionist army to invade the slave South and foment a general slave uprising — he would strike the first blow in a great war for liberation. The abolitionists with whom he first shared his plan came to be known as the Secret Six: Gerrit Smith, Thomas Wentworth Higginson, Theodore Parker, George Stearns, Franklin Sanborn, and Samuel Gridley Howe. Brown hoped to enlist their support for his upcoming grand plan.

Franklin Sanborn wrote to Higginson in February 1858: "Treason will not be treason much longer, but patriotism. . . . Write me if you can do anything for B____."[10] Although they raised money for Brown's cause, none of the six was willing to join him on the actual invasion. During the months and weeks before Brown's failed uprising, these Secret Six were part of an expanding crowd who learned of Brown's plans. In May 1858 Howe wrote Higginson with alarm: "Wilson as well as Hale and Seward, and God knows how many more have heard about the plot."[11] Brown had cast his net so far and wide that more than *eighty* individuals scattered across the North became aware of his impending invasion.

Most felt Brown's scheme was a fanatic's fantasy, especially his pipe dream to create an independent, interracial state along the southeastern corridor of the United States. He envisioned the establishment of a brand-new government, and spent three weeks in 1858 penning his provisional constitution at Frederick Douglass's home in Rochester. His preamble began:

> Whereas, Slavery, throughout its entire existence in the United States, is none other than a most barbarous, unprovoked, and unjustifiable war of one portion of its citizens upon another portion . . .[12]

Frederick Douglass recognized there was little he could do to dissuade Brown from this foolhardy scheme.

Douglass's hesitation was understandable. His own letters and speeches were consistently full of retribution and bloodshed, but Douglass never actually participated in any such activities. In Pittsburgh in 1850 he condemned the Fugitive Slave Act, arguing "to make a dozen or more dead kidnappers . . . carried down South would cool the ardor of Southern gentlemen, and keep their rapacity in check."[13] Douglass continued his violent rhetoric throughout the 1850s, but his own ardor cooled considerably when Brown urged him to join his armed rebellion.

At the same time, Harriet Tubman reinforced her role as a woman of action when Brown shared his plans with her. The Reverend Jermain Loguen, of Syracuse, wrote to Brown:

> My dear friend and Bro
> I have your last letter from Canada. I was glad to learn that you and your brave men had got on to Chatham. . . . Have you got Harriet Tubman of St. Catherines [sic]?[14]

Indeed, Brown had enlisted Harriet Tubman during his April 1858 excursion. On his first trip north of the border, John Brown was galvanized by his encounter with "Moses," of whom he had heard so much.

First and foremost, Tubman shared Brown's impassioned hatred of slavery, which gave them a strong emotional and intellectual bond. Tubman had long viewed slavery as a sin, but under Brown's influence, she came to perceive slavery as a state of war.

Brown disdained abolitionists who were unwilling to take direct action against the slave power, and Tubman shared this antipathy. She, of course, had a spectacular record of action, with her string of UGRR rescues. Brown advocated armed resistance, even bloodshed when necessary, to free slaves. To date, Tubman had never been associated with any kind of insurrectionary plots (except for mass escapes), but she was clearly ready to shift gears.

Tubman focused her considerable energies on plans of military action. To that end, she offered up her extensive knowledge of the Virginia countryside. As a conductor on the liberty lines, she had made scores of contacts over the years. She would be able to provide John Brown with practical information for his operation.[15] To get the ball rolling, Brown paid Harriet twenty-five dollars in gold to use to locate recruits for him in Canada.[16] He was clearly as taken with her as she was with him. John Brown dubbed her General Tubman and referred to her by this military title in correspondence and conversation.

While Douglass remained skeptical about Brown's plottings, Tubman endorsed his agenda. Brown was jubilant:

> I am succeeding to all appearance beyond my expectation. . . . Harriet Tubman hooked on his [sic] whole team at once. He [Harriet] is the most of a man naturally; that I ever met with. There is the most abundant material; & of the right quality, in this quarter beyond all doubt.[17]

The language of Brown's response is, of course, striking. It reflected his own peculiar views on gender. Brown was an Old Testament patriarch, who condemned the second-class status of blacks but accepted women's subservient role.[18] When Brown put out a call for his constitutional convention, to be held in Chatham, Ontario, in May 1858, nearly fifty blacks gathered. The "cover" for this meeting was the formation of a Masonic lodge — which could explain why there were no women among the thirty-four blacks and twelve whites who convened. But there may have been other reasons the audience was all male.

Brown advocated the shedding of blood to end slavery. Brown watched as many men quaked over his plans; he doubted women could ever fully embrace his plots for armed resistance. He believed it was against their feminine natures. Brown's attitudes toward the female sex were so absolute that when confronted with a blatant exception to his rigid rule, he merely ignored the fact that Tubman was a woman — "transubstantiating" her into a male. He desperately needed her, so much so that he could only view her as General Tubman, an invaluable recruit for his army.

Brown required comrades-in-arms, not doubters like Douglass. Fear of betrayal added concerns. Brown decided to make a trial expedition in late 1858. He took his men and conducted a raid into Vernon County, Missouri, to rescue eleven slaves and transport them to Canada. One of the slaveholders involved was killed. Murder signified there would be no going back. Brown once again felt bloodshed was justified. As in Kansas two years before, Brown would be judge and executioner. He wanted his volunteers to taste danger, accept the challenge, and commit themselves without reservation.

There is no evidence that Tubman ever advocated violence. But at the same time she stood firmly behind Brown — and was fully aware of what the consequences might be. She never qualified her support of him. Throughout the summer of 1858, Tubman devoted her energies to Brown's sketchy enterprise. Tubman was eager to accompany him on an armed raid, convinced military operations against slavery were long overdue. Yet postponements in Brown's operation caused lost momentum.

Tubman was in Auburn during the fall of 1858. By winter, she was able to rendezvous again with Brown, in Boston. Although neither party left any record of their meeting, the abolitionist leader Wendell Phillips recalled, "The last time I ever saw John Brown was under my own roof, as he brought Harriet Tubman to see me, saying 'Mr. Phillips, I bring you one of the best and bravest persons on this continent — *General* Tubman, as we call her.'"[19] By this time the two were deeply committed to each other's agendas to bring about slavery's downfall.

Because of his desperate need for funds, Tubman promised to promote Brown's cause around New England, to use her reputation and powers of persuasion to open pocketbooks. During the spring and into the summer of 1859, she spent time lecturing and soliciting donations. With Tubman making headway in the North, Brown was biding his time for a strike at the South.

Brown's repeated delays and wanderings from Kansas to Missouri to

Iowa to Canada — then to Pennsylvania, Massachusetts, and New York — kept even his closest allies in a constant state of anxiety. The Canadian recruits from the Chatham convention had been poised for action for well over a year, but were unsure where and when to join up with Brown. While on a visit to Gerrit Smith the first week of June 1859, Tubman suggested that July 4 would be a propitious date for Brown's southern invasion.

By the middle of June, Tubman had moved east to Boston. She was in Worcester visiting Thomas Wentworth Higginson, who wrote:

> We have had the greatest heroine of the age here, Harriet Tubman, a black woman, and a fugitive slave. . . . She has had a reward of twelve thousand dollars offered for her in Maryland and will probably be burned alive whenever she is caught, which she probably will be, first of last, as she is going again.[20]

Higginson presented Tubman as "Moses" when she spoke at a Fourth of July oration in Framingham.

The audience was introduced to "a black woman of medium size, upper front teeth gone, smiling countenance, attired in coarse but neat apparel, with an old fashioned reticule or bag suspended by her side."[21] Once she began to speak, she held her audience spellbound. The secretary of the Massachusetts Anti-Slavery Society reported: "The mere words could do no justice to the speaker, and therefore we do not undertake to give them; but we advise all our readers to take the earliest opportunity to see and hear her."[22] A plate was passed, with almost forty dollars donated to John Brown's campaign at this one venue.

She delivered a rousing address to the New England Colored Citizens' Convention in Boston on August 1, 1859. Tubman was introduced on this occasion as "Harriet Garrison." She presumably used a pseudonym to prevent any trouble with bounty hunters prowling the Massachusetts capital. She took the name Garrison, as it would be recognized for what it was, a tribute to the famed abolitionist who bore the name.

While Tubman was on tour in New England, Brown settled near

Harpers Ferry, Virginia, with several of his sons. On August 19, Brown met with Douglass in Chambersburg, Pennsylvania (his backup headquarters), making a last-ditch appeal to persuade Douglass to join the plot. When Brown revealed the federal arsenal at Harpers Ferry as his target, Douglass warned it would be a "perfect steel trap." Brown was not dissuaded. He returned to Virginia without Douglass, but instead came back with black recruit Shields Green, who had come all the way from Rochester.

Brown had wanted to strike at Harpers Ferry on Independence Day, as Tubman had suggested. But he put off the assault until more weapons arrived. However, time and money were running out. By autumn his "army" was only a handful of followers, rather than the legions he had envisioned. Sanborn wrote to Higginson:

> He [Brown] is desirous of getting someone to go to Canada and collect recruits for him among the fugitives, with H. Tubman, or alone, as the case may be, & urged me to go, — but my school will not let me. Last year he engaged some persons & heard of others, but he does not want to lose time by going there himself now. I suggested you to him. . . . Now is the time to help in the movement, if ever, for within the next two months the experiment will be made.[23]

Tubman remained in Massachusetts. Unfortunately for Brown, no one had been able to get word to Tubman about the revised timetable. Even if Brown had been able to locate her by October, Tubman had taken ill. She was felled by a flare-up of an illness associated with her head injury. Just when Brown was finally prepared to launch his assault — with fewer than two dozen black and white men in tow — Tubman was bedridden in New Bedford.

Early on the morning of October 16, 1859, John Brown's men cut telegraph lines leading into Harpers Ferry and moved swiftly to secure the arsenal. Brown left a man in charge of protecting the Shenandoah Bridge (the main rail and wagon access into town), while he personally took charge of the primary target, the arsenal. Brown sent his remaining volunteers out into the countryside to scare up slaves, to urge them to flee into town, seize weapons, and join the battle for liberation. This was a key component of his plan, but despite the months and months of preparation, Brown had failed to do the proper advance work.

Harriet Tubman's expertise was sorely missed. She had met with great success operating within the slave states by patiently laying the groundwork for her raids, studying options and alternatives. Tubman infiltrated a region, gained the confidence of local blacks, and then put out the word about an upcoming flight northward. Her careful preparations and her meticulous arrangements proved invaluable. And although there were many times when she resorted to prayer to rescue her from a tight spot, more often she had multiple escape routes lined up as fallbacks. Perhaps John Brown, as a white man, felt more complacent in this respect.

Brown's entire operation depended upon the hope that hundreds of slaves in the surrounding Virginia countryside would rise up on his request to join the fight and help his small band overcome overwhelming odds. His theory was flawed and untested. Given his failure at recruiting followers in the past, he had no reason to expect they would suddenly materialize this time.

To make matters worse, Brown's grasp of military strategy was abysmal. As Douglass predicted, Harpers Ferry proved a steel trap. Ironically, the first man to fall in the confrontation was a free black, the baggage master at the local train station — a terrible omen for Brown's tactical strike.

After forty-eight hours of armed struggle, only Brown and three comrades remained within the arsenal, holding hostages. His rebellion had not inspired slaves to join in. Reaction from the countryside had been swift and strong, but only from Virginia whites hell-bent to repel invaders.

On October 18, with sixteen of his men dead or wounded, Brown tried to negotiate his way out. He demanded safe passage from the town for himself and his three men in exchange for the hostages. His request was met with a volley of gunfire. Federal troops commanded by Robert E. Lee and J.E.B. Stuart stormed the building. Wounded in the final assault, Brown was led bleeding and defeated into jail.

News of the raid spread like wildfire, and after Brown was captured, the story headlined newspapers throughout the country. Even though she had no idea about the timetable, Harriet Tubman had a premonition about Brown's disastrous outcome. On the actual day of the Harpers Ferry raid, she felt "something was wrong — she could not tell what. Finally she told her hostess that it must be Captain Brown who was in trouble and that they should soon hear bad news from him."[24] Shortly thereafter, she discovered that he had been captured.

Brown's defense committee, funded by abolitionist philanthropists, failed to secure his acquittal. After a brief trial, Brown was found guilty of treason. On November 2 he was sentenced to be hanged. When Brown mounted the gallows on December 2, the eyes of the nation were upon him. Overnight he became the most famous martyr of the antislavery cause. For many involved in abolitionist campaigns, Brown was far more valuable in death than in life. But not to Harriet Tubman.

Although many questioned Brown's sanity, and even those who admired him might condemn his methods, Tubman never wavered in her support. Franklin Sanborn said that many years after Brown's death, when Tubman encountered a bust of Brown's head in his Concord parlor, she was transported into a rapturous state of "ecstasy of sorrow and admiration."[25] Her enthusiasm for Brown remained boundless and she mourned the loss of such a comrade.

As with the demise of Nat Turner, Harriet Tubman chose to see Brown's execution as both symbolic and sacrificial. But of course Tubman had not known Turner. Brown was someone with whom she had felt a special kinship, and someone whose loss was deeply personal. She confided, "When I think how he gave up his life for our people, and how he never flinched, but was so brave to the end; its clear to me it wasn't mortal man, it was God in him."[26] Franklin Sanborn remembered that she saw Brown as Christ-like.[27]

In the North, Brown's heroic stature blossomed between his conviction and his death — and grew exponentially when Yankee martyrdom followed. A newspaper in Kansas reported: "It is safe to say that the death of no man in America has ever produced so profound a sensation."[28] Brown became the focus of writers and poets alike.[29] Walt Whitman wrote: "I was at hand, silent I stood with teeth shut close, I watch'd, I stood very near you old man, when cool and indifferent, but trembling with age and your unheal'd wounds you mounted the scaffold."[30]

Certainly Brown's great dignity at the trial, and the scores of letters he wrote following his capture, especially those written in the days before his death, moved many northern sympathizers. On the question of his "sanity," Brown's arrest granted him a composure he had never had as an agitator. His calm defeated critics who called him a crazed fanatic. He wrote to friends on this point:

> I may be *very insane;* (and I *am* so, if insane at all). I am not in the least degree conscious of my ravings, of my fears, or of any terrible visions whatever; but *fancy* myself entirely composed, and that my *sleep, in particular,* is as sweet as that of a healthy, joyous little infant. . . . I have scarce realized that I am in prison, or in irons, at all. I certainly think I was never more cheerful in my life.[31]

Brown's response to his impending martyrdom won thousands of admirers. Only four days before his execution, he wrote:

> It is a great comfort to feel assured that I am permitted to die for a cause, — not merely to pay the debt of nature, as all must. . . . My whole life before had not afforded me one half the opportunity to plead for the right. In this, also, I find much to reconcile me to both my present condition, and my immediate prospect.[32]

Many white southerners responded caustically to the prospect of Brown's martyrdom. A southern commentator in Kentucky's *Frankfort Yeoman* warned: "If old John Brown is executed, there will be thousands to dip their handkerchiefs in his blood; relics of martyr will be paraded throughout the North."[33]

The religious symbolism of Brown's death had a powerful effect on Harriet Tubman. Not only the power of his example moved her, but his death in some way reinforced her own prophetic powers, as she had witnessed his demise in a dream, when she saw the crowd of men striking him down.[34] Tubman took Brown's death as a sign that the time was drawing near for liberation. "When I think of all the groans and tears and prayers I've heard on plantations, and remember that God is a prayer-hearing God, I feel that his time is drawing near. He gave me my strength, and he set the North Star in the heavens; he meant I should be free."[35]

She found, however, like Brown, that others doubted the nearness of a reckoning. On a visit with black abolitionist Henry Highland Garnet in 1860, Harriet sang out, "My people are free. My people are free."

Garnet admonished, "My grandchildren may see the day of emancipation of our people, but neither you nor I."

Tubman retorted, "I tell you sir, you'll see it, and you'll see it soon."[36]

In the months following Brown's death and the death of his dream, it was difficult for Tubman to maintain optimism. She had spent over a decade on the liberty lines, watching North and South grow farther and farther apart. She had rescued hundreds, while millions still groaned under the lash. Tubman had hoped a charismatic leader like John Brown might lead the way out of the wilderness, but he had been struck down, executed by the slave power Tubman so hated.

Tubman knew his message could not be silenced: America would have a reckoning, because, as Brown preached, slavery was war. To honor his memory, Tubman vowed to carry on his legacy, to act in his stead. No matter how much Brown's death dispirited her, the fact that one white man was willing to die to free the slaves was a powerful psalm, one that could provide her Godspeed on the long journeys ahead.

During the spring of 1860, Gerrit Smith invited Harriet, at home in Auburn, to abolitionist meetings in Boston. While en route, Tubman stopped off in Troy, New York, to visit a relative. Her visit was serendipitous, as she became involved in her first public rescue of a fugitive slave.[37] She had labored long and hard, but Tubman felt God directed her always to do more. In the wake of Brown's passing, she vowed she would do more and, if necessary, proclaim what was right in the light of day, rather than under cover of darkness.

On April 27, Charles Nalle, an African American coachman, was being held by Troy authorities.[38] He had escaped from Virginia in 1858. By spring of 1860 his luck ran out when a Virginia slavecatcher came to reclaim him. This slavecatcher was none other than Nalle's own brother, a free black, paid to do dirty work for his slaveholding father. Nalle was being held in a federal commissioner's office at the Mutual Bank Building, at the corner of First and State Streets, when a large group of antislavery protestors began to gather.

As a precaution, observers were barred from the commissioner's courtroom, but Harriet Tubman had made a plan. She wrapped herself in a shawl and sought admission to the proceedings carrying a food basket. Her props helped her to appear elderly and innocuous (she was only thirty-four at the time), and gained her entrance to the second-floor proceedings. (It has been suggested that she might have been mistaken for a scrubwoman employed by the bank.)[39] She was standing at the back of the room when the decision was announced to ship Nalle back to Virginia.

When he heard his fate, Nalle scrambled out onto the window ledge high above the road, with a sea of supporters gathered below. However, bailiffs hauled him back indoors before he could jump. While Nalle's attorney rushed out to try to file an appeal, the presiding judge demanded that Nalle's guards keep a tight hold on the prisoner until transportation south might be arranged.

The crowd surrounding the bank building began to swell.[40] Harriet Tubman decided to test the commitment of the good people of Troy: would they rise to the occasion and help her strike a blow for freedom? She worried about getting Nalle down to the river. She did not know how to transport him safely to the dock. Shortly after Nalle was manacled, Tubman maneuvered herself into a position to take action.

In the blink of an eye, the frail old woman transformed herself, taking the guards by surprise. Whirling out of her shawl and grabbing hold of

Nalle, she wrenched him free and dragged him down the stairs into the waiting arms of comrades assembled below. This was no easy feat, and an eyewitness reported: "She was repeatedly beaten over the head with policeman's clubs, but she never for a moment released her hold . . . until they were literally worn out with their exertions and Nalle was separated from them."[41]

Bleeding and half-conscious, Nalle was carried down to the river and across the water on a skiff, followed by a ferry full of nearly four hundred abolitionists bent on protecting him from recapture. However, authorities on the other side apprehended Nalle again and he was dragged back into custody.

The battle seemed lost, until Tubman herself landed and rallied her followers. On her signal, the mob of abolitionists stormed the judge's office where Nalle was being held. Bent on liberation, this human battering ram caused all hell to break loose. The *Troy Whig* described the scene:

> At last, the door was pulled open by an immense Negro and in a moment he was felled by the hatchet in the hands of Deputy Sheriff Morrison; but the body of the fallen man blocked up the door so that it could not be shut.[42]

This gave the antislavery mob its opportunity.

"When the men who led the assault upon the door of Judge Stewart's office were stricken down," a participant reported, "Harriet and a number of other colored women rushed over their bodies, and brought Nalle out, and putting him into the first wagon passing, started him for the West."[43] A *Tribune* correspondent reported that this incident "has developed a more intense Anti-Slavery spirit here, than was ever known before." The *Troy Times* weighed in:

> The rescuers numbered many of our most respectable citizens, — lawyers, editors, public men and private individuals. The rank and file, though, were black, and African fury is entitled to claim the greatest share in the rescue.[44]

Tubman's prominent and public role in the Nalle rescue symbolized her gladiator status. She had become the general John Brown envisioned. From this time forward, she was not just Moses but had finally taken on the mantle of the warrior Joshua as well. Tubman later recalled that "shot was flying like hail above her head,"[45] but she felt the thick of public battle was where she belonged.

## Chapter Ten

# Arise, Brethren

*She must be regarded as the first heroine of the conflict.*
— *Samuel J. May*

————◄○►————

ONE OF TUBMAN'S FAVORITE PARABLES was the tale of a man who sowed onions and garlic on his pasture to increase the output of his dairy cows. The butter came out too strong and would not sell. He then decided to sow clover instead — but the wind had already distributed the garlic and onions throughout all his fields. Tubman suggested that "just so, the white people had got the Negroes here to do their drudgery, and now they were trying to root them out and ship them to Africa, but they can't do it. We're rooted here and they can't pull us up."[1]

Harriet Tubman always felt the depth of her American roots. She knew that no matter how hard white southerners tried to sweep aside black rights, African Americans and their antislavery allies would never give up the fight against slavery. She had been in the trenches and had entrusted her life to scores of men and women connected with the UGRR. She believed in the ideas set forth in the Declaration of Independence and the Constitution. Although deprived of any formal education, she had learned from experience to cherish her liberty, and to extend this newfound sense of entitlement to all American blacks.

When John Brown raised the abolitionist stakes, North and South proceeded even more quickly down a collision course. Frederick Douglass explained that the time for compromise was over:

> Moral considerations have long since been exhausted upon slaveholders. It is vain to reason with them. One might as well hunt bears with ethics. . . . Slavery is a system of brute force. . . . It must be met with its own weapons.[2]

Harriet was confident she would see jubilee (the slaves' term for general emancipation) within her own lifetime. She wanted to bring her family back to the United States, and other American-born blacks out of Canadian exile. She decided it was time to step up the pace, to promote a more direct opposition to slavery. During her treks south, she had repeatedly faced down the slave power and her own fears. But she did fear indifference and resignation in the face of the increasing influence of white supremacists, who would stop at nothing to get their way. After all, slavery was war.

After the Nalle rescue in Troy, in late May 1860 Tubman arrived in Boston as a celebrity guest at the New England Anti-Slavery Society Conference. She also attended a special session on women's suffrage on June 1, where she gave a speech. *The Liberator* reported that "Moses" spoke; her "quaint and amusing style won much applause."[3]

She addressed her audience from the same platform as other distinguished speakers — among them Wendell Phillips and William Lloyd Garrison. Tubman alone was compelled to use a pseudonym. Following John Brown's insurrection, slavecatchers had become more emboldened.

By the summer of 1860, slaveowners felt even more under siege when a Black Republican and damned abolitionist, Abraham Lincoln, was nominated for president. Slaveholders, particularly in the border states, girded for battle. Proslavery advocates in Maryland gathered in Baltimore to demand legislative relief. This was a movement spearheaded by Eastern Shore delegates. Maryland newspaper notices illustrated the growing alarm of Chesapeake slaveholders trying to hold on to their property:

> *Stampede of SLAVES* — On the night of the 24th ult., twenty-eight slaves made their escape from Cambridge, Md. A reward of $3,100.[4]

Many felt this exodus was symptomatic of deeper disturbances.

Maryland slaveholders, fretting over their loss of control, decided to levy stiffer fines for anyone found guilty of aiding and abetting fugitives. They decided that, above all, Moses must be stopped. They imagined she roamed unimpeded through their countryside, rousing slaves to flee, mocking their impotence with her every abduction. They hoped by offering incredible sums, they might coax someone to betray her. The price on Tubman's head was anywhere from $12,000 (allegedly the legislature's top offer) upward to $40,000 (reputedly the total of all rewards put forward to capture her).[5]

Her friend and admirer Thomas Wentworth Higginson feared for Harriet's safety, as Maryland slaveholders debated the "various threats of the different cruel devices by which she would be tortured and put to death."[6] He viewed her as a kind of modern-day Joan of Arc, sure to be burned at the stake if she were ever caught. Since Nat Turner's head was allegedly put on a pike in 1831 for his role in slave uprisings and, most recently, John Brown had swung from the gallows, there was every reason to believe that Tubman would be executed if caught, whether by a party of slaveholders or the courts of Maryland.

That she was a woman no doubt elicited special venom from proslavery advocates. None was more vituperative than Philadelphian John Bell Robinson, who attacked Tubman in his book, *Pictures of Slavery and Anti-Slavery*. Robinson was aghast, reading about her 1860 appearance where she was identified as "Harriet Tupman, who has been eight times South, and brought into freedom no less than forty persons, including her aged father and mother, over seventy years old."[7] His response was livid: "What could be more insulting after having lost over $50,000 worth of property by that deluded negress, than for a large congregation of whites and well educated people of Boston to endorse such an imposition on the Constitutional rights of the slave States."[8] Robinson was as offended by the delusions of the antislavery audience as he was by the "negress" who held their attention.

His invective became even more lethal when he launched into a diatribe about her removal of her aging parents from a slave state. Robinson's reasoning was that of a quintessential proslavery apologist:

> Now there are no old people of any color more caressed and better taken care of than the old worn-out slaves of the South. . . . Those old slaves had earned their living while young, and a home for themselves when past labor, and had sat down at ease around the plentiful board of their master whose duty it was to support them through old age, and see them well taken care of in sickness, and when dead to give them a respectable burying.[9]

Robinson painted slavery as a cradle-to-grave welfare system that whites shouldered for the benefit of blacks who could not take care of themselves. His portrait of Harriet railed against her "diabolical" and "fiendish" powers. He regretted that her parents were cheated out of the comfort and consolation of their master's care. If they had remained behind, the "laws of the State compelled him [their owner] to give them that support righteously due them the balance of their days."[10]

Even though Harriet had done the slaveholder a "kindness" by removing the burden of this expense, Robinson pointed out, she remained guilty. He supposed the elderly couple was carried off to Canada, "where they have nearly six months of severe winter out of twelve" and "no master's woodpile to go to." His lament continued: They will have "no rich white man or woman to call them 'Uncle Tom, and Aunt Lotta.'"[11]

Robinson argued that life imprisonment would be "inadequate" punishment for Tubman, considering her crime. He concluded that hers was "as cruel an act as ever was performed by a child toward parents."[12]

Of course, all of these arguments ignore the fact that Ben Ross had already been manumitted by his master, and that he had purchased his wife's freedom by the time they left Maryland. It suited both proslavery and abolitionist camps to portray Harriet's parents as an elderly enslaved couple. One side claimed their dependence upon some fictive master's goodwill, while the other painted the harsh cruelties of whips and chains if they did not escape.

Robinson's inflammatory tone was not unusual for his time. Between John Brown's raid (October 1859) and the firing on Fort Sumter (April 1861), the country experienced a convulsive series of political shifts. These wrenching episodes reflected the growing ideological divide between North and South. Southern states had long threatened to secede, and slaveholders had persuaded themselves that the South would be allowed to simply withdraw. If they could not get along with the North, why not go their separate ways?

Following Lincoln's election, South Carolina passed an Ordinance of Secession in December 1860. These fire-eaters (as radical secessionists were called) urged other states to join them in forming a new and independent Confederate nation. This proposed "legal separation" was not taken lightly in Washington. Any bid for southern independence would be met by armed resistance.

No matter how much Tubman welcomed war, unleashing the furies was also something she dreaded. What would happen to all of those families trapped within slavery's borders? She decided to make one last quick trip south before it became even more dangerous to smuggle people out. She set off to rescue a couple and their two children from Dorchester County in December 1860 — and in typical Tubman fashion collected two other fugitives along the way.[13] Garrett wrote to Still in Philadelphia about her chances:

> There is now much more risk on the road, till they arrive here, than there has been for several months past, as we find that some poor, worthless wretches are constantly on the look out on two roads, that they cannot well avoid.[14]

But with her usual aplomb, Tubman guided these fugitives all the way to safety in Canada. When she returned to St. Catharines this time, friends insisted that she must not go back to the States.[15] Having spent nearly ten years as a conductor on the UGRR, Harriet reluctantly agreed to suspend her activities. She took refuge among her several siblings: James Isaac, Robert, Henry, William Henry, and Ben were scattered around Ontario. Her niece Mary Anne (Kizzy) was settled in Chatham with her four children. While in exile, Harriet had several family homes from which to choose.

By early 1861 sectional tensions in the United States were roiling, as the southern rebellion proceeded apace. Several seceding states declared their collective sovereignty as the Confederate States of America. The upstart nation inaugurated its own president, Jefferson Davis, in February 1861 in its new capital of Montgomery, Alabama. By this time, the chasm between North and South seemed unbreachable.

Abraham Lincoln struggled to hold his fractured nation together. But within weeks of his own inauguration, following the Confederates' firing on Fort Sumter on April 12, 1861, he could no longer stave off the inevitable. The federal commander at the South Carolina fort surrendered on April 14. Lincoln responded with a call to arms on April 15, requesting 75,000 volunteers to put down the rebellion. After months of tense speculation, North and South were finally at war. Harriet Tubman crossed back into the United States.

The streets of every American city were soon filled with soldiers marching off to enlist. The South could draw on 900,000 eligible white men, while the North had a pool of more than 4 million. Girls encouraged fiancés to join up, while mothers and wives endured separation from loved ones. Family circles became casualties of war when men young and old registered for military service.

In the North, patriotism was the order of the day, as Yankee children fashioned newspaper hats and waved miniature flags. In Harriet's former home, Philadelphians were caught up in recruitment fever. Sarah Butler Wister described the city on April 17:

Chestnut Street is a sight; flags, large & small flaunt from every building, the dry-goods shops have red, white & blue materials draped together in their windows, in the ribbon stores the national colors hang in long-streamers, and even the book sellers place the red, white, and blue bindings together.[16]

Within a month more than 90,000 males in Philadelphia had placed their names on the state's militia rolls.

Even radical abolitionists who had so long denounced the federal government changed their tune overnight. Wendell Phillips spoke at a rally in Boston on April 21: "Now for the first time in my antislavery life, I speak under the stars and stripes, and welcome the tread of Massachusetts men marshalled for war."[17] Gerrit Smith and William Lloyd Garrison, among other founding members, abandoned the American Peace Society, a group that had formed in the 1840s to oppose America's aggression toward Mexico and the U.S.-Mexican War (1846–48). Even pacifist abolitionists shifted gears, and advocated supporting Lincoln and the fight to save the Union. Garrison had branded the U.S. Constitution "a covenant with death and an agreement with hell," but he removed this slogan from the masthead of *The Liberator* in favor of a new motto: "Proclaim Liberty throughout all the land, and to all the inhabitants thereof."[18]

African Americans throughout the nation responded to the declaration of war with unbridled enthusiasm, having waited not just months but rather decades for this reckoning. Enslaved African Americans were determined to abandon their shackles, and northern free blacks consistently framed the Union cause as a battle to defeat slavery. Frederick Douglass crowed that Lincoln's presidency would break the "exacting, haughty and imperious slave oligarchy."[19] This was a view shared by many whites as well. Charles Francis Adams (son and grandson of the second and sixth presidents, respectively) proclaimed: "The country has once and for all thrown off the domination of slaveholders."[20] Many white abolitionists enjoyed the fantasy that Confederate rebellion would rally the North around their cause. Blacks suffered no such illusions.

The earliest known photograph of Tubman, taken when she was already established as the Moses of her people. *Library of Congress*

A studio portrait of Tubman taken in Auburn, New York. © *Cayuga Museum of History and Art*

Tubman nearly always wore a white ruff and lace-edged blouses for her portraits. Admirers commented on her neat and ladylike appearance. © *Cayuga Museum of History and Art*

## Look out for the Kidnappers.

A FREE NEGRO MAN, named Solomon Sharp, sometimes called Solomon Atkins, was kidnapped by persons unknown, from the house of William D. Atkins, in Indian River hundred, Sussex county, Delaware, on the night of the 22d of February. The said Solomon is the son of Rosannah Chippy, is aged about 22 years, about 5 feet 7 inches high and well made, light complexion for a negro, has but little to say, slow of speech and civil in his deportment; his eyes are large and full, lips thick and nose large and flat  He served his time as a bound boy with Isaac Atkins. It is supposed he has been taken towards Salisbury, and from thence to Norfolk. Any information that may lead to the recovery of this man from the fangs of a set of wretches, will be gratefully received by his distressed mother. Editors to the South, friendly to the rights of humanity, are requested to insert the above in their papers.          March 16.

Free blacks frequently posted notices to warn of abductors and to find out information about loved ones who had been stolen away. *Historical Society of Delaware*

Shipley Street in Wilmington, Delaware, wh Thomas Garrett maintained his UGRR headquarters. *Historical Society of Delaware*

Thomas Garrett, one of Tubman's most faithful partners on the Underground Railroad. *Historica Society of Delaware*

Northern papers frequently featured images of slaves on the run. This image depicted a mass escape of twenty-eight from Maryland's Eastern

After rescue, kidnapped blacks tell their story. *Library of Congress*

A stylized image of a fugitive family crossing into Canada. *Library of Congress*

Idyllic images of St. Catharines in Ontario, where Tubman and many of her family settled during the 1850s. *Author's collection*

In this portrait, the effects of Harriet's childhood injury are apparent from the droop of her left eye. © *Cayuga Museum of History and Art*

John Brown, the man who called his comrade "General Tubman." *Library of Congress*

A reproduction of the scene at the Harpers Ferry arsenal, where Brown and his men were finally captured. *Library of Congress*

The image of Tubman serving during the Civil War, which appeared in the first edition of her authorized biography, *Scenes in the Life of Harriet Tubman* (1869). *Schomburg Center for Research in Black Culture*

A gallery of antislavery portraits, including Gerrit Smith, who was a particular friend of Tubman's. *Library of Congress*

An imagined confrontation between slavecatchers and runaway slaves, entitled "A Bold Stroke for Freedom." *Library of Congress*

The home of William Seward in Auburn, New York. Seward was Tubman's patron, friend, and neighbor. *Seward House, Auburn, New York*

William Seward. This portrait was taken after an attempted assassination on April 14, 1865, the night Lincoln was murdered. (Seward's right cheek drooped the rest of his life as a result of his injuries.) *Seward House, Auburn, New York*

A studio portrait of Tubman taken in Auburn, New York, after the Civil War. *Library of Congress*

The Civil War victory arch in Auburn, New York.
© *Cayuga Museum of History and Art*

AME Zion Church, Parker Street, Auburn, New York. Tubman worshipped there during the last few decades of her life. *Cayuga Historical Society*

A group portrait (circa 1885) of Tubman (far left), her husband, Nelson Davis (seated, pipe and walking stick), and residents of her home, which she opened to charity cases. *Schomburg Center for Research in Black Culture*

Margaret Lucas, Harriet Tubman's adopted daughter, with her own daughter, Alice, in Auburn, New York, circa 1907. *Schomburg Center for Research in Black Culture*

The last portrait of Harriet Tubman, circa 1910. *Library of Congress*

Plaque erected on Cayuga County Courthouse in Auburn, New York, to honor Tubman in 1914. *Cayuga Historical Society*

The Harriet Tubman Home in Auburn, New York, today. *Courtesy of the author*

Even though he would eventually become known as the Great Emancipator, Abraham Lincoln entered the war without any intention of freeing the slaves. Lincoln would even propose colonization for free blacks.[21] At the outset of the war, restoring the Union was Lincoln's primary goal. Yet African Americans believed it was only a matter of time before the federal government recognized that the war would bring about slavery's demise. They knew blacks must be given the opportunity to serve as soldiers. After being tested by combat, would they not be given their rights as citizens?

Following Lincoln's call to arms, black men rallied in Pittsburgh to form the Hannibal Guards. Black drill companies assembled in Cleveland, Boston, and throughout the North, responding to war fever. The government received their efforts coolly, as Lincoln's administration prohibited black volunteers from enlistment. Black leaders such as Frederick Douglass, Jermain Loguen, and William Wells Brown advocated the enlistment of black soldiers. Douglass complained: "Men in earnest don't fight with one hand, when they might fight with two, and a man drowning would not refuse to be saved, even by a colored hand."[22]

Tubman prophesied that a Union victory would deliver slavery's death blow. With the political machinery in motion, Tubman and her African American comrades threw themselves into the fray to help shape the war as well as to help win it. She began by informally attaching herself to Massachusetts troops in May 1861, returning to familiar territory by slogging with General Benjamin Butler's men through her home state of Maryland.

Benjamin Butler, a Democrat, had been a member of the Massachusetts delegation to Congress when the war broke out. He was a stout, blustery man with crossed eyes, which made him a figure of ridicule among his enemies. But he was a tough opportunist, underestimated by many until his bully tactics began to pay off. Commissioned a brigadier general, Butler led his Massachusetts troops into Maryland, where he threatened to arrest any legislator who attempted to vote for secession. He even went so far as to confiscate and hold hostage the state's great seal. He was banished to Fort Monroe, Virginia, by his commanding officer, General Winfield Scott, who resented his headline-grabbing tactics. Butler quickly took advantage of his new position, and ruffled Confederate feathers by offering protection to runaway slaves, claiming they were "contraband" of war.

Although Butler championed the seizure of Rebel slaves, he was not known as any "friend of the Negro," as was his political rival in Massachusetts, Governor John Andrew. At first Butler was very skeptical of the idea of using former slaves as soldiers. But, as with many Yankee generals, his attitude shifted radically during the course of the war. Indeed, in appreciation of black troops' bravery at the storming of New Market Heights in Virginia in September 1864, he commissioned Tiffany's (of New York City) to design and manufacture two hundred silver badges (which became known as Butler Medals) inscribed with the motto "Distinguished for Courage," for presentation to his men.

Trailing along with Butler's all-white troops in May 1861, Tubman arrived at encampments near Fort Monroe. The fort, completed in 1834, was mistakenly called Fortress Monroe throughout the Civil War: a fort is a fortification containing a garrison, while a fortress encloses a town within its walls — which Fort Monroe never did. This sixty-three-acre military garrison on the western shores of Chesapeake Bay at the mouth of the James River was bounded by water on three sides.

This fort became the major magnet for escaping slaves throughout the region. At first Annapolis had received a flood of runaways, but because Maryland remained loyal to the Union, its slaveholders were able to secure federal assistance to retrieve their property.[23] Thus the slave grapevine advised fugitives to make their way to Fort Monroe for safety.

Fugitives also had to maintain that they were escaping Rebel masters to secure protection. Groups from as far away as North Carolina evaded detection for nearly two hundred miles and finally arrived safely. Fugitives who came into Union camps with tales of impressment by the Confederate army were welcomed with open arms — offered food and rations, and then handed a pick or shovel and put to work.[24]

While she was at Fort Monroe, Tubman's role was neither official nor directly related to military operations. But civilian volunteers became vital when "contrabands" flooded into the federal camps. Military authorities reported, for example, more than one hundred slaves arriving on one morning, just a month into the war. Three months later, over a thousand contrabands resided at Fort Monroe. By February of 1862, less than a year after war had been declared, the fugitive population had tripled.[25]

Unlike free blacks, contrabands were denied wages, and one critic suggested, "They are still slaves, having merely changed masters."[26] Simon Cameron, secretary of war, instructed General Butler to "keep an account of the labor by them performed, of the value of it, and the expenses of their maintenance. The question of their final disposition will be reserved for future determination."[27]

In the meantime, although these fugitive laborers drew soldier's rations, men often arrived accompanied by families and required much more. A northern missionary at Fort Monroe reported that the ex-slaves were "supplied with provisions, but quite destitute of clothing and bedding, especially of shoes."[28] Tubman found working with these refugees familiar terrain. Her skilled assistance reflected winters in St. Catharines, where scores of runaways had been in similar need of instruction and material support. As Union commanders debated their fate, African Americans who fled behind "enemy" lines grasped the strategic importance of their mass movement.

By August 1861 Congress passed the First Confiscation Act, which called for the seizure of all property in aid of rebellion — including human property. Rapidly quartermasters and engineers, treating the ex-slaves like indentured labor, put black refugees to work as manual laborers, ditch-diggers and dike builders. Slave women were drafted into roles as cooks and washerwomen. The war was less than six months old, but a growing and potent black labor force demonstrated its worth to the Union cause.

Tubman interpreted flight from the Confederacy as the rising of a race. She welcomed the tide of refugees and took on the challenges of caregiving without complaint — as cook, as laundress, as nurse. During the war's earliest weeks, even if Tubman had more militaristic aspirations, she devoted herself to domestic duties. Like most others caught up in war's momentum, she was not yet sure exactly where it might take her, but she was grateful, at long last, that the journey had begun.

For the Underground Railroad, the changes brought even graver obstacles for those struggling to escape. Some found that the presence of soldiers added greater risks during nighttime travel. Fugitives were forced to evade pickets and sentries as well as the usual dangers. But the Civil War could not block off the liberty lines.

A Virginia slave named John Parker, like many other bondsmen in the Chesapeake, was drafted to serve with the Confederate army. Parker was assigned to Rebel artillery at the First Battle of Bull Run, on July 21, 1861. During combat, with bullets flying all around, he later said, blacks wanted to switch sides but feared being shot by their Rebel officers. Parker eventually escaped his Confederate masters. With help from Union soldiers at Alexandria, he walked all the way to Pennsylvania — and freedom.[29]

Tubman was on a visit to New England from Fort Monroe when news arrived about the capture of Port Royal, South Carolina, on November 7, 1861. Yankees viewed this as a great victory, and one with enormous potential. First and foremost, they hoped that Lincoln's naval blockade of the Confederacy might actually succeed. Second, since South Carolinians had "started" the war, both with the Ordinance of Secession and with their attack on Fort Sumter, the Union greeted news of any defeat of Palmetto forces with riotous enthusiasm.

Further, abolitionists were buoyed by accounts that Union troops found scores of abandoned plantations and hundreds of slaves left behind. The seacoast of South Carolina and Georgia boasted some of the most fertile land in the region, where the finest cotton, known as Sea Island cotton, was grown. Immediately after its capture, Port Royal, a barrier island south of Charleston, became a magnet for hundreds of black refugees heading for Union sanctuary. This flood of ex-slaves became the federal army's number one problem. They were put to work.

By December northern papers reported that "the cotton upon these islands is being picked by contrabands, under the direction of our officers. About two million dollars of cotton has already been secured."[30] By March

1862 the Union had conquered enough territory that the new secretary of war, Edwin Stanton, designated Georgia, Florida, and South Carolina as the Department of the South.

A leading African American newspaper, *The Christian Recorder,* suggested: "If there is any class of people, who at this crisis, demand the sympathy and immediate notice of the colored citizens of the North, it is assuredly the contraband."[31] Articles in William Lloyd Garrison's *Liberator* also harped on the fugitives' desperate needs:

> Abandoned to themselves, they are now suffering from the lack of clothing hitherto provided by their masters. . . . The people of the North owe at least this much to the subject-people of the South that their condition shall not be the worse for our invasion.[32]

He argued that donations must pour in to assist ex-slaves. Garrison also suggested it would take a regiment of volunteers to make a success of these black communities, which needed positive leadership to become self-sufficient.

The U.S. Treasury Department, in combination with private enterprise — the Freedmen's Aid Society of Boston, the National Freedmen's Relief Commission of New York, and the Pennsylvania Freedmen's Relief Association — organized an important relief campaign. This organization sought volunteer teachers who would do much more than provide instruction in the classroom. Many young idealists heeded the call to become part of "Gideon's Army." They were prepared to educate, train, and assist former slaves to become self-supporting. A young Harvard law school graduate, Edward Pierce, spearheaded the effort.[33] New England reformers, intending to demonstrate that freedpeople would become industrious when given half a chance, launched their Port Royal Experiment.[34]

In the winter of 1861–62, Tubman decided she could do much good by returning to Virginia from Boston. She had already spent considerable time there and knew the countryside and its people. But she also knew about new schools for freedpeople being built around Fort Monroe. She welcomed the arrival of Catholic Sisters of Charity and the boxes of donations flowing in from freedmen's aid societies. She knew there were plenty of volunteers and unobstructed avenues into occupied Virginia to help the contrabands there.[35]

Massachusetts governor John Andrew, a staunch abolitionist, asked Harriet instead to join the contingent of his state's volunteers heading for South Carolina, and promised sponsorship. Tubman decided she would go to Port Royal, joining the nearly ninety Yankee volunteers who departed for the Sea Islands that spring and summer. She would be assigned to a region where thousands of slaves were seeking escape routes and Union sanctuary. Fugitives collected along the Carolina coast and were shepherded to Hilton Head and Port Royal, two barrier islands nestled between Savannah and Charleston. Tubman's new undertaking would more closely resemble the life she had been used to leading — creating lifelines for blacks trapped within slavery.

Before heading to this new assignment, Tubman made a tour of upstate New York to say her good-byes to Frederick Douglass, Jermain Loguen, and Gerrit Smith, among others.[36] She made sure her elderly parents, living in her home on South Street, would be looked after by Auburn neighbors during her absence. This sweep of friends and family suggested that she knew the risks of traveling so deeply within slave territory.

For Harriet, much more than for other volunteers, it was the natural course of events to burrow deeply into enemy terrain. Yet even so, this was a dangerous proposition: she was still a wanted woman in the slave South.

Before she sailed for Carolina, Boston abolitionists sponsored a "donation festival" at the Twelfth Baptist Church to underwrite her trip. Tubman's journey would be officially sponsored by the New England Freedman's Aid Society. As she was illiterate, Tubman was listed as a teacher of "domestic arts." The Massachusetts Aid Society teachers were required to file monthly written reports, something that Tubman could not easily promise. She later prevailed upon others to write down messages to be sent back to Boston. Doubtless it did not matter to Tubman who sponsored her, simply that she went.

Once she had taken care of her household affairs upstate, she headed for Manhattan, where Governor Andrew obtained military passage for her on a federal ship, the *Atlantic*. Tubman was eager to extend the liberty lines into the Deep South — or as far into the Deep South as she had ever been.

On April 7, while Harriet was preparing for South Carolina, Americans learned the bloody outcome of one of the Civil War's deadliest battles thus far. The showdown at a small crossroads in Virginia named Shiloh shocked the nation. In two days, 4,000 soldiers were killed and more than 27,000 were wounded. That same month General George B. McClellan, Lincoln's top commander, assembled the largest army ever to fight in the Western Hemisphere — 150,000 strong. McClellan's force would try to capture Richmond, the new Confederate capital, by circling round and approaching from the south.

Confederate general Robert E. Lee, possessing a much smaller force, defended the city with vigor. In what became known as the Peninsular Campaign, Lee's army claimed a string of victories against McClellan's men. The Rebel armies lost 20,000 men, compared with Union casualties of 16,000.

Union troops perched along coastal South Carolina were in a difficult position. They were essentially encircled; the enemy surrounded them on three sides, with the ocean on the fourth. Nevertheless, the newly appointed Union commander of the region, General David Hunter, had ambitious ideas about how to expand the Department of the South.

Hunter earned the nickname Black Dave because of his enlightened views on race. Born the son of a District of Columbia Presbyterian minister, he had graduated from West Point in 1822 and intended to become a career military man. Hunter's hopes were dashed when he was court-martialed after killing three men in duels. President John Quincy Adams intervened and was able to restore Hunter to active duty.

Although Hunter resigned from the army in 1836, he returned to serve during the U.S.-Mexican War. A series of letters to the newly elected Abraham Lincoln in 1860 led to his commission as a brigadier general and his posting to head the force guarding the White House. Seriously wounded at Bull Run, Hunter first served in the Department of the West before being given command of the Department of the South in March 1862.

Hunter was perhaps being rewarded for his staunch abolitionist politics. As early as 1861, he had complained about delays in enlisting slaves as soldiers:

> We have wasted time enough. . . . I would advance south, proclaiming the negro free and arming him as I go. The Great God of the universe has determined that this is the only way in which this war is to be ended, and the sooner it is done the better. If I am the instrument, I shall not stop short of the Gulf of Mexico, unless laid low by his Almighty hand.[37]

His evangelical fervor had natural appeal for Tubman when she joined him in Port Royal.

Hunter detested planters who came into Union camps complaining about runaway slaves. Some Union officers turned fugitive slaves back over to owners willing to beg for them. Hunter insisted that the military put a stop to this practice.

He was not alone among the Union command to hold such strong abolitionist views. Many Yankee politicians and black activists opposed Lincoln's appeasement policy. They wanted an unambiguous condemnation of slaveholding, to bring things to a head. These radicals hoped to shift the goals for Union triumph from a purely military realm into a moral one as well.

On May 9, 1862, after less than two months on the job, Hunter took matters into his own hands and proclaimed, "The persons in these three States [South Carolina, Georgia, and Florida] . . . heretofore held as slaves are therefore declared free."[38] Hunter directed officers to begin rounding up able-bodied African Americans for federal army use. He was passionate about his dream of "negro regiments" and determined to move ahead, even if the government dragged its feet.

Months before, Lincoln had been forced to slap down another Union general for jumping the gun on emancipation. In his jurisdiction in Missouri, General John C. Frémont declared martial law and abolished slavery in August 1861.

After Lincoln objected, the policy was modified on September 11, emancipating only those slaves who "aided Confederate military forces." Lincoln explained his reluctance, that "to arm the Negroes would turn 50,000 bayonets from the loyal Border States against us."[39] In response to Hunter's mandate, politicians in Washington called for the general's resignation, while Union slaveholders demanded his head.

Whatever his personal feelings about slavery at the time — and many scholars believe that by this point he was tilting toward emancipation — Lincoln did not want military men dictating policy. A declaration on May 19, 1862, voided the Department of the South's emancipation edict. Hunter licked his wounds and, bowing to pressure, disbanded all but one of the black South Carolina regiments he had organized from fugitive slaves in the region. He insisted that since he was never officially censured, he was just a victim of bad timing.

Doubtless Hunter felt partially vindicated when Congress passed a Confiscation Act in July 1862, which "freed all slaves whose masters were rebels," and a Militia Act, which allowed these "forever free" blacks to be enlisted by the military as paid laborers.

By then Washington had finally begun to warm to the idea of stealing away Rebels' slaves, even if it resisted the idea of slaves as soldiers. Again, Hunter did not want the army to employ ex-slaves just as laborers, but wanted them, as Frederick Douglass advocated, with muskets on their shoulders and eagles on their buttons. His zealotry on the topic of slave soldiers eventually derailed his military career.[40]

When Tubman first landed along the South Carolina seacoast in May of 1862, the heat was as oppressive as any she had encountered during her thirty-seven years.[41] Palmettos and lush island foliage surrounded her. Acacia and jasmine were in bloom. This was the very climate that had swallowed up her two sisters years before.

Tubman was greeted with chaos when she landed at Beaufort, South Carolina. A white volunteer from Boston, Elizabeth Botume, described the scene upon docking:

> Negroes, negroes, negroes. They hovered around like bees in a swarm. Sitting, standing, or lying at full length with their faces turned to the sky. Every doorstep, box, or barrel was covered with them, for the arrival of a boat was a time of great excitement.[42]

Most volunteers found it overwhelming to provide care and instruction for the swelling numbers of ex-slaves collecting at Port Royal, Ladies Island, and Hilton Head.

Tubman complained that at first it was as if she were among some strange, foreign people. By the time she arrived in South Carolina, she had been living in the urban North for over a decade. Sea Island blacks spoke in the Gullah dialect of their forebears (a blend of African languages that was a distinctive patois). Both their vocabulary and thick accents made communication difficult.[43] Many of these children of African parents wove sweetgrass baskets, carrying them on their heads.

Shortly after her arrival in South Carolina, Tubman was drafted to work alongside Dr. Henry K. Durant, the medical director of the freedman's hospital at Port Royal. A note from Durant dated August 28, 1862, detailed: "Will Captain Warfield please let 'Moses' have a little Bourbon whisky for medicinal purposes."[44]

Port Royal soldiers quickly learned they were dealing with the famed conductor of the Underground Railroad. When they recognized the woman known as Moses, William Wells Brown reported, Union officers "never failed to tip their caps when meeting her."[45]

The dearth of food for refugees on the Carolina coast was a pressing problem, growing with each passing month. Even though there had been no formal provision made to regularize her attachment to the army, Tubman collected government rations. During the first weeks after Tubman's arrival, refugee slaves saw her collect government provisions and, with little understanding of her role there, were jealous of her privilege. As a consequence, she "voluntarily relinquished this right and thereafter supplied her personal wants by selling pies and root beer — which she made during the evenings and nights — when not engaged in important service for the Government."[46] Tubman worked in solidarity with the freedpeople, making herself much beloved by these gestures of goodwill.

Tubman's blackness set her apart from the vast majority of northern volunteers settled on Port Royal. Most of these northern teachers formed their own tightly knit communities, keeping themselves purposely aloof. They might fraternize with army doctors and officers, participating in the upper strata of camp social life, but they limited contact with freedpeople, remaining supervisors and instructors. This was neither Tubman's style nor preference.

Harriet came into intimate contact with contrabands by her role as a nurse. The Port Royal nurses and doctors fought a constant battle against malaria, typhoid, yellow fever, cholera, "spotted fever" (typhus), and the dreaded dysentery, striking civilian, contraband, and soldier alike. One officer complained as he watched his men struck down: "There is hopeless desperation when one is engaged in a contest with disease. . . . The evening dews fall only to rise again with fever in their breath."[47]

Tubman's skills as a root doctor were formidable at a time when disease was the army's number one enemy. Three out of five Civil War soldiers who died during the war were killed by disease unrelated to wounds. Because keeping soldiers free of disease was a military aim, Tubman's medical proficiency took on an enhanced urgency. Tubman used local plants to concoct her remedies.

Once Tubman was summoned to Fernandina, a Union outpost on Amelia Island, several miles south of the Georgia border, in Florida. A Union officer, alarmed at his men "dying off like sheep" from dysentery, hoped she might help. Tubman journeyed south to give her time and energy to the soldiers as well as to contrabands, seeing them through this severe outbreak. She also tended men with smallpox and other "malignant fevers," without being felled herself.[48] Once again, miraculous powers were ascribed to her, as her healing powers became legendary among her Union comrades.

Tubman undertook special projects on her own initiative. She supervised the building of a laundry house, so she might train local African American women to become laundresses, financing this project with money from her own pocket. She also undertook protection of some of these women, as when she discovered a "pretty, white colored girl" still being held as a slave.

Tubman asked one of the Union doctors about to embark on a furlough to accompany this young woman northward and to deliver her to friends. Yankee colleagues in the North promised to provide for the girl's care and education. But until she could find suitable chaperonage, Tubman felt it was "best that she remain with her Misstress [sic] rather than to break loose from all restraint."[49] Tubman knew all too well what might happen to a vulnerable and attractive female in the midst of an army camp.

Tubman despised the licentious atmosphere that plagued towns where Civil War soldiers gathered. As one of the Union doctors complained, the mistreatment of black women was a shame and scandal of occupied Carolina, where lawless conditions reigned during the first year of occupation.

> No colored woman or girl was safe from the brutal lusts of the soldiers — and by soldiers I mean both officers and men. . . . Mothers were brutally treated for trying to protect their daughters, and there are now [October 1862] several women in our little hospital who have been shot by soldiers for resisting their vile demands.[50]

The doctor went on to point out that the arrival of General Rufus Saxton in the summer of 1862 improved matters considerably, as Saxton "has made it somewhat disgraceful to be caught abusing women."[51] Tubman, considerate of the enslaved girl's vulnerability, only provided a rescue after she had arranged for the young woman's removal from camp.

The arrival of Saxton in South Carolina in the summer of 1862 heralded a new regime in other ways as well. Rufus Saxton was born in Massachusetts and educated at Deerfield before he graduated from West Point in 1849. He was an artillery officer in St. Louis when the war broke out, and was sent to Port Royal as a chief quartermaster in 1861. He was posted to Virginia, where he achieved distinction at Harpers Ferry, protecting the arsenal and town during Stonewall Jackson's Shenandoah campaign in the spring of 1862. He then was posted permanently to the Department of the South. While serving in St. Augustine, Florida, Saxton required townspeople who wished to remain behind to take an oath of allegiance, which created a massive exodus, including scores of women and children. His order was later overturned, but it signaled Saxton's lack of sympathy when dealing with Confederates.

Like Hunter, Saxton was an early and persistent advocate of enlisting ex-slaves in the army. He believed that shifting black men into the ranks was a vital solution to the shortage in military manpower. Saxton also felt this would ease the economic burdens on fragile refugee communities crowding the South Carolina shoreline.

In July 1862 Lincoln confided to members of his cabinet his plans to reverse himself and pave the way for the emancipation of southern slaves. He hoped to publicly proclaim his new policy following a Union military victory, so as not to appear to be taking this measure out of desperation. Unfortunately, his generals gave him no opportunity for several weeks. Then McClellan's Army of the Potomac turned back General Robert E. Lee's push into Maryland at Antietam Creek on September 17. Despite its being such a bloodbath, Lincoln decided to claim a victory. On September 22, he issued his Preliminary Emancipation Proclamation: all slaves in areas still in rebellion on January 1, 1863, would be declared forever free. He also pledged the enlistment of former slaves into the federal armed forces.

Both of these provisions were intended to pressure slaveholders into urging their state to rejoin the Union before the end of the hundred days' deadline. Lincoln's proclamation did no such thing. His announcement, however, did transform the Union cause into a war for liberation as well as unification.

Saxton quickly drafted the distinguished New Englander Thomas W. Higginson, a colonel in the Union army, to organize and lead a black regiment at Port Royal. Higginson, an old friend and admirer of Tubman's, arrived in South Carolina in October 1862 as part of the coterie of Yankee abolitionists determined to showcase the crucial role black soldiers could play. He wrote to his mother on December 10: "Who should drive out to see me today but Harriet Tubman, who is living at Beaufort as a sort of nurse and general caretaker."[52] (Higginson added that Harriet asked to be remembered to his mother, indicating the closeness of their friendship.)

African Americans north and south avidly anticipated general emancipation and blacks' enrolling in the military. Frederick Douglass addressed a Rochester audience on December 28:

> It is difficult for us who have toiled so long and hard to believe that this event, so stupendous, so far reaching and glorious is even at the door. It surpasses our most enthusiastic hopes that we live at such a time and are likely to witness the downfall of slavery in America. It is a moment for joy, thanksgiving and Praise.[53]

Emancipation Day itself became a time of jubilation — not just a new year but a whole new era. On January 1, the Reverend Henry Turner, an AME pastor in the District of Columbia, grabbed a freshly printed broadsheet of the proclamation, hot off the press, and ran down Pennsylvania Avenue, "as for my life," to read it to the gathered crowd near the White House. Turner, brandishing his copy, was met with "a cheer that was almost deafening."[54]

Douglass and Turner would doubtless have been moved by the ceremony organized on January 1 by General Saxton in South Carolina to celebrate the official reading of the proclamation.[55] He anticipated a group of over five thousand — and ordered a feast of twelve oxen to be roasted, as well as bread, molasses, and other provisions. Crowds were ferried in by boat to the former Smith plantation, where the First South Carolina tented at Camp Saxton. Soldiers at the wharf escorted guests to the middle of a large grove, where a platform had been set up for speakers. A regimental band played and spirits were high when festivities commenced shortly before noon. This three-hour program of prayer, presentations, hymns, and speeches washed over the assembled crowd.

The formalities proceeded with invited speakers and included the presentation of a regimental flag. Up on the platform, as Higginson took the flag in hand, a quavering voice from the audience unexpectedly broke into song — "My country, 'tis of thee" — and soon the entire crowd joined in for several verses.[56] When the singing ended, Higginson was so moved it was difficult for him to continue, but he collected himself and went on with his speech.[57] The formal presentations resumed and soldiers sang other songs, including one of Tubman's favorites, "John Brown's Body."

The purest moment of the day remained when black voices rose spontaneously to overtake the occasion. Thousands of former slaves — Harriet Tubman included — could finally embrace America truly as their own "sweet land of liberty." It was a turning point on the road to freedom, and one few would ever forget.

## Chapter Eleven

# Bittersweet Victories

There are few captains, perhaps few colonels, who have done
more for the loyal cause since the war began.
—*Wendell Phillips*

————◄○►————

WHEN THE WAR FIRST BEGAN, Tubman was reluc-
tant to support Abraham Lincoln. She found the Republican president's cautious policy toward slavery frustrating. As the war dragged on,
she feared the North might "use up all the young men." And what's worse,
she asserted, it was to no avail to send the "flower of their young men down
South" because "God won't let Mister Lincoln beat the South till he does
the right thing." She wanted an end to slavery.

With faith and simplicity, Tubman confided to abolitionist Lydia Maria
Child: "I'm a poor Negro; but this Negro can tell Mister Lincoln how to
save the money and the young men. He can do it by setting the Negroes
free." Tubman had been dealing with slavery her whole life and told her
abolitionist ally:

> Suppose there was an awfully big snake down there on the floor.
> He bites you. You send for the doctor to cut the bite; but the
> snake, he coils up there, and while the doctor is doing it, he bites

you again. The doctor cuts down that bite, but while he is doing it the snake springs up and bites you again, and so he keeps doing it till you kill him. That's what Mister Lincoln ought to know.[1]

At long last, Union politicians and military advisers were finally forced to see the wisdom of Tubman's vision. With the Emancipation Proclamation in January 1863, Lincoln killed the snake.

Considering Tubman's extraordinary talents and track record, she was vastly underutilized during her first several months in Carolina. With her proximity to the front lines, her gifts of dissemblance, her ability to blend in and live by her wits, this former UGRR conductor was an untapped resource. Tubman was eager to take on more challenging work.

With the arrival in the region of Thomas Wentworth Higginson (in the fall of 1862) and James Montgomery (in the spring of 1863), both Union colonels in charge of black regiments, Tubman had influential advocates among the Union brass. Because of her association with Higginson in Massachusetts, she had a personal friend on her side at headquarters. Colonel James Montgomery had been with John Brown in Kansas and knew Tubman only by her reputation (and she his), but this bond made them allies as well.

Montgomery was a veteran of the border wars in Kansas, where he earned a reputation as bloodthirsty. He had ridden to South Carolina from the west to command the Second South Carolina Volunteers. He was a tall man with a weather-beaten face, and his looks matched his rough-hewn personality. His vigor and abolitionist ire recommended him to Tubman. He had also been one of Brown's most trusted lieutenants.

Harriet's abolitionist comrades and military admirers made the case to Saxton for a spy network to be established in the region. It would be useful to extend federal tentacles into the interior, pushing beyond occupied territories. Tubman had established such clandestine networks in the upper South during her Underground Railroad days and felt confident she might make similar headway in wartime Carolina.

By early 1863, after ten months spent ministering to the sick, Tubman had been given the authority to line up a roster of scouts, to infiltrate and map out the interior. Most of her agents were men recruited directly from the surrounding low country. Several were trusted water pilots, like Solomon Gregory, who could travel upriver by boat undetected. Her closely knit band became an official scouting service for the Department of the South: Mott Blake, Peter Burns, Gabriel Cahern, George Chisholm, Isaac Hayward, Walter Plowden, Charles Simmons, and Sandy Suffus.

Tubman's espionage operation was under the direction of the secretary of war, Edwin M. Stanton. Stanton had wanted to postpone the use of black soldiers and had sided against commissioning black officers, fearing the wrath of northern public opinion: what if a white man would have to salute a black? Stanton's and others' reservations prevented integration of the officer corps. Although he might block African Americans from holding advanced rank, the secretary of war was not opposed to allowing them to risk their lives as Union spies. He wished to break the back of the Confederacy, and welcomed Tubman's spy ring. Listed as commander of her men, Tubman passed along information from her network of agents, reporting directly to either General David Hunter or General Rufus Saxton.

In March 1863 Saxton wrote confidently to Stanton concerning a planned assault on Jacksonville, Florida: "I have reliable information that there are large numbers of able bodied Negroes in that vicinity who are watching for an opportunity to join us."[2] A few days later Montgomery led an expedition to capture the town and met with quick success. Tubman's advance intelligence and Montgomery's bravado convinced Union brass that extensive guerrilla operations would be feasible.

This led to the famed Combahee River Raid in June 1863 — a military operation that would mark a turning point in Tubman's career. Up until this point, all of her attacks upon the slave power had been anonymous strikes by a "woman named Moses." Though she had been a ringleader in the successful assault to rescue fugitive slave Charles Nalle in 1860, she still remained unidentified. However, with her prominent role in this military operation, she would not remain nameless.

\*       \*       \*

South Carolina's low-country rice plantations, fanning out from the Atlantic shore, sat on some of the richest land in the slave South, yielding a crop that became known as Carolina gold. During the eighteenth century, rice, Sea Island cotton, and slaves combined to make millionaires out of the tightly knit circle of coastal Carolina planters. They married their cousins, combining estates and bloodlines. They made the most of political connections, ruling their beloved Carolina and exerting a disproportionate influence within the national arena. They feared that the North's mounting hostility to their precious slaveholding economy would upset the applecart, and closed ranks. South Carolina slaveholders were the staunchest of Rebels, belligerent for independence and ready for blood.

The night of this Union raid, June 2, 1863, as the moon played hide-and-seek with the clouds, three federal ships moved cautiously out of St. Helena Sound. The boats headed up the Combahee River shortly before midnight, loaded with the soldiers of the Second South Carolina. The entrance to the Combahee River was approximately ten miles north of Beaufort, where Tubman and her comrades were stationed.

The waters slapped against the sides of the gunboats as they made their way into enemy territory. The band of 150 black soldiers knew that on this mission their fates rested not just in the hands of their commander, Colonel James Montgomery, but had been entrusted as well to the famed Moses, as she guided troops upriver.

A sneak attack in the dead of night, to catch slaveholders off guard in their own backyards, was vintage Tubman. It resembled the days when she would return to Maryland under the nose of her former slaveholder and steal her brothers to freedom. Tubman had provided the location of Rebel torpedoes (stationary mines planted below the surface of the water) and guided the ships to avoid them. She had found slaves willing to trade information for liberation, information that would insure the raid's ultimate success.

On scouting expeditions, Tubman had moved with ease through and among white southerners. As an illiterate, Tubman was unable to write down any vital data she collected, but after years of practice, she was able to commit to memory critical information.[3] This made her intelligence gathering even more impressive.

On this journey she was liberating more than the handfuls at a time she had freed during her conductor days. On the lookout, Tubman guided the boats to designated spots along the shore where fugitive slaves had hidden. Once given the all clear, they would approach the waterline to be loaded onto ships to cast their lots with "Mr. Lincoln's army."

The response of the Combahee River slaves was astonishing. Tubman described the scene when Union boats approached the riverside in the wee hours of June 3:

> I never saw such a sight. . . . Sometimes the women would come with twins hanging around their necks; it appears I never saw so many twins in my life; bags on their shoulders, baskets on their heads, and young ones tagging along behind, all loaded; pigs squealing, chickens screaming, young ones squealing.[4]

The Confederate ranking officer in the area, a Major Emmanuel stationed inland near Green Pond, only a few miles away, was alerted during the early hours of June 3. But by the time Confederate headquarters got wind of the incursion, Union gunboats had steamed far upriver, continuing their raid.

A landing party of over a dozen Union soldiers, relatively inexperienced black troops, disembarked near Field's Point, where a Confederate officer on picket duty, a Colonel Newton, sighted them. He immediately sent one of his men to warn comrades at Chisholmville, ten miles upriver. After dispatching his courier, Newton and the five other Confederates fell back to allow the Union scouting party to advance without incident.

The Union operation proceeded like clockwork. Near dawn, said a Confederate witness,

> [Tubman's vessel] passed safely the point where the torpedoes were placed and finally reached the . . . ferry, which they immedi-

ately commenced cutting way, landed to all appearances a group
at Mr. Middleton's and in a few minutes his buildings were in
flames.[5]

The horror of this attack on the prestigious Middleton estates drove
the point home. This distinguished family owned several estates in the region and was one of the wealthiest clans in the state. Robbing warehouses
and torching planter homes was a bonus for former slaves sent as soldiers,
striking hard and deep at the proud master class.

Eventually a company of Rebels, under the command of a Lieutenant
Breeden, arrived near Combahee Ferry with orders from Emmanuel to re-
pulse the Yankees. Breeden's men failed to make any substantial dent in
Union activities. They reportedly stopped only one lone slave from escaping, shooting her in flight.

Emmanuel led his own contingent to the river's shoreline, commanding a single piece of field artillery. He staged a fruitless attack after sighting
enemy ships steaming back toward the sound. Hard charging to the water's
edge, the Confederate commander could only catch a glimpse of escaping
gunboats, pale in the morning light. In a fury, Emmanuel pushed his men
into pursuit — and got trapped between the riverbank and Union snipers.
In the heat of skirmish, Emmanuel's gunners were able to fire off only four
rounds, booming shots that plunked harmlessly into the water. Frustrated,
the Confederate major cut his losses after one of his men was wounded and
ordered his troops to pull back. The Union invaders and their human
cargo escaped entirely unharmed.

More than 750 slaves were spirited onto Union gunboats that night,
shepherded by 150 black soldiers. The estates of the Heywards, the Mid-
dletons, the Lowndes, and other Carolina dynasties were left bereft and
humiliated. Tubman's plan was triumphant.

Official Confederate reports laid blame squarely on Emmanuel and his
men, claiming they "were neither watchful nor brave . . . allowing a parcel
of Negro wretches calling themselves soldiers, with a few degraded whites,

to march unmolested, with the incendiary torch, to rob, destroy, and burn a large section of the country."[6] Certainly Confederate ineptitude contributed to Union success. But credit must be given to Tubman and the spies who provided her information. The official Confederate report concluded: "The enemy seems to have been well posted as to the character and capacity of our troops and their small chance of encountering opposition, and to have been well guided by persons thoroughly acquainted with the river and country."[7]

Tubman later provided the comical highlights of this rescue. She described a woman with two pigs in tow — a white one nicknamed Beauregard (after the Confederate general at Bull Run) and a black one jokingly referred to as Jefferson Davis (after the Confederate president). Tubman wrestled with the woman's livestock, stepping on the hem of her dress and falling while trying to get back to the ship. She vowed never again to wear a skirt on a military expedition.[8] Upon her return to Port Royal, she asked her friend Franklin Sanborn to tell the ladies of Boston about her wardrobe problems so that they might send her some bloomers.[9] Sanborn also commented that if Tubman were ever sent a new wardrobe, "even this she will probably share with the first needy person she meets."[10]

By the summer of 1863, Union commanders were willing to risk sending men into the interior, even greenhorn colored troops, based on Tubman's assessment of enemy strength and positions. These men were untested by combat, but because of the hard fight to get them into the ranks, Union commanders in South Carolina were eager to push them to perform. The previous March, Tubman had described slaves as a fifth column, restless on low-country plantations, eager to anticipate the Union invasion. Many slave men wished to join the Union army, but would do so only after federal troops transported their families to safety. On the Combahee operation, General Hunter feared ambush. Tubman reassured him that if Montgomery prepared the troops, she and her scouts would take care of the rest.

Robbing the Cradle of Secession was a grand theatrical gesture, a headline-grabbing strategy that won plaudits from government, military, and civilian leaders throughout the North. African Americans had long endured doggerel in Dixie:

> *May these northern fanatics, who abuse their southern neighbors,*
> *Approach near enough to feel the point of our sabres.*
> *May they come near enough to hear the click of a trigger*
> *And learn that a white man is better than a nigger.*

Blacks were satisfied to be able to throw some of this scorn back at the enemy — and to prove to northern white comrades that colored troops were well worth the trouble. After the Combahee River Raid, critics north and south could no longer pretend that blacks were unfit, as this was a well-executed military operation. Using colored troops provided a double bonus: reminding the enemy of what was to come with defeat.

Official military reports credited Montgomery with the Combahee River Raid's triumph, yet soldiers recognized this victory as Harriet Tubman's. As the Union raided the homes of the Carolina planter class, colored troops stole more than property: they ripped away the veil, exposing the hypocrisy of Confederate claims of "loyal darkies."

In the immediate aftermath of this raid, Tubman felt keenly the burdens imposed by hundreds of new refugees. Women and children were dropped unceremoniously into her lap back at Port Royal headquarters. The liberated families were settled chock-a-block onto an abandoned estate christened Montgomery Hill. One of the civilian volunteers stationed at Beaufort described conditions:

> Each house was divided into four rooms or compartments, and in each room was located one family of from five to fifteen persons. In each room was a large fireplace, an opening for a window, with a broad board shutter, and a double row of berths built against the wall for beds. Benches, tables, dippers, and articles of wearing apparel somewhat filled out the interiors. It was rough and crude living and compact and hasty, but the Negroes were free and they preferred this to the slightly larger cabins of the plantations they had quit.[11]

Flush with success, Hunter wrote jubilantly to Secretary of War Edwin Stanton later on the day of June 3, boasting that Combahee was only the beginning. He also wrote to Governor Andrew of Massachusetts, promising that Union operations would "desolate" Confederate slaveholders "by carrying away their slaves, thus rapidly filling up the South Carolina regiments of which there are now four." Andrew had been a longtime champion of black soldiers and was a supporter of Hunter's campaign to put ex-slaves in uniform. The North did well to enjoy their triumph.

The Confederacy discovered overnight what it took the Union's Department of the South over a year to find out — Harriet Tubman was an effective and formidable secret weapon whose gifts should never be underestimated. In the weeks following the Combahee success, the uncommonly reticent Tubman was straining. Ever since African Americans became eligible for enlistment in the Union army, the press and the nation had focused on the weighty responsibilities falling on the shoulders of black soldiers. The pressures they carried into battle were enormous. Even black advocates of slave soldiers feared the consequences. What if blacks in combat fulfilled the prophets of doom, running scared at the first signs of enemy fire?

Black troops were under severe scrutiny during this crucial period. The newly assembled colored troops in Louisiana were sent into combat at the Battle of Port Hudson, Louisiana, and on May 27, 1863, black soldiers under the Union flag once again won praise from white commanding officers. General Nathaniel Banks commented:

> Whatever doubt may have existed heretofore as to the efficiency of Negro regiments, the history of the day proves conclusively to those who were in condition to observe the conduct of these regiments that the Government will find in the class of troops effective supporters and defenders.[12]

Indeed, another Confederate defeat was courtesy of the valor of colored troops who "rallied with great fury and routed the enemy" on June 7,

1863, at the Battle of Milliken's Bend, Mississippi, four days after the Combahee River Raid.

These Louisiana veterans earned headlines in the *New York Times* and other Yankee papers. Tubman was distressed that her own noble comrades, formerly enslaved South Carolina black soldiers who had been willing to crawl back into the belly of the beast — in some cases to the very plantations from which they had escaped — were not being given their due. She felt that black troops who had sailed with Montgomery deserved similar encomiums. Tubman suggested that "we colored people are entitled to some of the credit."[13]

Tubman dictated a letter to Franklin Sanborn:

> We weakened the rebels somewhat on the Combahee River by taking and bringing away *seven hundred and fifty six* head of their most valuable live stock, known up in your region as "contrabands," and this, too, without the loss of a single life on our part, though we had good reasons to believe that a number of rebels bit the dust.[14]

This is all the more remarkable because having been born a slave, Tubman had always observed a strict code of silence within the slave community. Whippings and punishments were too often traced back to loose talk. Slave conspiracies or rebellions (notably Gabriel's Revolt in Richmond in 1800 and Denmark Vesey's conspiracy in 1822 in Charleston) were reputedly foiled by slave informants. Imprudence might lead to betrayal, and Tubman, above all, was prudent. During Tubman's many years as a conductor on the Underground Railroad, secrecy had served her well. Advertising one's triumphs, even to taunt the enemy, was not her style. War did little to change Harriet's attitudes, since discretion had so long been a matter of life and death in her line of work.

Historical knowledge of spy rings during the American Civil War remains sketchy and circumstantial, but most often Union spies were white men. Black men were actively recruited and played important roles as agents throughout the war. Many a Union commander attributed his awareness of enemy strength and location to African Americans who made their way across army picket lines to volunteer crucial information.

Several white women gained fame during or after the war as spies or smugglers, such as the celebrated Washington society hostess Rose Greenhow (who passed information to the Confederacy and was credited with helping the Rebels win at the First Battle of Bull Run), or the intrepid Virginia horsewoman Belle Boyd (who spied for the Confederacy and ended up eluding her Union warden before escaping abroad), or actress Pauline Cushman (a double agent, posing as a southern sympathizer, while sneaking secrets to the Union command), and a dozen other intriguing characters whose stories have been only partially verified.

Fewer than a handful of black women can be credibly labeled Civil War spies. Mary Elizabeth Bowser was a free black woman in Philadelphia whose former mistress, Elizabeth Van Lew, got Bowser placed as a servant within the household of Jefferson Davis, in the White House of the Confederacy. Bowser was instrumental in passing vital information along to a Union spy ring in Richmond, Virginia, during the war. There are only a few instances when Bowser's activities can be corroborated, and evidence about her — before, during, and after the war — remains sketchy at best. A wartime diary she kept was allegedly still in family hands into the twentieth century but has reportedly since been destroyed.

Tubman's wartime accomplishments fit into the pattern of resistance and achievement she had followed from early childhood. When the slave power extended its tentacles with the Fugitive Slave Act of 1850, Tubman relocated to Canada along with thousands of other refugees. While her fellow fugitives remained safe above the border, Tubman risked return again and again, not just to the North, but into the slave South. Her activities became even more notorious when Tubman became a staunch supporter of John Brown. She condoned rather than condemned his zealotry, which earned her the nickname General Tubman long before Lincoln began handing out commissions. With war under way she became a secret weapon, and only *pretended* to fade into the landscape of the Deep South in order to continue her mission.

Tubman's gift was, again and again, to make her appearance when the enemy least suspected, working behind the scenes. Federal commanders came to depend on her, but kept her name out of official military documents. Her missions were clandestine operations, and as a black and a woman she became doubly invisible. Much of the information available about her war work was written up later when she applied for a pension, and, again, much was lost.

By July 1863, after spending so many frustrating months trying to make headway in South Carolina, Yankees trumpeted the Combahee River conquest. With the first public account of the raid on July 10, Tubman's anonymity was preserved:

> Col. Montgomery and his gallant band of 300 black soldiers, *under the guidance of a black woman,* dashed into the enemy's country, struck a bold and effective blow, destroying millions of dollars worth of commissary store, cotton, and lordly dwellings, and striking terror into the heart of rebeldom brought off near 800 slaves and thousands of dollars worth of property, without losing a man or receiving a scratch.[15]

When the story of the Combahee raid blossomed onto the pages of Yankee papers on July 10, 1863, it heralded a new era: Moses was alive and well — and "above ground" in the war to end slavery.

But any cover she might have maintained was completely blown when Sanborn wrote a biographical sketch of Tubman on July 17. Using her full name, he highlighted her significant accomplishments and featured her key role in the Combahee military victory. Sanborn's front-page article in *The Commonwealth,* an antislavery journal in Boston, suggested that the nation had too long been "deaf to her cries" while she was guiding fugitives to freedom; he believed the whole world should finally sing her praises. In this lengthy essay, Harriet Tubman was heralded by name, and linked with her clandestine reputation as Moses.

Sanborn's feature catapulted Tubman into the international spotlight as, once again, fans in Great Britain were awed by her exploits. In December 1863 the Reverend Moncure Conway — at an anniversary memorial to John Brown in London — quoted Harriet and exalted her for keeping Brown's legacy alive.

After the Combahee River Raid, all eyes turned once again to coastal Carolina, where a proud regiment of African American soldiers from the Bay State had been sent to fight. The Massachusetts Fifty-Fourth Regiment was a project spearheaded by Tubman's ally and patron Governor Andrew. He had thrown all his energies into showcasing this black regiment from Massachusetts, which included soldiers recruited by black leaders such as James Forten, John Mercer Langston, and Frederick Douglass — whose two sons joined the regiment. A grandson of Sojourner Truth's also enlisted in this elite corps.

From January through April 1863, nearly one thousand black men had been drilling outside Boston, preparing for combat duty under the supervision of white officers. Governor Andrew had fought to enlist black officers but relented under pressure from Washington and instead drafted the cream of the Bay State's abolitionist aristocracy for command.

Robert Gould Shaw, scion of wealthy Boston Brahmins, was an extremely calculated but inspired choice to head the regiment. Born into a wealthy antislavery clan in Massachusetts, educated in Switzerland and Germany before matriculating at Harvard, young Shaw was related to the Cabots, Lodges, Parkmans, and Lowells. With his impeccable credentials and zealous ideals, the twenty-four-year-old Shaw enlisted once the war broke out. He was wounded at Antietam and gained the rank of captain. This dashing and handsome young officer fit the governor's bill. At first Shaw was reluctant to leave his own regiment, even to participate in such a noble experiment, but his mother's pride that he would be "willing to take up the cross" proved persuasive.[16]

Shaw was promoted to colonel when he agreed to train and lead the Massachusetts Fifty-Fourth. He drafted officers from other prominent Boston families, such as Garth Wilkinson James, known as Wilky, a younger brother of William and Henry James. Shaw married his sweetheart the first week of May, but his honeymoon was abbreviated when the men of the Fifty-Fourth were ordered to South Carolina.

On May 28, black men in blue and their officers proudly marched through the streets of Boston with their Enfield rifles over their soldiers. The men of the Fifty-Fourth sang "John Brown's Body" as they passed the site where African American Revolutionary hero Crispus Attucks had fallen, the first to die at the Boston Massacre.[17]

A Boston paper reminded its readers of a very different scene nearly a decade before, when Anthony Burns was deported.[18] Boston had stood by while this fugitive slave was shipped south, but now the city cheered as African American soldiers shipped out to defeat the slave power. The regiment was accompanied by the high hopes of radical Republicans, and the moral and financial support of Boston's abolitionist aristocracy.

The year before, men and women from Boston's upper crust had volunteered to serve at Port Royal as teachers and educators. Some would even die there — as did Wendell Phillips's nephew Samuel, felled by disease in the summer of 1862. But those who elected to join the military campaign knew risks were even higher, and in combat many more would be left behind.

The 650 men of the Fifty-Fourth landed in Beaufort, South Carolina, on June 3 — just in time to savor the news of the Combahee raid. Shaw met up with fellow Bostonian Thomas Wentworth Higginson, also commander of a black regiment. Higginson's troops were as southern as Shaw's men were Yankee, showing the remarkable diversity of Union soldiers, even within black ranks.

Shortly thereafter, Shaw was transferred to St. Simon's Island, off the coast of Georgia, posted to the command of Colonel James Montgomery. Shaw, the bookish and youthful commander, did not get along with the more rough-and-tumble Montgomery. Shaw was bitterly disappointed by his men's first military foray under Montgomery's orders.

This raid on Darien, Georgia, on June 10 resulted in the burning of the town. Montgomery explained to Shaw that "Southerners must be made to feel that this was a real war, and that they were to be swept away by the hand of God like the Jews of old."[19] Shaw wanted to disassociate himself from blatant disregard for civilian safety, a policy of which he disapproved. Further, he was aghast at Montgomery's bland response to the reports of arson and looting committed by black soldiers.

It was particularly painful to the men of the Fifty-Fourth when northern journalists derided the soldiers' behavior at Darien. Even a proabolitionist journal, *The Commonwealth,* described the town as a "plain of ashes" following the invasion of "Yankee negro vandals" who poured turpentine and applied the torch with abandon. Soldiers attempted to burn down a Methodist church. Shaw was humiliated at Yankee press reports that called his men "brigands."[20]

The men of the Fifty-Fourth hoped to redeem themselves with a planned assault on Fort Wagner. This crucial fort was located on the northern tip of Morris Island, a few miles south of Charleston. The Union command believed this bastion held the key to the harbor. If the Yankees could take control, they might cripple blockade running along the coast and pave the way for conquest of Charleston.[21]

The Fifty-Fourth was expected to play only a small role, assigned the task of holding the line at nearby James Island. Yet during a Confederate attack on July 16, three of Shaw's companies performed bravely, protecting the retreat of a white regiment. While the men of the Tenth Connecticut abandoned their position, Shaw's men fought with bayonets, in hand-to-hand combat, suffering forty-three of the forty-six losses during the Confederate raid.[22] Shaw commended, "They fought like heroes."[23] A journalist concurred: "Dark-skinned heroes fought the good fight and covered with their own brave hearts the retreat of brothers, sons, and fathers of Connecticut."[24] Shaw used this success to curry favor. General George Strong, a brigade leader, requested that the Massachusetts Fifty-Fourth join him in leading the assault on Fort Wagner. The invitation was considered a great honor.

The Union command faced extraordinary obstacles in plotting their assault, as the fort was practically impregnable. Waves washed up to the eastern wall at high tide, and marshes and bogs covered the ground leading to the other three walls. Further, the Rebels ringed the fort's walls with a moat as well as a rifle pit.[25] With more than seventeen artillery guns aimed outward, the fort seemed invincible — but it was a prize Yankees eagerly sought. The chief battle strategist, General Quincy Adams Gillmore, underestimated both the Confederates' artillery and the resolve of the 1,600 Rebel soldiers within the battery.

When invited to lead the Union charge, Shaw's men were weary from the previous days' fighting and marching without rest. Rain on the seventeenth postponed the battle by a day. Shaw asked his soldiers "to prove themselves as men," and promised to carry the regimental flag himself if the color bearer fell.[26] Tubman reported that she served Shaw his breakfast before he went off to battle on July 18 — a meal that would prove his last.

By noon, nearly 9,000 shells had been lobbed into Fort Wagner, from ironclads at sea and artillery on land. When the fort's Confederate flag was shot away, the Union soldiers thought it meant surrender. They ceased fire and began to cheer — prematurely, as a Confederate officer mounted the rampart to display their battle flag, and shelling resumed.[27] At sunset, General Gillmore wanted to send in the infantry.

Shaw's men were dispatched to the head of the Union column, in formation with two lines of two men deep and one wing of five companies in the front, and another battalion bringing up the rear.[28] Eighteen-year-old Wilky James confided to a fellow officer, "We have the most magnificent chance to prove the valor of the colored race now."[29]

Shaw and his men moved out at 7:45 P.M. They had to wade through water and sand to begin to move onto a narrow strip of land where the marsh cut across the island toward the ocean. As they moved along this corridor toward the fort's moat, Confederate guns began their deadly attack: howitzers and canisters mowed down the Union army's charge. Physical logistics and the gross underestimation of Confederate strength contributed to the Union's heavy casualties.

After hours of bloody battle, lasting well past midnight, the Union assault failed — although federal units, especially African American soldiers, had fought bravely and well. By the wee hours of July 19, scores of Union soldiers lay injured on the beach; when the tide came in, many drowned before they could be rescued by litter bearers coming to collect the wounded.

When July 19 dawned, an eyewitness reported the gruesome scene:

> Blood, mud, water, brains and human hair all melted together; men lying in every possible attitude . . . their limbs bent into unnatural shapes by the fall of twenty or more feet; the fingers rigid and outstretched, as if they had clutched the earth to save themselves.[30]

Of the 5,000 Union men engaged at Fort Wagner, more than 1,500 (including 111 officers) were killed, wounded, or captured. The Massachusetts Fifty-Fourth lost 272 soldiers out of 650, including Shaw — a casualty rate of over 40 percent.

Wounded whites, including Wilky James, were evacuated to Hilton Head and placed in the care of nurse Clara Barton, while black soldiers were transported to Beaufort, where Harriet Tubman awaited survivors.

Although Tubman was horrified by the carnage, she took pride in the glory black soldiers earned that day. The *New York Tribune* suggested that Fort Wagner would be "such a name to the colored race as Bunker Hill has been for ninety years to the white Yankees."[31] Private Lewis Douglass, Frederick Douglass's son, survived the battle and confided:

> Not a man flinched, though it was a trying time. Men fell all around me. A shell would explode and clear a space of twenty feet, our men would close up again, but it was no use, we had to retreat, which was a very hazardous undertaking. How I got out of that fight alive I cannot tell.[32]

Clara Barton commented bitterly: "We have built one cemetery, Morris Island."[33] While the bodies of all other Union officers killed were returned by the enemy, the lifeless Robert Gould Shaw, riddled by seven bullets, was withheld. Confederate gravediggers chose to bury the colonel "with his niggers," as a Rebel commander ordered.[34] To strip Shaw's body and pile twenty dead black soldiers on his white corpse was intended as a gesture of southern dishonor. To undercut the insult, Shaw's family discouraged attempts to recover their son's body and expressed their pride that he had died among and been buried with his men.

The Fifty-Fourth colorbearer did fall during the battle. A black sergeant from New Bedford, William Carney, rescued the regiment's national banner. He planted the flag on the Confederate works, and then, once retreat was sounded, rescued the flag and carried it back to Union lines, sustaining several wounds in the process. For his valor that day, Carney would be the first African American soldier to earn the Medal of Honor.

Tubman offered the most moving assessment of battle to the historian Albert Bushnell Hart:

> And then we saw the lightning, and that was the guns; and then we heard the thunder, and that was the big guns; and then we heard the rain falling, and that was the drops of blood falling; and when we came to get in the crops, it was dead men that we reaped.[35]

Although the Union would continue to bombard the fort and scheme to capture both Morris Island and Charleston Harbor, it would take years to achieve this elusive goal. But the renown won that day by black soldiers at Fort Wagner would endure.

The war continued to inflict staggering casualties with no apparent end in sight. The Confederate defeat at Gettysburg on July 4 was a particularly bloody outcome, occurring simultaneously with the surrender of Vicksburg to Ulysses S. Grant after a protracted siege. Though the Union wrenched these two major victories from the Rebels, draft riots in New York signaled a souring mood on the war. Lee and his generals refused to back down. As the war became one of attrition, generals on both sides were as concerned with filling the ranks as they were with winning the battles.

In the first year of the war the Department of the South's sick list included more than 52,000 incidents, which meant that each Union soldier serving in the southern theater of war had been ill, on average, several times a year. Union surgeons recommended measures to reduce the sick list and prevent epidemics. These included digging wells for fresh water whenever possible, providing fresh vegetables for meals, requiring men to move their tents at least once a week, demanding that they bathe once a week, adding soil daily to latrines, burying kitchen refuse in deep holes, and burning dead animals. All of these preventive actions demonstrated a relentless struggle against war's deadliest foe.

Summer was the peak season for sickness, and Harriet's nursing duties became more constant. During the summer of 1863, she faced the challenge of nursing African Americans wounded at Wagner back to health, as well as the even larger number of black soldiers who succumbed to South Carolina's debilitating and often deadly climate.

More than the summer season concerned Tubman. She confided to Sanborn in July that she was also worried about her parents: "I have now been absent two years almost, and have just got letters from my friends in Auburn, urging me to come home. My father and mother are old and in feeble health and need my care and attention."[36] But, Tubman explained, she could not leave just yet, because of the important work she was doing. She trusted the good people of Auburn would look after her family for her — perhaps hinting to the New England Freedmen's Aid Society that they would need to do more for the family she had left behind.

During the fall of 1863 Harriet's own health went into decline, and by the following spring she knew she could not endure a third Carolina summer. Tubman wanted to make a trip home in May 1864 to recover her health. She requested leave. Her commanding officers, both surgeon Henry Durant (who supervised her work in the hospital wards) and General Saxton (who had sent her into the field) commended Tubman's service. They signed a certificate that enabled her to obtain military transport from South Carolina to New York — and authorized her return after her furlough.

Tubman made the long journey back to upstate New York in the summer of 1864, finding her parents well, considering their advanced age, and living peacefully at her home on South Street in Auburn.

During her own convalescence, Tubman became fast friends with Sarah Hopkins Bradford, a staunch abolitionist from Geneva, New York. Bradford's brother, the Reverend Samuel Miles Hopkins, had befriended Tubman while he was a professor at the Auburn Theological Seminary. Sarah Bradford had regularly copied down letters for Ben and Harriet Ross (both illiterates) to send off to Harriet while she was away at war. They were addressed via her commanding officers, and reached her down south. When Tubman returned home to Auburn in June 1864, Bradford showered her with care.

Bradford was not alone among those in Auburn to herald Tubman. The community pitched in to praise their adopted daughter. Elsewhere too the Yankee press turned her into a freedom fighter, a Union heroine, and a celebrity known now by her own name.

When she felt well enough to travel from upstate New York, Harriet made a pilgrimage to see New England friends who had supported the launch of her military mission. On August 12, 1864, *The Commonwealth* announced: "This heroic woman whose career we described last summer, when she was engaged in the military service, in the Department of the South, has lately arrived in Boston." The article, under the heading "Harriet Tubman," further informed readers that she had been "inadequately recompensed by the military authorities" and was using her own limited resources for the good of others. As a result donations would be welcome. An address was provided for those who could contribute clothing and money, which would be distributed "for the good of the colored race."[37]

As in previous visits to Boston, Harriet was given first-class treatment. It was during this period that she was introduced to another abolitionist stalwart, a black woman who was becoming, in her own way, equally legendary: Sojourner Truth.

Truth had been born a slave, Isabella Baumfree, in Ulster County, New York. Her birth year is unknown, but estimated as 1797. During her youngest years, Truth, like Harriet, was farmed out to local families by her owner, families who subjected her to rough treatment. English-speaking masters abused her, as her native tongue was Dutch. She was sold in 1810 to an owner named Dumont.

Over the course of the next sixteen years she grew into a towering woman (six feet tall), married, and gave birth to five children. Like Harriet, Truth performed heavy-duty labor for her masters — hoeing corn, scutching flax, and other challenging physical chores. When Dumont reneged on his promise to free her, Truth took matters into her own hands and emancipated herself in 1826. In 1828 she moved to New York City and ended up living with a religious cult. By 1843, Isabella decided to strike out on her own and took the name Sojourner Truth. She began to preach as she traveled throughout the North.

As was the case with Harriet Tubman, this phase of taking on a new name was a milestone. And like Tubman, Truth remained illiterate. But she confided: "I cannot read a book, but I can read the people."[38] Although their lives took very different paths, these two women had much in common.

During Truth's intense involvement with antebellum reform, she lived in a variety of communes, preached spiritual perfectionism, and became most closely associated with both feminism and antislavery during the late 1840s. Her *Narrative of Sojourner Truth* was published in 1850 with a fiery introductory essay by William Lloyd Garrison. Truth's narrative ended with her confrontation with a slaveholder, her former owner, who finally acknowledged slavery's evils. In many ways, Sojourner's conclusion represented the "truth and reconciliation" ideals of Tubman's youth.

During most of the 1850s, Truth was on the road, mainly on the speakers' platform. In 1857, the same year that Tubman settled in Auburn, New York, Truth made Battle Creek, Michigan, her permanent home. In 1863 Harriet Beecher Stowe penned an embellished biographical sketch of

Truth, a piece for the *Atlantic Monthly*, which catapulted Truth from relative obscurity. Previously she was known only within abolitionist circles, but this essay turned her into a figure of national reputation. Unfortunately Stowe's essay was full of factual errors, including the misstatement that Truth was dead. But Truth seized on this notoriety and began a renewed round of public appearances. When she spoke, she would always offer copies of her autobiography or portraits for sale. It was during this bubble of publicity that Truth crossed paths with Tubman in the fall of 1864.

Truth had left her home in Michigan accompanied by a grandson, bound for her first visit to Washington. Along the way, she offered speeches to promote Lincoln's reelection. She hoped to gain an audience with the president when she arrived in the District of Columbia.

Truth doubtless knew of Tubman's work among the soldiers in the Carolinas, and her exploits before and during the war. Equally, Tubman would have been curious about Truth, the compelling speaker whose lectures always opened with her singing spirituals. The article on Tubman in *The Commonwealth* in July 1863 suggested that "her religious experiences are as startling as those of Sojourner Truth."[39] Thus it was not uncommon for these two women to be linked in the public imagination.

Little is known about their first encounter, except that it allegedly took place in Boston. At the time the women had conflicting views on Lincoln, for whom Truth was stumping. The topic of the president and his policy toward blacks surfaced during their discussions. Harriet had witnessed the second-class status of African American soldiers fighting in the Union army, and blamed the commander in chief for this failing.

When black men in blue were first recruited, they were offered a lower pay scale than white soldiers and asked to buy their own uniforms out of pocket, while white soldiers were given a clothing allowance on top of their higher wages. This was an enormous sacrifice, especially for many of the soldier's families, who needed money to survive once husbands and fathers left for the army. When black soldiers protested by refusing to draw any pay, they continued to perform their military duties. They demonstrated their loyalty but rejected discriminatory wages on principle, thereby humbling the U.S. government into pay equity. Tubman fumed that these brave soldiers had to fight the enemy on two fronts.

Tubman became embittered over the fact that white soldiers injured at Fort Wagner were sent to Hilton Head while black soldiers were transported to Beaufort. The separate evacuation plans for handling the wounded, not to mention burying the dead in segregated graves, added insult to injury. She could not reconcile these injustices. She blamed Lincoln, even as Truth sang his praises. Tubman told Truth that she had no interest in meeting Lincoln — something she came to regret in later years.[40] Their disagreements may have prevented them from cementing a deeper bond with each other — as sisters committed to a common cause.

During her stay in Boston, close friends may have been even more solicitous of Tubman. She was only thirty-nine but appeared much older because of her deteriorating physical condition. One of her confidantes later reported that the fracture of her skull at the hands of a Maryland overseer when she was younger continued to undermine her health. During her time in Auburn in the summer of 1864, she suffered frequent spells.

No description of these spells and seizures has turned up in any medical records, so speculation about Tubman's condition is based on sketchy eyewitness reports. One observer reported that she would, "to her deep mortification, [drop] into a heavy sleep even when conversing, from which she will after a time arouse and resume the thread of her narrative where she left off."[41]

Everyone who commented on Tubman's disability suggested that her symptoms mimic what we today would call narcolepsy, a disabling neurological disorder. A narcoleptic will frequently drop off to sleep at inappropriate times — even midsentence — then slip back into wakefulness with no memory of this blackout period.

Narcolepsy was first identified in 1877, and doctors studying the illness believed both that the disorder was genetic and that these episodes were triggered by emotions. But over time it became clear that many sufferers experienced effects unrelated to psychological issues, and that symptoms might occur if a person suffered specific brain irregularities, mainly lesions in the posterior hypothalamus. The hypothalamus is the region of the brain that regulates wakefulness.

Since narcolepsy usually begins its onset between the ages of fifteen and thirty, it is not even possible to tell if this condition was related to Tubman's adolescent head injury or was merely attributed to it. Without any contemporary data and perhaps even with it, there is no way of knowing her exact medical condition.

Tubman's disorder might well have been an inherited condition called cataplexy: sudden brief episodes of muscle weakness or paralysis. This condition is brought on by sudden, strong emotions — anger, fear, and anxiety. It seems that if this were the case, Tubman would have been severely plagued during her UGRR career, but there are few comments about her disability from fugitives. Also Harriet did not seem to suffer two of the most common effects of the disease: "sleep paralysis" and daytime sleepiness. No one ever accused Tubman of excessive daytime sleepiness, a prevalent symptom, and Harriet never complained of "sleep paralysis" — an inability to move when first waking or while falling asleep.

However, during her fits Tubman would have wakefulness invaded by short bouts of unconsciousness. Also narcoleptics can suffer from hypnagogic hallucinations — vivid images that emerge at the onset of sleep. Both of these characteristics were described in detail by Tubman herself or those commenting on her illness. She was especially forthcoming about the remarkable dreams that visited her. But it is impossible to say if there was some physiological or neurological root cause of her visions.

Victims of this disorder are taken out of themselves by irresistible attacks of sleep, which last from thirty seconds to thirty minutes. During Tubman's lifetime the disease was barely diagnosed, and effective treatments came much, much later. Doctors nonetheless treated this illness by surgical means — most commonly cerebrospinal fluid removal.

Perhaps her illness led her to see a specialist while she was in Boston. In any case, during one of her later visits to Boston, Tubman underwent an operation to relieve her symptoms. Whatever the source of her increasing discomfort, Tubman constantly sought medical relief. The surgical procedure she underwent at Massachusetts General Hospital somehow reduced her discomfort, although it reportedly did not completely cure her spells.[42]

In the spring of 1865, she overstayed her military leave and was not able to return to South Carolina as she had planned. She arrived too late in New York to catch her designated ride back to occupied South Carolina. But Tubman was eager to return, especially after the Thirteenth Amendment, officially abolishing slavery, was passed by Congress in February 1865 and sent to the states for ratification. This act may have been the beginning of Tubman's changing attitude toward Lincoln, as she would eventually hold him in high regard.

In March 1865 she went to Washington, where she obtained permission for military transport, which read:

> Pass Mrs. Harriet Tubman (colored) to Hilton Head and Charlestown, S.C., with free transportation on a Gov't transport. By order of the Sec'y of War March 20 1865.[43]

On her journey to New York to find a ship to take her back to South Carolina, she stopped off in Philadelphia. Representatives of the Sanitary Commission, the agency responsible for the care and treatment of the Union wounded, urged Tubman to abandon her plans for Carolina and instead to return to Virginia.[44] They begged her to return to the James River hospitals near Fort Monroe, where authorities were in desperate need of her skills. It was this pleading that caused Tubman to relinquish her plan to return to the Department of the South. She did not realize what the bureaucratic consequences of this absence might mean. Rather, as always, Tubman responded to immediate needs, part of the reason that her status remained unofficial, ad hoc, and so difficult to document in later years.

Since Tubman had left Fort Monroe in the fall of 1861, more than 10,000 contrabands had passed through the garrison seeking assistance.

Several thousand remained in residence, and a nearby school in Hampton boasted more than five hundred pupils. Hospitals were filled with military patients, although black and white soldiers were treated at separate facilities.[45] In March 1865 Harriet returned to the trenches, serving in the hospital wards of Union-occupied Virginia.

Tubman rejoiced over Lincoln's visit to Richmond on April 4 and was roused by the news of Confederate surrender five days later, after four years of war. Like most northerners, she was stunned by grief when Lincoln was shot in Ford's Theater on April 14 and died the next day.

With the official conclusion of wartime hostilities, Tubman and her fellow ex-slaves recognized another turning point, just as crucial as the emancipation, as they sought the brass ring of citizenship. Impassioned rhetoric began even before the war ended, as Frederick Douglass thundered: "If he [the black man] knows enough to take up arms in defence of this government and bare his breast to the storm of rebel artillery, he knows enough to vote."[46] Henry Highland Garnet, speaking in front of the House of Representatives in 1865, suggested that blacks would end their crusade for justice "when emancipation shall be followed by enfranchisement, and all men holding allegiance to the government shall enjoy every right of American citizenship."[47]

Tubman had experienced a righteous sense of anticipation, especially with the amendment to abolish slavery in February 1865. However, Harriet knew the struggle was not over. She remained in Virginia, working doggedly on behalf of soldiers and freedpeople through April, May, and June of 1865, in worsening conditions. Supplies were so limited and circumstances so dire by July that she was compelled to go to Washington to solicit help from her allies in the District of Columbia. She went to see the powerful men with whom she could obtain an audience and made an appeal for improved conditions at the military hospital where she served. As a result, "so great was the confidence of some officers of the Gov't in her, that Surgeon Gen'l Barnes directed that she be appointed 'Nurse or Matron.'"[48] This was a high honor and one that had not been granted to a black woman thus far.

She returned to Fort Monroe on July 22, 1865. But the bureaucracy, weighed down by the postwar chaos, was slowing everything to a halt. Tubman's Washington contacts failed her, as neither any official appointment nor the promised supplies materialized. By this time the forty-year-old Tubman had given years to the Union effort — with no regular salary, no back pay, no recognition of her valuable contributions. Now that the war was over, the pull of home overwhelmed her.

Harriet Tubman rationalized that "the country's need had ceased." She could in good conscience return to her parents, "entirely dependent on her."[49] She made her way back to Auburn, where family and community eagerly awaited her. In this last trip north, Tubman was part of the thousands who came "marching home" in the summer of 1865. Like many towns, Auburn built a victory arch to commemorate the triumph over Confederate foes. But it was a bittersweet victory, as the country mourned more than 600,000 soldiers who died during the four long years of war.

Walt Whitman, who had also served as a nurse in Union hospitals — and would later become the war's unofficial poet laureate — observed:

> The camp, the drill, the lines of sentries, the prisons, the hospitals (ah, the hospitals) — all have passed away, all seem now like a dream . . . and in the peaceful strong, exciting fresh occasions of today, and of the future, that strange sad war is hurrying even now to be forgotten.[50]

Indeed, in the postwar rush to reunion, only one Confederate was hanged for any actions taken during the War of the Rebellion — Captain Henry Wirtz, the Swiss-born officer in charge of Union prisoners at Andersonville, Georgia. Only a handful of Confederate leaders spent any time inside a prison. Even the Confederate president, Jefferson Davis, was rapidly rehabilitated in post–Civil War America. So much so that a Confederate veteran could declare as early as 1865:

> We Rebs, "so called" have been "overwhelmed," "crushed out," "subdued," "defeated," or by whatever other name you please to

call it except disgraced. In the face of the civilized world the honor of the South stands untarnished and her sons will live in the world's memory as a chivalrous, gallant and brave people.[51]

It was Harriet Tubman's hope that the noble and brave among African Americans might not be forgotten as well. But after the American Civil War, chivalry and gallantry would be reinvented and racialized by advocates of the Lost Cause, the Confederates' cult of nostalgia. These vigilant campaigns would cost African Americans dearly — especially during the prolonged battle to claim rights guaranteed by new constitutional amendments and federal enforcement of the law. The rise of the Ku Klux Klan, vigilante violence, and other campaigns of terror swept the postwar landscape.

During Reconstruction, southern freedpeople and blacks in general became scapegoats, suffering a violent backlash in war's aftermath. Tubman wanted African Americans to be granted the freedom and dignity they deserved, as well as the legal status they had won. For those who could not care for themselves or claim what they had a right to, Tubman would become a friend and protector. She would dedicate her remaining years to this important mission.

Tubman herself fell victim to the backlash, even as she was returning home a war hero.[52] On the train heading north to Auburn from Virginia, she was roughed up while passing through New Jersey. The conductor decided that Harriet's papers must have been forged or illegally appropriated, finding it incredible that a black woman could carry a soldier's pass. She was asked to leave her seat.

Tubman politely refused. When she failed to move, the conductor called in assistance. Her stubborn resistance took four men altogether to eject her from her seat. She was dumped unceremoniously into the baggage car for the rest of her trip, let out of her imprisonment only when she reached her destination.[53] Tubman suffered additional physical injuries from this incident, injuries that plagued her for several months, suggesting the seriousness of her resistance and the implacable contempt of the rail-way functionaries.[54]

This was Harriet Tubman's homecoming. Like so many of her fellow black soldiers, she found no road rising to greet her as she made the long journey home. She and other ex-slaves could only imagine the harsh struggles ahead. The land of Egypt might be behind them, but they were not in the promised land.

In the months and years to come, Harriet Tubman would enjoy only the most bittersweet of victor's spoils.

## Chapter Twelve

# Final Battles

She is the greatest woman of the age.
—*Thomas Wentworth Higginson*

————◄○►————

AFTER THE WAR Tubman retired her guns and gave up life on the road. She traded in campfires for her own hearth and returned to the home for which she had so long struggled. She created a household that was not only home to members of her own extended family, but a refuge for the forgotten and abandoned. Over the years Harriet Tubman's charitable endeavors became a symbol for reformers, and her accomplishments the proof that individual dreams can shape a collective reality.

When questioned by a white woman after the Civil War about whether she believed females should have the vote, Tubman replied with characteristic bluntness: "I suffered enough to believe it."[1] During the postwar decades Tubman became a grand old lady on the suffrage circuit. After addressing an audience, she was often described as spellbinding. Preacher and reformer James Freeman Clarke commented on her "great dramatic power" as an orator.[2] A longtime Auburn friend wrote, "As a raconteur, Harriet herself, has few equals."[3]

She attended women's suffrage meetings faithfully in upstate New York.

In 1897 the New England Women's Suffrage Association gave a fete in Boston to honor Tubman. There she enjoyed all the praises heaped upon her, and was interviewed by Wilbur Siebert for his history of the Underground Railroad.[4]

Suffragist Susan B. Anthony introduced her as a living legend at the twenty-eighth annual convention of the New York State Women's Suffrage Association, held in 1904. The *Rochester-Democrat* described the scene: "The old woman was once a slave and as she stood before the assemblage in her cheap black gown and coat and a big black straw bonnet without adornment, her hand held in Miss Anthony's, she impressed one with the venerable dignity of her appearance."[5] At this impromptu occasion, Tubman made her famous remark, "I was conductor of the Underground Railroad for eight years, and I can say what most conductors can't say — I never ran my train off the track and I never lost a passenger."[6]

In 1896, at the founding meeting of the National Association of Colored Women in Washington, D.C., Tubman was warmly embraced by the crowd and heralded as the oldest member of the National Federation of Afro-American Women.[7] By the turn of the century, none could rival Tubman's accomplishments or outdraw the esteem felt by an audience of black clubwomen.

In war's immediate aftermath, Tubman's commitment to her race remained steadfast. She continued solicitations for the freedpeople of the South and recognized the long, hard road toward reconstruction. She collected funds for freedpeople's schools and hospitals. But soon after settling in Auburn, Tubman began to focus her energies on those around her, extending a hand to the needy and poor within the Finger Lakes region. Her focus on aged and indigent Negroes was appreciated by the white citizens of Auburn, who were relieved that African Americans would have their own champion.

Tubman channeled donations into projects to help the less fortunate people of color within the town — orphans, disabled veterans, the blind, and others requiring assistance. Like most of the North, upstate New York offered only segregated social services. There were few opportunities for African Americans, especially in communities with small black populations. Without Tubman's solicitations, too many would have fallen by the wayside. She took in the poor, she took in the needy, without questioning how she could provide for these strangers as well as her own family.

During Reconstruction, Tubman launched another crusade — one that turned into a thirty-year battle. She struggled to obtain compensation for her military service. Like her campaigns before the Civil War, this was not undertaken strictly for personal gain but rather as part of something larger, symbolic of higher purpose.

Tubman knew her own contributions to the Union cause had been considerable. Soldiers, whatever their color, and loyal citizens, regardless of sex, deserved just compensation for wartime sacrifice. The government, as a matter of principle, should honor its commitment and repay those who made verifiable sacrifices. Just because her services had not been properly documented during wartime did not mean Tubman should be disqualified from collecting the wages she deserved. She only wanted fair treatment.

While in Union service, Tubman assisted the army with housing and hygiene for the hundreds and eventually thousands of contrabands who fled behind Union lines. When she ventured into occupied Carolina, it was no longer Tubman's private war against slavery; she operated within the theater of war to save the Union, under the auspices of the secretary of war.

In July 1865, before leaving Washington, Tubman had applied to her good friend and patron William Seward for assistance. Favorably disposed, Seward referred the matter to General Hunter; but at that time "no pay whatever was obtained."[8] Doubtless Tubman was unwilling to press her legitimate claim during the chaotic immediate postwar era. She was especially loath to pester Seward, who was preoccupied with affairs of state in the wake of Lincoln's assassination and was himself recovering from stab wounds inflicted during a thwarted assassination attempt on the night Lincoln was shot.

Tubman postponed her official appeal, believing that her powerful patrons would eventually prevail. One of her white friends confided that "while Harriet has never been known to beg for herself, the cause of the needy will send her out with a basket on her arm to the kitchens of her friends, without a show of hesitation."[9] But two years after the war, she felt more the burdens of being the sole support of her aged parents, trying to make ends meet with occasional handouts and selling her own homegrown produce and pies.

Not surprisingly, Tubman fell on hard times and was forced to beseech former abolitionist friends for loans. A sixty-dollar gift from Wendell Phillips late in 1867 allowed Tubman's South Street household to be stocked with food and fuel to last during the harsh winter ahead.

In October 1867 she learned that John Tubman had been murdered in Cambridge, Maryland, leaving behind his widow, Caroline, and their four children. A white man, Robert Vincent, had shot him in cold blood. The murder was committed on a lonely stretch of road, with only John Tubman's thirteen-year-old son as a witness. A Baltimore paper reported, "The murderer has not yet been arrested and we question whether he ever will. . . . No effort, that we are aware of, has been made to overtake and bring him to justice."[10] However, by December 16 Vincent was apprehended and put on trial. The defendant claimed self-defense and his all-white jury returned a verdict of not guilty after ten minutes of deliberation.[11]

This was a disheartening blow to Harriet: both the violent death of someone whom she had loved, and the callous disregard for justice that followed his murder. The *Baltimore American* editorialized:

> As no one but a colored boy saw him commit the deed, it was universally conceded that he would be acquitted, the moment it was ascertained that the jury was composed exclusively of Democrats. The Republicans have taught the Democrats much since 1860. They thrashed them into at least a seeming respect for the Union. . . . They forced them to recognize Negro testimony in their courts. But haven't got them to the point of convicting a fellow Democrat for killing a Negro. But even that will follow when the Negro is armed with the ballot.[12]

Harriet had little leisure to mourn, as the pressing needs of her household weighed on her.

By November 1867 Tubman decided she must take her financial case to the federal government again. She visited Gerrit Smith at Peterboro in hopes he might help with her claim. She brought along "a letter from William H. Seward to Maj. Gen. Hunter, dated 1865 in which Mr. Seward says, 'I have known her long and a nobler, higher, spirit or truer seldom dwells in human form.'"[13]

Local advocates began to advertise Tubman's plight, to promote her case. A Mr. R. Fisk reported, "A few warm, appreciative friends in Auburn help her [Tubman] from time to time." But, he complained, "more ought to remember her . . . and do for her what so many years in a much larger and with a far more deserving spirit than our own she did for the oppressed and needy, the suffering and afflicted in slavery and war."[14]

By 1868 former abolitionists in upstate New York mobilized on Tubman's behalf. When her financial crisis was revealed to Republican friends, community leaders penned endorsements for her to attach to her claim. One wrote a letter to the editor of the *Auburn Daily Advertiser,* complaining, "She hasn't yet succeeded in procuring any assistance from the Government for the acknowledged services, especially in securing the scouts in South Carolina who were so very successful in piloting our army about Port Royal, Hilton Head and Beaufort."[15]

Her champions tackled the problem on more than one front. They sponsored an authorized biography — selling her story to raise funds, a common tactic from antislavery days. Her friend Sarah Bradford was drafted to prepare the manuscript for publication. Besides interviewing her subject, she amassed stories about Harriet from prominent statesmen, soliciting testimonials on Harriet's behalf.

Bradford wove Harriet's own tales together with statements from luminaries such as William Seward, Frederick Douglass, and Wendell Phillips. Gerrit Smith and other wealthy donors underwrote all printing costs. A January issue of Boston's *Commonwealth* announced the book's publication in 1869.

Mrs. Sarah H. Bradford, of Geneva, New York, has made quite an interesting memoir of this devoted woman, which has been published in neat book-form and the proceeds of the sales of which go to her support, she being now very old [Tubman was actually forty-four at the time] and quite infirm. The price is $1 only, and copies can be procured at the rooms of the Woman's Club and the Freedman's Aid Society, or they will be forwarded post-paid, upon receipt of price, by addressing "Box No. 782" Boston Postoffice.[16]

Advertising paid off, and the volume eventually yielded Tubman a windfall of over $1,200.

Simultaneously, an Auburn banker named Charles P. Wood prepared a narrative of Tubman's war service, with an appendix of available documentation. Copies are still on file at the National Archives. The result of Wood's research was originally scheduled to be included in Bradford's book, but it instead became part of the official claim sent to the House of Representatives. Faithful supporters like Gerrit Smith chimed in: "During the late war, Mrs. Tubman was eminently faithful and useful to the cause of the country. She is poor, and has poor parents. Such a servant of the country should be well paid by the country. I hope the Government will look into her case."[17]

Congress was supplied with a detailed account of Tubman's military assignments. Wood attached only a few of her orders and passes, explaining that because she was "unconscious of the great value of the official documents she had from the several officers at different times, Harriet has lost some of them."[18] Although she possessed very little paperwork from the period, those Union officers contacted were willing to supplement the record with letters commending her wartime service: David Hunter, Rufus Saxton, James Montgomery, and Dr. Henry Durant.[19] All provided Wood with detailed testimonials.

Wood lamented that during more than three years of service, she received only $200, and "with characteristic indifference to self" Harriet used this amount to build a laundry facility at Beaufort, where she taught the freedwomen to take in wash to become self-supporting. This altruistic effort was dealt a cruel blow when "during her absence with the important expedition in Florida this wash-house was destroyed or appropriated by a Reg't of troops fresh from the north to make shelter for themselves but without any compensation whatever to Harriet."[20]

When she liberated several hundred slaves during the Combahee River Raid, she brought soldiers into the ranks, a service the Union regularly rewarded. Bounties for enlisting soldiers could run as high as $300 per recruit (for substitutes), depending upon the state. Tubman recalled that she took roughly one hundred of the adult male refugees to Hilton Head to the "recruiting officer and they enlisted in the army." She commented that "Colonel Whittle said I ought to be paid for every soldier as much as a recruiting officer, but laws! I never got nothing."[21]

Wood carefully added that Tubman "is known throughout this State and New England as an honest, earnest and most self-sacrificing woman" and that all statements are "obtained from her lips" and from "original papers in her possession," of which he offered copies. He confidently concluded "that Harriet is entitled to several thousands of dollars pay — there can be no doubt." Wood conceded "that she held no commission, and had not in the regular way and at the proper times and places, made press and applications of and for her just compensation."[22] Nevertheless, his lengthy narrative insisted that she finally be given her due. Wood's document took years to work its way through the federal bureaucracy.

Sometime late in 1866 or early in 1867, a young black soldier whom Tubman had known during her wartime service in the South reappeared in her life. Private Nelson Charles had been born a slave near Elizabeth City, North Carolina, but escaped his master, Fred Charles, and removed to upstate New York.[23] In September 1863 at Oneida, he joined the ranks of the New York Eighth Regiment, Company G.

After training in Philadelphia, the nineteen-year-old Charles moved south with his unit in January 1864. He landed in South Carolina, where he met Harriet Tubman. He accompanied an expedition to Jacksonville, Florida, in February 1864, where black Union troops occupied the town.

On February 20 Charles fought at the Battle of Olustee. His regiment retreated to Jacksonville, where he remained until April. Harriet departed to Auburn for a furlough in June 1864, while Charles was posted to Virginia shortly thereafter. Theirs was an acquaintance of only a few months, and it is not known if he kept in touch with Tubman after she returned to Auburn.

Nelson was honorably discharged from the army in November 1865 at Brownsville, Texas, and he made his way to Auburn, arriving in upstate New York in the winter of 1866–67. Now using the name Nelson Davis, the twenty-two-year-old moved into Tubman's home on South Street, presumably to convalesce during a bout of tuberculosis. But he seems to have remained in her home even after he recovered. Davis found work as a bricklayer and became a boarder in Tubman's expanding household. Despite his ill health, the veteran was described as a tall, strapping man.

Davis surely would have sympathized with Harriet in the fall of 1867 when she learned that John Tubman had been gunned down in the streets of Cambridge. Once she was a widow in the eyes of God, she was finally willing to entertain the possibility of remarriage. Sometime in the next fifteen months, Nelson and Harriet decided to wed.

It was doubtless satisfying to Tubman that both her parents, now extremely elderly, as well as at least one brother and several other kin, were together to help her celebrate this joyous event. Tubman would have been pleased at the contrast between her first, unrecorded marriage ceremony while a slave, and her second wedding, in a prominent church, with local dignitaries as well as family members in attendance.

On March 18, 1869, the Reverend Henry Fowler married the couple at Auburn's Central Presbyterian Church. At the time, Davis was only twenty-five and Harriet was at least twenty years older — if not twice the groom's age. The age difference may appear striking, but was perhaps negligible upon meeting them in person. Census data and photographs suggest that they looked to be much closer in age. In the 1870 census, Davis was identified as forty years old (although he was not yet thirty), and Harriet was likewise listed as forty (although she was older). In 1880 Davis was again listed as forty — perhaps aging very well as a married man. In this same census, Harriet was identified as being forty-four, although by this time she was well over fifty. By all accounts, the difference in their ages was insignificant to them.

The wedding announcement in the *Auburn Morning News* misidentified the groom as "William Nelson." He used the name Charles Nelson Davis on the church marriage registry. But he was known to the townspeople as Nelson Davis, and afterward, in local newspaper articles, the name Davis often was attached to the more famous name of Harriet Tubman, by which the bride continued to be known. But "Mrs. Davis" was also used, a postwar gesture of goodwill toward this respected woman. African Americans were too often dismissed as "aunty" in person and in the press; thus "Mrs. Harriet Davis" signaled the esteem Tubman elicited among whites as well as blacks.

These name changes seemed inconsequential compared with the real transformation that the ceremony symbolized. A reporter at the wedding wrote:

> The audience was large, consisting of the friends of the parties and a large number of first families in the city. Ladies and gentlemen who were interested in Harriet, and who for years had advised and assisted her, came to see her married. After the ceremony Rev. Mr. Fowler made some very touching and happy allusions to their past trials and apparently plain sailing the parties now had, when the ceremony ended amid the congratulations of the assembly, and the happy couple were duly embarked on the journey of life.[24]

This "journey of life" was certainly one she had long anticipated — to be married and have a home and a large circle of family and friends within her community.

One of Tubman's descendants lumped John Tubman and Nelson Davis together, calling them both "colorless creatures."[25] Yet the union between Harriet Tubman and Nelson Davis was longer, and had a much happier outcome than Harriet's first marriage. Tubman and Davis were married for nearly twenty years.

Harriet and Nelson lived quietly in her house on South Street, sur-

rounded by her parents and other family. One of her grandnephews, Harkless Bowley, visiting from Maryland, remembered his great-grandfather
Ben with delight. Harkless's grandmother was one of Harriet's disappeared
sisters. Her grandson was born free in Canada. After the war, Harkless's
mother, Mary Anne, a former fugitive slave, was able to return to both her
Maryland birthplace and her former name, Kizzy (Keziah). Family reunions,
however marred by those missing, must have been satisfying accomplishments for Tubman.

Harriet and her husband had much to be grateful for, yet still they
struggled. Money was chronically short, and Tubman was always making
solicitations for charity cases. Once when she requested a contribution for
southern freedmen from William Seward, he told her, "You have worked
for others long enough. . . . If you ask for a donation for *yourself* I will give
it to you, but I will not help you to rob yourself for others."[26] Despite
Seward's advice, Tubman never gave up — continually making appeals for
freedmen's schools, for the Salvation Army, and for her church, the AME
Zion Church on Parker Street.[27]

Seward remained a supporter and adviser to Harriet on his visits home.
The loss of his wife in 1865, and the death of his twenty-two-year-old
daughter, Frances, the following year were terrible sorrows for the secretary
of state to shoulder. His own demise at the age of seventy-one, in 1872,
was a blow to Auburn. The loss of the town's most celebrated native son was
deeply mourned. The massive funeral preoccupied the county, and was recounted at length in the press:

> Just before the coffin was to be closed, a woman black as night
> stole quietly in, and laying a wreath of field flowers *on his feet,* as
> quietly glided out again. This was the simple tribute of our sable
> friend and her last token of love and gratitude to her kind pro-
> tector.[28]

Harriet had paid her last respects to her longtime patron.

Tubman's financial worries multiplied after Seward's death. Although
the Seward family forgave other debts, she had to pay off her mortgage to

settle Seward's estate. On May 29, 1873, Frederick Seward, William's son and executor, collected $1,200 from Tubman.[29] Although she now owned, free and clear, her South Street home on seven acres, her savings were gone. Her household was overflowing with charity cases and she had barely enough money to get by.

Her financial woes allowed Tubman to become prey to a criminal swindle in 1873. The "gold scam" was all too common during the postwar era. In late September 1873 a pair of black men appeared in Auburn and first approached Harriet Tubman's brother John Henry Stewart with a proposition: they would give him a trunk full of gold — coins worth $5,000 smuggled north from South Carolina — in exchange for $2,000 in greenbacks. These con artists explained that they could not be "seen with the gold, as all coin belonged to the Government, whose agents would seize it."[30]

Although Tubman was described as shrewd by most who knew her, sadly these men were able to con her. Tubman had been in Beaufort when gold and silver had been hidden away by wealthy whites in the surrounding countryside during Union invasion. She knew firsthand that African Americans were frequently the ones on shovel detail, and they might well have been able to locate slaveholders' hidden valuables before whites themselves made it back to recover buried treasures. So to Tubman the men's story was not so far-fetched.

Eventually one of Tubman's longtime friends, merchant and Republican politician Anthony Shimer, furnished her with $2,000 in greenbacks. He expected to be given, in exchange, the same amount in gold, which would realize a handsome profit. Not surprisingly, the trade of paper for coin was to take place during the cover of night. The two con men were able to separate Harriet from those who had accompanied her — her husband, her brother, Shimer, and one other white man. After being lured on her own deep into the woods, Harriet was knocked out with chloroform and injured, relieved of her purse, and left bound and gagged.[31] Shimer was able to rescue Harriet sometime before dawn, but the scoundrels were long gone, as was the money.

This episode, splashed into the Auburn headlines, created a terrible scandal, and wild rumors blossomed throughout upstate New York. Apparently, two years before, these same confidence men had committed a similar fraud along the Canadian border, ironically near St. Catharines. The entire upstate New York community was in an uproar, especially because Tubman had been left to die. She recuperated with her friends the Howlands, who nursed her back to health.[32]

Many commented on Tubman's simplistic approach to matters involving money — her intuition that God would deliver. This hangover from her UGRR days now failed her. Perhaps after years of battling illnesses and struggling for survival, the forty-eight-year-old Tubman had lost some of her sharpness. Whatever the case, the misadventure was a setback.

Outraged, local townspeople recognized that Harriet had been preyed upon. They concluded she would never have been involved in such a risky scheme if she had not been so economically vulnerable. Thus town fathers renewed their campaign to get Tubman the financial help she needed. Her government claim seemed to be stuck in the Capitol's bureaucratic entrails. New York congressman C. S. MacDougall, a former Union general, pressed the issue in Congress. Representative Gerry W. Hazelton of Wisconsin, a member of the Committee on War Claims, finally endorsed bill H.R. 3786, which appeared in 1874 in the official report of the *Congressional Record:*

> The whole history of the case establishes conclusively the fact that her services in the various capacities of nurse, scout, and spy were of great service and value to the Government, for which no compensation was paid her beside the support she was furnished. . . . Your committee are of the opinion that she should be paid for these services and to that end report back the accompanying bill as a substitute for H.R. 2711, appropriating the sum of $2,000 for services rendered by her to the Union Army as scout, nurse, and spy, and recommend its passage.[33]

However, there were thousands of such requests pouring into Congress. Tubman's bill, H.R. 3786, passed the House but not the Senate.

During the years of his marriage to Tubman, Nelson Davis became active in Union veterans' organizations, a member of the Crocker Post of the Grand Army of the Republic (GAR). He shared his wife's religion and was a founding trustee of St. Mark's AME Church in July 1870.[34] He was by his wife's side during the burial of her father in the early 1870s,[35] and again when her mother was laid to rest in 1880.

Nelson Davis would also be the one to help his wife rebuild their home, purchased from Seward, after it was destroyed by fire in 1886. He did extensive repair work by replacing the original wooden structure with a largely brick one, still standing in Auburn today.

Davis would encourage his wife in her philanthropic endeavors. Her dream of building a charity home adjacent to their South Street house was thwarted by their constant lack of funds, but her benevolence made Tubman the pride of the town. In 1873 the Auburn paper identified her as "the celebrated colored philanthropist."

One of the white ladies of Auburn who would empty her pantry for Tubman's cause recalled:

> All these years her doors have been open to the needy. . . . The aged . . . the babe deserted, the demented, the epileptic, the blind, the paralyzed, the consumptive all have found shelter and welcome. At no one time can I recall the little home to have sheltered less than six or eight wrecks of humanity entirely dependent upon Harriet for their all.[36]

In a photograph taken at Harriet's South Street home circa 1885, six African Americans (besides Harriet and Nelson) are identified as household residents. Harriet is standing in the back row next to Gertie Davis Watson and three children — Lee Cheyney, Walter Green, and Dora Stewart (Tubman's grandniece). Seated in front are Nelson Davis (smoking a pipe), Pop Alexander, and Blind Aunty Parker.[37]

By this time, Harriet's favorite, her adopted daughter Margaret, had married Henry Lucas, a local caterer, and moved out. But she would bring her own children to Harriet's house for long afternoons filled with stories and reminiscences. Margaret's youngest daughter, Alice, fondly remembered her frequent visits to the South Street home. Once while she was playing in the long grass, Alice was taken by surprise when her great-aunt suddenly popped up in the meadow beside her. Harriet had left her rocking chair, flattened herself against the ground, and silently slithered up to the little girl to surprise her — a trick she had learned from her days with the Underground Railroad.[38]

Tubman kept her household filled with family, but also with strangers who needed her support. This hospitality was critical for "the friendless of her race" who were elderly, because "few if any of the homes for the aged between Auburn and Greater New York [New York City] admit colored people."[39] With her husband's failing health in 1886, Tubman decided she must renew her appeal for government subsidy. Veterans' pensions were being lavishly dispensed during this period. Indeed Ohio congressman Benjamin Harrison (who would serve as Republican president from 1889 to 1893), himself a Civil War veteran, had been criticized for sponsoring so many private bills to benefit veterans — even for some, it was later discovered, who had been declared deserters.

In January 1887 Tubman was granted permission to withdraw the papers submitted to Congress in 1874 on behalf of her private bill.[40] These documents were sent to Philip Wright of Medford, Massachusetts, who advised: "If I knew any body in authority I should try to do something for you about getting you your pension. Unfortunately, I do not. *The petition for a pension should properly come from a representative from New York.*"[41]

By the late 1880s Tubman's reluctance to reveal the severity of her circumstances spurred the ladies of Auburn to devise a system whereby their servants would deliver baskets of food to the porch of Tubman's South Street home — anonymous donations to help her out. She might wake up with the cupboard bare, wondering how to provide for the motley group collected under her roof, and discover a bounty on her front steps when she opened her door.

When Theodore Pomeroy, a former mayor, prominent legislator, and great friend of the Sewards, died in 1905, Harriet paid a mourning call at the Pomeroy home. There she was "cordially received by all the members

of the family [the younger ones she had rocked and tended in infancy],"
the newspaper commented.[42] She was given a place of honor in the funeral
cortege, and the family carriage took her home.[43] Apparently there were
several prominent families in Auburn who had employed Tubman at one
time or another in a domestic capacity, most likely as child tender.

This kind of work, which completely dominated opportunities for
black female wage earners during this era, seems to have been the exception rather than the rule for Harriet while in Auburn. Serving as a children's nurse for the Pomeroys was perhaps undertaken only as a means of
securing continued patronage by Auburn's elite, whose favor Tubman required. Or she may have been forced into this domestic role when she lost
her husband's income, first due to his illness and then, finally, his death.

Harriet Tubman buried Nelson Davis, her husband of nineteen years,
at Fort Hill Cemetery in October 1888. Her brother John Henry Stewart,
a teamster in Auburn, who also resided on South Street, died the next year.
Tubman must have felt considerably alone once again.

In June 1890 Congress passed a law providing for widows of war veterans to receive modest payments. Tubman applied for the $8 per month
available. Her application offered a number of facts, to which she swore,
including her birth year as 1825. But Tubman's pension application was returned to her with specific queries about her claim. For example, the government requested some proof about the true identity of Nelson Davis.
Like many ex-slaves, black veterans and their relatives found their appeals
challenged or rejected because of mix-ups concerning slave names and free
names.

In May of 1892 Tubman tried to clear up the matter with another
round of documentation. She offered a new deposition and swore again
that she was born in 1825. Tubman confirmed the name of her late husband of nearly twenty years was Nelson Davis. But she explained that in
bondage he was known as Nelson Charles. She testified that her husband
served in the Union army and was discharged under the name of Nelson
Charles, but by the time he settled in Auburn in 1866, he had taken the
name Nelson Davis. When he married, he used a combination of names:

Charles Nelson Davis. In her statement Tubman "positively and unequivocally swears that the Nelson Davis who was married under the name Charles Nelson Davis and who died as Nelson Davis was the identical person who served in Co. 'G' 8th U.S.C. Infantry as Nelson Charles."[44] She supplied a church marriage certificate and provided affidavits from two witnesses (one was Maggie Lucas) who confirmed Davis's identity. These deposed witnesses testified that Harriet and Nelson's was a proper and legal union, that Davis had no other wife, and so on. Finally Harriet was able to prove her case, and by the end of 1892 she was granted her monthly widow's pension of $8.

Not only was this the first time Tubman had secured government support since the war, but it was the first time in her entire life that she had any reliable income.[45] Although it was a very small sum, this lifetime pension represented some measure of security to Harriet, who had spent such a hardscrabble life.

Many would have expected Harriet Tubman to savor the moment. She owned her own home and now had a small but steady income to maintain her household. She was nearly seventy years old and had surely earned the right to retire from the challenging pace she had undertaken since her return from war. But this was never Tubman's style.

She steadfastly held on to her dream: to establish a separate charitable institution in Auburn for the needy and neglected of her race.[46] She surveyed an enviable parcel of land from her porch: she coveted a large, ten-room, brick building next door, with another plain house nearby. Both structures were surrounded by smaller outbuildings. One observer commented that this property in many respects reminded her of a picturesque southern setting, with a Big House, an overseer's cottage, and slave cabins.[47] Purchasing this twenty-five-acre lot would quadruple Tubman's real estate holdings but also saddle her with debt. Yet the acquisition of this parcel and its buildings could move her closer to her lifelong objective of creating a permanent charity home.

Although a small circle knew of her ambitions, most townsfolk were taken aback when Tubman showed up at a public auction in 1896 and bought 130 South Street. The property, known as the old Beardsley estate, had once belonged to Seward's father-in-law and in 1864 was sold for over $2,000.[48] When the estate came back on the market, Tubman made a winning bid of $1,450.[49]

Tubman contacted elders of the AME Zion Church and persuaded them to help her secure a bank mortgage for $1,000 and to raise funds for the remaining sum to provide a down payment. An AME Zion minister, Rev. G. C. Carter, took on this cause, and in a little over a week, donations funded the down payment for the project so Tubman could expand her charity for Auburn's needy. Her leap of faith in buying this property shamed fellow citizens into yet another push to secure Tubman money for her own postwar government claim.

An article appeared in July 1896 in *The Chautauquan* that chided, "It seems strange that one who has done so much for her country and been in the thick of the battles with shots falling all about her, should never have had recognition from the Government in a substantial way."[50] Harriet often echoed this lament: "You wouldn't think that after I served the flag so faithfully I should come to want under its folds."[51]

Prominent Republicans offered to lead the charge once again. In 1897 a petition requesting that Congressman Sereno E. Payne of New York "bring up the matter again and press it to a final and successful termination" was circulated and endorsed by Auburn's most influential citizens. This appeal included signatures from the Garrisons, Sedgwicks, and other prominent upstate and New England families. An affidavit from Tubman and other supporting documents were sent along with the petition to Washington.[52]

Payne's first gambit was a request for review by the Committee on Invalid Pensions, as the chair of the committee was his fellow delegate from New York, George Ray. Payne hoped a straightforward soldier's pension could be obtained on the basis of Tubman's war record. The inquiry omitted any reference to the issue of back wages — just a simple pension request.

Payne's new bill proposed that Congress grant Tubman a "military pension" of $25 per month, the exact amount received by surviving soldiers.

A staff member of the National Archives, later researching background on this claim, pinpointed problems with supporting documentation; no extant evidence in government records supported Tubman's persistent claim that she had been working under the direction of the secretary of war. The archivist conceded that Tubman might have been "a confidential agent of the Department of State or of Secretary Seward, rather than of the War Department," but cautioned, "The records which we have received from the Department of State contain no reference to her."[53] Providing her with funds without any corroborating evidence was a bureaucratic red flag.

Some on the committee believed that Tubman's service as a spy and scout, which was supported by valid documentation, justified such a pension. Others suggested that the matter of a soldier's pension should be dropped, as she could more legitimately be pensioned as a nurse. At the same time, $25 was more than double the pension nurses received.

One of the members was W. Jasper Talbert of Parkesville, South Carolina. Some have suggested this South Carolina politician vindictively tried to block Tubman's pension — that it was a point of honor to this white southern statesman that a black woman not be given recognition as a soldier. After all, she was a fugitive slave much of her life, with a high price on her head imposed by southern magistrates and even the legislature of Maryland. Perhaps a South Carolinian's stubborn resistance was as much a part of war's legacy as was Harriet's unwavering claim.[54]

Regardless, a compromise was finally achieved. Tubman's pension as a widow would be increased on account of special circumstances. The House authorized raising the amount to $25, while the Senate amended to lower this to only $20 — which was finally passed by both houses and signed into law by President William McKinley in February 1899.

After thirty years of struggle, this represented a tremendous victory. First and foremost, details of Tubman's wartime service became part of the *Congressional Record*. It was publicly acknowledged that hers was a "double claim."[55] Although she may have only been given an increase for her widow's pension, the record asserted that "in view of her personal services to the Government, Congress is amply justified in increasing that pension."[56]

It must have been with great personal satisfaction that she finally received her due — that her persistence had paid off. She had been committed to Union veterans and had participated with enthusiasm in Grand Army of the Republic veterans' activities, with or without any government pension. When interviewed in 1907, she insisted that the journalist from the *New York Herald* highlight her affiliation with the veterans' group.[57]

She would be bankrolled by pension checks of $240 per year instead of the less than $100 she had been receiving. But even with her increased pension, Harriet, nearing eighty, was finding that her ambitions outdistanced her abilities. She felt overwhelmed by the administration of her own and extended households. She was daunted by the burdens associated with her additional charitable property and its residents. One year she did not have the cash to cover the taxes on her twenty-five-acre parcel and had to surrender cows to pay the debt.[58]

By 1903 she decided to donate the property she had purchased at auction to the AME Zion Church, with the stipulation that she would hold a lifetime deed and that the place would be maintained as a home for "aged and indigent colored people." In this way her dream would outlive her. A newly appointed board christened one of the buildings on the grounds John Brown Hall, to honor their donor's wishes, but they insisted upon calling their project the Harriet Tubman Home. Although it took five more years to raise sufficient funds to properly equip and fully staff the home, there were several residents before the official opening. This feat was only accomplished with the organizing talents of the Board of Lady Managers, the dedicated clubwomen who helped Harriet realize her dream.

On June 23, 1908, Tubman was guest of honor at the daylong opening celebration, which included a parade, prayers and speeches, a band concert, a dinner, an evening reception, and a dance. The Harriet Tubman Home became the only charity outside New York City dedicated to the shelter and care of African Americans in the state. The main brick building, John Brown Hall, also known as the John Brown Infirmary, was filled with "comfortable furniture, plenty of clean white linen, enameled beds," and surrounded by bountiful orchards. The newspaper recorded:

> With the Stars and Stripes wound about her shoulders, a band playing national airs and a concourse of members of her race gathered about her to pay tribute to her lifelong struggle on behalf of the colored people of America, aged Harriet Tubman Davis, the Moses of her race, yesterday experienced one of the happiest moments of her life, a period to which she has looked forward for a score of years. . . . The Harriet Tubman Home is today an accomplished fact and her 95 years have at last been crowned with success.[59]

Again, Harriet's age was always a matter of speculation; at this time, she was closer to eighty-five than ninety-five. She had been hospitalized just the year before, but with the opening of her home, Tubman demonstrated that even at her advanced age she was both sound and spry.

That June afternoon was a glorious one for Tubman. She circulated among the crowds, telling stories to rapt listeners. She made time for those who would lean close to catch her every word, especially the children. This is just one of the dozens of occasions over the years where she spun her stories — tales of the UGRR, daring during the Civil War, meeting and greeting the great men of her day — recounting her unique adventures to an enthralled, mainly white audience.

Her quick wit and sharp response charmed the crowds. When she was asked to give a speech to the assembled visitors, Tubman spoke extemporaneously, at length, and, as always, entertained her listeners. Harriet explained, "I did not take up this work for my own benefit, but for those of my race who need help. The work is now well started and I know God will raise up others to take care of the future."[60] All knew that this was a landmark occasion, because "the dream of Moses for herself and for her people was at last realized."[61]

Even with the establishment of the home, there remained battles to wage with its overseers. The fees required by church supervisors disgruntled Tubman. The cost of room and board was $3 a week, or for a fee of $150 a resident was given "life privileges." She accepted the church's regulations, but knocked on doors and solicited contributions for those who could not afford these charges. Wealthy patrons such as the Osborne family continued to heed Tubman's charitable calls. Although she was officially retired from funding the home that bore her name, she never passed up the opportunity to pry open the pocketbooks of those she visited, offering some story of a forlorn but deserving case to which they might want to contribute.

Whenever health permitted, she toured on behalf of the home that bore her name. She was especially pleased when Julia Henderson established a "home for colored women" on Holyoke Street in Boston, and named the facility after her. Tubman was the center of attention and most honored guest at the home's dedication in 1904.

Tubman was even more pleased when the world came to her. Over the Christmas holidays in 1903, Harriet had a reunion with Susan B. Anthony. On New Year's Day, Anthony reported with delight that Tubman was "still alive":

> I saw her the other day at the home of Eliza Wright Osborne, the daughter of Martha C. Wright — in company with Elizabeth Smith Miller — the only daughter of Gerrit Smith. Miss Emily Howland — Rev. [illeg.] H. Thaw — and Miss Ella Wright Garrison, the daughter of Martha C. Wright & wife of William Lloyd Garrison, Jr. — all of us were visiting at the Osbornes — a real love feast of the few that are left — and here came Harriet Tubman.[62]

Tubman's devotion to women's rights was legendary as well. She would always take advantage of reunions with women friends from her abolitionist days, many of whom transferred their considerable energies to fighting for women's rights after slaves were freed. Whenever suffrage advocates gathered in upstate New York, Tubman would grab her shawl and hat and head for the Auburn train station. Friends commented that she rarely concerned herself with a schedule, but simply would make her way to the depot and take the next train going the right direction.

On October 23, 1905, Emily Howland and Harriet Tubman shared a train ride to Rochester for a suffrage meeting the next day, but parted upon arrival in Rochester. While Howland spent the night comfortably, Tubman sat up all night at the station — knowing, perhaps by experience, that there would be "no lodgings which would take in a woman of color."[63] The next day, when they met up at the conference and Howland discovered how Tubman had spent the night, she was horrified, especially at her own thoughtlessness.

First, Howland offered to share her room with Tubman for the duration of the meeting. Second, she confronted convention organizers and pointed out the leadership's responsibility to black delegates, insisting that they provide lodgings for women of color who attended future meetings.[64] It was typical that these kinds of demands for reform came from Tubman's friends, but not from her personally. She was extremely modest and would rarely advance agendas that might be construed as self-promoting. Even when forced to sit up all night in a train station, Tubman's restraint and self-sacrifice were on prominent display.

Tubman especially enjoyed offering advice and inspiration when visitors arrived on her doorstep. Perhaps she appreciated a reunion with an old friend she had met during the war, Sojourner Truth, when she spoke at a local Friends meeting on August 18, 1878.[65] Booker T. Washington often paid his respects during stopovers in upstate New York.[66] Tubman also became a confidante and friend to some of the most powerful black women leaders of her day: Women's Christian Temperance Union leader Eliza Peterson (of Texarkana, Texas) and Mary Talbert of Buffalo, New York, who became president of the Empire State Federation of Colored Women's Clubs and led a protest of exhibits demeaning to blacks at the 1901 Pan-American Exposition. Talbert's club gave Tubman and her home substantial financial support.

Tubman enjoyed regaling journalist interviewers, such as Frank Davis, whose 1907 Sunday magazine piece in the *New York Herald* featured a profile of her.[64] In 1911 eminent author James B. Clarke published a pamphlet, *An Hour with Harriet Tubman,* to promote the cause of her charitable home. Clarke's tribute suggested, "When her voice is forever stilled, her soul, like the soul of him whom she calls her dearest friend, will later be 'marching on.'"[68]

By this time, Harriet Tubman had slowed her pace but not her determination, working on behalf of her dream right up until her demise. Following a lengthy hospitalization in 1911, she moved out of her own house and into the charity facility next door. The minister of the AME Zion Church would conduct services there if she was unable to attend Sunday worship. By 1912, although her spirit was still joyful and her faith still abundant, her body was giving out.

In November 1912 she summoned a local lawyer and prepared a will. She named three women as heirs: her niece Mary Gaston (one of her brother John Henry's descendants), her grandniece Katy Stewart (the adopted daughter of her brother James Isaac), and Frances Smith, the matron of the Harriet Tubman Home, to whom she felt indebted for her dedication and personal care. These three would inherit Tubman's personal home and its seven acres.

In early March 1913 Tubman lapsed into a final illness and announced to bedside attendants that she knew she was going to die soon. Friends and family gathered, and notices in local papers, as well as in the *New York Times* and *New York Tribune,* notified readers that Harriet Tubman was dying.[69] All praised her work with the Underground Railroad and mentioned her connection to the Civil War.

It was as if some grand historic eye were slowly closing. Harriet Tubman had witnessed the burials of Frederick Douglass, William Lloyd Garrison, William Seward, so many of the great statesmen and politicians, all her colleagues in the struggle to free the slaves. She survived the deaths of Civil War comrades — Generals Saxton, Gillmore, and Montgomery, and so many of the officers and soldiers she knew during the war. She outlived several siblings, nieces, and nephews, as well as two husbands. Tubman was clearly ready to die, and all who visited her deathbed described her as a powerful spirit, one who would join in the singing of hymns and felt "ready to meet her maker."

Shortly before she died, on the evening of March 10, 1913, in loving remembrance she told the assembled mourners, "I go to prepare a place for you."[70]

## *Epilogue*

# Harriet Tubman's Legacy

———◄o►———

IN MARCH 1913 Harriet Tubman was buried with military honors in Auburn's Fort Hill Cemetery. A photograph of the event shows a handsome coffin at the grave site, while black and white mourners crowd around. Shortly after her death, the town of Auburn decided to dedicate a plaque in her honor to be placed on a public building. The town organized such an event a little over a year after Tubman died.

The memorial service was held in the midst of a period described as the nadir of American race relations, an era when the gains of Reconstruction were edged out by the losses to Jim Crow. That the town of Auburn would sponsor such a tribute demonstrated Tubman's exalted status within her upstate community. The bronze tablet was funded by the Auburn Business Man's Association and the Cayuga County Historical Society. Booker T. Washington, the most prominent race leader of his day, traveled to upstate New York to make the keynote address. Mary Talbert, a close friend of Tubman's and chair of the board of the National Association of Colored Women, spoke on Tubman's life and work. Alice H. Lucas, listed in the program as Harriet's grandniece, was invited to perform the unveiling. On June 12, 1914, church and civic leaders, black and white alike, convened in a civic auditorium for the dedication ceremonies, as the mayor presided over this historic and integrated event.

Tubman was lionized by those who gathered to pay tribute. At the same time, the souvenir program bore a cover quote from Booker T. Washington, which carried his photograph and a two-page promotion of his Tuskegee Institute inside. Certainly the Tubman Home, still a local Auburn institution, received its due — but the charity was already falling on hard times, and it would close its doors in little over a decade, when the last of five remaining residents died. But it was the bronze tablet, meant to herald Tubman's achievement, that most clearly revealed hints of problems to come.

It began promisingly:

CALLED THE "MOSES" OF HER PEOPLE, DURING THE CIVIL WAR,
WITH RARE COURAGE, SHE LED OVER THREE HUNDRED NEGROES
UP FROM SLAVERY TO FREEDOM, AND RENDERED INVALUABLE
SERVICE AS NURSE AND SPY.

But it went on to proclaim:

SHE TRUTHFULLY SAID "ON MY UNDERGROUND RAILROAD
I NEBBER RUN MY TRAIN OFF DE TRACK AND I NEBBER LOS' A
PASSENGER."

The use of dialect on the plaque was creative license, reflecting the way in which white projections and racist shadings shaped "Negro" achievements. In this, as in so many other cases, the alleged authenticity of dialect undermined and overshadowed any purported attempt to convey Tubman's exact words. Such distortions began almost as soon as Tubman was laid to rest and continue well into the present day. Similarly, while she was credited with seeing three hundred slaves to freedom as a conductor, those she freed during her service in wartime South Carolina (more than 750 in the Combahee River Raid alone) were left uncounted.

Trying to untangle the web of misinformation and plumb the rich reservoir of memories associated with Harriet Tubman presents major challenges to her biographers. Those who cherished her while she was alive — and perhaps Tubman herself — would be both pleased and puzzled by current-day efforts to extend her legacy.

How would Tubman respond, knowing her name was attached to contemporary hot lines and shelters for fugitive women and children, those who seek protection from abusive spouses?[1] In her former home of Canada, she is associated with a recently opened *digitized* research facility at York University in Ontario: the Harriet Tubman Resource Centre on the African Diaspora.

Although the charitable home that bore her name in Boston has long since folded, a life-size group of bronze figures commemorating her role in the Underground Railroad, "Step on Board," was recently dedicated in Boston's South End. This monument was the first statue of a woman erected on the city's public grounds. An equally impressive statue of Tubman (larger than life) stands in Battle Creek, Michigan, Sojourner Truth's longtime home.[2]

In the Battle Creek representation, Tubman is holding on to a rifle. In her birthplace state of Maryland, plans to paint a billboard-size portrait of Tubman showing her with a rifle have been stalled. Protests within the state have prevented any public art of Tubman in the familiar guise of handling her Civil War musket. The image has sparked considerable controversy within contemporary debates: issues of political correctness, gun culture, black violence, and feminist heroics all come into play.[3]

Lynne Cheney, former head of the National Endowment for the Humanities (1986–93), led an attack on the National History Standards released in 1994. Tubman's name was frequently invoked as an example of flaws associated with the guidelines. After a protracted public debate in which opponents like Cheney railed against political correctness and hammered away at "revisionism," these commissioned standards failed to gain congressional approval. Overnight, Tubman's name became a hot button for conservative critics, and she became a symbolic "whipping girl" for political correctness.

Tubman's overlapping legacies and enduring impact within American culture could not be more firmly established.

Tubman's membership and association with Auburn's Parker Street

AME Zion congregation sustained her. For most of her years in Auburn, she was an exuberant enthusiast during church services, shouting in the aisles and stirring up the congregation. She was identified with favorite hymns such as "Swing Low, Sweet Chariot."

In Maryland, the Bazzel Methodist Episcopal Church of Dorchester County has hosted summer celebrations to commemorate her life, and the Harriet Tubman Museum of Cambridge hosts an annual event in observance of Harriet Tubman Day (March 10). Her association with the British Methodist Episcopal Church in St. Catharines, Ontario, merits a double-sided bilingual historical marker (in French and English) on church grounds, dedicated in 1993.

By far the largest pilgrimage gathers in May in Auburn, New York, on Memorial Day weekend. The AME Zion Church (which still owns both her house and the charity home property) calls together the faithful to celebrate her moral example and legacy. One wonders what Tubman would make of the group's Miss Harriet Tubman Contest, in which high school students nominated by their church congregations vie for the title. Surely, the extensive prayer meetings, gospel program, and elaborate meals would be reminiscent of similar celebrations during her lifetime, even if the annual coronation of a teenaged girl is not. Many of her relatives, descendants of nieces and nephews, flock to Auburn to join in the festivities, both at the home and at the grave site. Two headstones have been erected at Tubman's grave since her burial, the second by the Empire State Federation of Colored Women's Clubs in 1937.

After the Harriet Tubman Home was abandoned, the remaining structures fell into ruin. In the 1940s the property was slated for public auction, to satisfy back taxes. But due to the efforts of the AME Zion Church, funds were raised to preserve and partially restore this historic site. Now the Harriet Tubman Home is run by its church owners as a house museum and education center. In the 1990s the church purchased the adjacent property on which the actual house in which Tubman lived still stands. At present, plans are under way for desperately needed repairs and restoration.

Scores of public schools scattered across the country bear Tubman's name, as do at least two additional public buildings. Cambridge, Maryland, is the nearest town to Tubman's birthplace, a rural site where a state marker has been placed. Cambridge supports a storefront facility established and maintained by the Harriet Tubman Museum and Educational Center. The museum is a relatively new addition, but the band of volunteers promotes its annual commemoration, while offering year-round tours of Tubman sites in Dorchester and, in recent years, a monthly forum for exchange of information about Tubman's world. In May of 2000 a Harriet Tubman Memorial Garden was dedicated along the town's highway and a pilgrimage from Maryland to upstate New York was conducted.

The Cambridge facility is an attempt to involve the local community in preserving a native daughter. This facility now boasts only schoolchildren's dioramas and a souvenir shop. Both the Harriet Tubman Home in Auburn, New York, and the Harriet Tubman Museum in Cambridge, Maryland, are underfunded and understaffed, and reflect the hard times they have endured. But these institutions also reflect the spirit of dedication that embodied Tubman's own life.

In Macon, Georgia, a brand-new multimillion-dollar facility will soon open, yet another museum to honor Tubman. But this museum and its collections have no substantive connection to Harriet Tubman. The founders decided in 1981 to build a cultural center in adjacent abandoned warehouses, and named this new venture the Harriet Tubman Center for Spiritual and Cultural Awareness. The original building (1985–2004) displayed Harriet Tubman's name on an exterior plaque, which explained the tribute. Yet visitors would search in vain inside for any information about Tubman. The several exhibits — including one on Macon natives William and Ellen Craft, famed fugitive slaves — made no mention of her at all. The governing board renamed their galleries the Tubman African American Museum and styled themselves as a cultural center for middle Georgia. While her name is not being taken in vain with these tributes, by being invoked, it will continue to raise the question, Who was Harriet Tubman?

For countless American blacks living today, Harriet Tubman was not just a mythical figure but a flesh-and-blood liberator who delivered their ancestors to freedom. There are by now *thousands* of African Americans whose grandparents or great-grandparents trace their freedom to Tubman: the list of those whose lives were forever changed by her work with the Underground Railroad or Union army will grow through the generations. Their deliverance was a concrete gift of freedom, as Tubman offered new lives in liberty, not just for those she rescued, but also for their descendants, and their descendants' descendants as well.

Tubman died the same year that Rosa Parks was born. For the rest of the teens, the twenties, and well into the thirties, Tubman's life fell into literary obscurity. But a biography in 1943 and then, in the 1950s, a handful of books sympathetically reexamined Harriet's life — most notably juvenile biographies by Dorothy Sterling and Ann Petry.[4] By the 1960s, interest in her accomplishments was reflected in a steady stream of children's books and juvenile novels: six in the 1960s, five in the 1970s, six in the 1980s. In the 1990s a whopping twenty-one young adult and picture books were published on Tubman. And with sixteen new children's titles appearing between 2000 and 2003, the revival flourishes.

But Tubman has been maternalized by her role as one of the most popular heroines of the elementary school set. The true tale of Tubman's career following the North Star by now may have surpassed the folkloric popularity of George Washington's "chopping down the cherry tree" confession, "I cannot tell a lie," a fabrication dreamed up by Washington biographer Mason "Parson" Weems. Highlighting Harriet Tubman is not meant to *replace* George Washington but to insist that she take her rightful place within the pantheon of American patriots.

Generations of American schoolchildren have been treated to performances of *Freedom Train* and other dramas based on Tubman's life and career. Even if these stage productions are sprinkled with inaccuracies, they usually include the essential truths of Tubman's experience as a UGRR conductor. The lessons of following the North Star, of standing up for what is right — that individual actions can change the world — sends a powerful message to America's young people, especially when performed under the banner "Based on a true story."

Tubman cherished her freedom and her citizenship more than most, certainly more than those who had never been in bondage. Besides a commitment to racial justice and a passion for liberty, Tubman preached the power of persistence. Throughout her UGRR career, she offered the following refrain: "If you are tired, keep going; if you are scared, keep going; if you are hungry, keep going; if you want to taste freedom, keep going." Along with the inspirational spirituals for which Moses became so beloved, this motto has been handed down to the present generation as part of her enduring legacy.

Born into an age of darkness, an age when America was in thrall to slavery, Harriet Tubman freed herself and was reborn. She renamed her liberated self — and hoped to lead others into Canaan as well. This was not because she saw herself as a hero, but because she believed she was doing the Lord's bidding. Not unlike Joan of Arc, with whom she was frequently compared, Harriet Tubman viewed herself as an instrument of God. However, Tubman did not manifest any messianic qualities, nor did she particularly see herself as "chosen." She did not trust in fate as much as in the power of prayer, and in the individual's ability to seize her own destiny.

Tubman embraced a much more universalist view: each and every person has the light of God within. And just like the song, she was going to let hers shine. In 1868 Frederick Douglass lauded Tubman by lamenting that while his role in the antislavery crusade brought him applause and encouragement, " 'God bless you' has been your only reward. The midnight sky and the silent stars have been the witnesses of your devotion to freedom and of your heroism."[5]

But history is also a witness to Tubman's heroic deeds and sacrifices along the road to freedom. And although historians may have too long ignored it, her past remains before us, all around us, and urging us, in her own words, "Keep Going."

# Acknowledgments

E VERY BOOK IS A JOURNEY, and this has been one of
the most challenging and one of the most satisfying for me to pursue. A subject like Harriet Tubman has proved incredibly inspiring, even
as, completing this project, I faced what seemed insurmountable ordeals:
the loss of two of my closest confidantes, Barbara Uhlmann and Bobbie
Simms. Their personal integrity and deep faith still offer me shining ex-
amples.

The kind and considerate professionals who have given of their time
and assistance generously have made this project a great road to travel. First
and foremost, I wish to thank Paul and Christine Carter of the Harriet
Tubman Home, Auburn, New York, and Pauline Copes Johnson, also of
Auburn. They had seen many people writing books on Harriet Tubman,
and I am sure they will meet many more, but their insights and encouragement were extremely important over the years. Kyra Popiel, Christina
Ericson Hansen, and Pat Anderson were wonderful research assistants: ef-
ficient, enthusiastic, and detail oriented. Jim Downs of Columbia University took time out from his own Civil War archival research; his insights
and generosity proved invaluable. Ted Widmer of the Starr Center at
Washington College in Chestertown, Maryland, and his colleague John
Seidel have both been obliging hosts. Thanks to the Tubman Study Task
Force of the National Park Service.

While finishing my fieldwork, I was given wonderful tours by individuals from two remarkable groups on Maryland's Eastern Shore: J.O.K. Walsh and Pat Guida of the Caroline Economic Development Corporation in Denton, Maryland, and John Creighton of the Harriet Tubman Museum in Cambridge, Maryland. Both kindly provided follow-up information, and I want especially to thank Jay and Susan Meredith of the Bucktown Village Foundation.

I wish to thank the staffs of the Schomburg Center at the New York Public Library (especially Michael Roudette), the Seymour Library (Auburn), the Rare Books and Manuscripts Division at Columbia University, Manuscripts and Rare Books at the University of Rochester, the Philadelphia Historical Society, the Library Company of Philadelphia, and the New York Historical Society.

I wish to express appreciation to the following persons, who extended themselves on my behalf: Ellen McHugh of the Cayuga Museum (Auburn), Peter Wisbey of the Seward House (Auburn), Kris Wilhelm and D'Ann Blanton (National Archives), Malcolm Goodelle (Cayuga County Historian's Office), Michael Wayne (University of Toronto), Connie Cooper (Delaware Historical Society), Monique Gordy (Talbot Free Library, Easton, Maryland), Mary Louise DeSarran (Maryland Historical Trust Library), Monique Roach (Cornell University), Rocky Rockefeller and Chris Haley (Maryland State Archives), Larry Hudson (Frederick Douglass Institute, University of Rochester), Lesley Hermann (Gilder Lehrman Institute), Edward Ayers (University of Virginia).

Three other friends deserve special mention for their cheer and collegiality during this project: Tom Appleton, David Blight, and Ken Greenberg. Finally, for more than twenty years David Donald, Eric Foner, and Craig D'Ooge have given me their sage counsel and unwavering support. I want each of them to know how much I appreciate remaining in their debt.

Several of my sister scholars have given me support that I can never repay (especially the phone bills), but I wish to acknowledge the ongoing encouragement they offered as I struggled with this project: Virginia Meacham

Gould, Christine Heyrman, Carol Berkin, Carol Bleser, Margaret Ripley Wolfe, Susanna Delfino, Jean Baker, and, as ever, Michele Gillespie.

My ongoing access to Sterling Library in New Haven remains so very crucial to my work; I remain grateful for affiliation with the Gilder Lehrman Center for the Study of Slavery, Resistance, and Abolition at Yale University. Two crucial fellowships enabled me to complete my research for this book in a timely fashion. I wish to thank the Gilder Lehrman Institute for American History (2001) and the National Endowment for the Humanities (2002–03).

I salute Kris Dahl, agent extraordinaire, who was there from the beginning and whose endearing finesse and anchoring wisdom have become more precious to me with each passing year. As for my editor, Deborah Baker, who has been unflagging with her enthusiasm and brilliant with her insights, I stand in awe. She has both shared a vision of Harriet and helped me to reshape my own hopes for this project — which has made our collaboration both a privilege and a pleasure. Allison Markin Powell has been a stellar and steadying influence on the project, Sophie Cottrell provided early and essential guidance, and Peggy Leith Anderson's improvements were much appreciated.

As always, friends offering hospitality when I was on my road trips made the time away from home bearable: Stan and Judy Engerman, Christine Heyrman and Tom Carter, Bricks and Jean Baker, Craig and Fran D'Ooge.

And finally I come to the trio of fellows — my sons, Drew and Ned Colbert, and my husband, Daniel Colbert — who have been so very understanding of my quest. To Drew, who accompanied me on my first pilgrimage to Harriet's birthplace on Maryland's Eastern Shore, to Ned, who tagged along on several trips to upstate New York and Canada, and to Dan, who was always there for me at Sheephill Road — I can never thank you enough for the gift of freedom you have given me, and for all you continue to mean to me.

*Riverside, Connecticut*
*July 2003*

# Notes

## PREFACE

1. Unfortunately, Jean Humez's very informative monograph, *Harriet Tubman: The Life and the Life Stories* (Madison: University of Wisconsin Press, 2003), appeared after my manuscript was completed.

## CHAPTER ONE: BORN INTO BONDAGE

1. Samuel Ringgold Ward, *Autobiography of a Fugitive Negro: His Anti-Slavery Labors in the United States, Canada, and England* (London: John Snow, 1855), 4.

2. On a pension application in 1890, Tubman declared she was sixty-five, and again in another petition in 1892, she testified she was sixty-seven years old — which shows consistency in her claims about her birth year. A congressman trying to help her secure the funds declared in 1893 that Tubman did not know her true age, and he believed she was *eighty* years old. So the mystery surrounding Tubman's true age remains, and there is no way to determine the year — although Tubman, being the most interested party, is most likely to have made the best educated guess about her year of birth.

3. Emma Telford, "Harriet: The Modern Moses of Heroism and Visions," as dictated to Emma Telford, 1911, on deposit at Cayuga County Historical Society, Auburn, New York, 3. Hereafter cited as Telford Memoir.

4. Her name is variously spelled "Green" or "Greene," but I am using the name as it was described in Paul Touart, "Monograph on Harriet Tubman," Maryland Historical Trust Library. Hereafter cited as Touart MSS.

5. Telford Memoir, 3.

6. "The Moses of Her People," *New York Herald*, September 22, 1907.

7. The name "Modesty" has been found in white records, but without any corroboration in Tubman family lore. See Touart MSS, 3.

8. See Family Letters in Harriet Tubman Collection, Schomburg Center, New York Public Library, and also Copy of Will of Atthow Pattison (January 18, 1791), filed

in Dorchester County Chancery, Case 249, October 7, 1853, Maryland State Archives. In *History of Cayuga County, New York* (1901), Harriet Green Ross is listed as age 107 at her death in 1880, which would have made her year of birth 1773. Anthony Thompson, giving testimony in court, claimed Rittia was "about 64" in 1853, which would have meant she was born in 1789. We know she was born before Atthow Pattison listed her as part of his granddaughter's inheritance in 1791. But an exact year is impossible to determine.

9. Anne Fitzhugh Miller, "Harriet Tubman," *American Magazine* 74, 4 (August 1912), 420.

10. Copy of Will of Atthow Pattison.

11. Calvin W. Mowbray and Maurice D. Rimpo, *Close-ups of Early Dorchester County History* (1987; 2nd ed., Silver Spring, Md.: Family Line, 1988), 40–49.

12. Richard H. Steckel, *Economics of U.S. Slave and Southern White Fertility* (New York: Garland, 1985).

13. Daisy Anderson Leonard, *From Slavery to Affluence: Memoirs of Robert Anderson, Ex-Slave* (Steamboat Springs, Colo.: Steamboat Pilot, 1927), 7.

14. Christopher Phillips, *Freedom's Port: The African American Community of Baltimore, 1790–1860* (Urbana: University of Illinois Press, 1997), 23.

15. Interview with J.O.K. Walsh, Caroline Economic Development Corporation, Caroline County, Maryland, November 15, 2002.

16. Telford Memoir, 6.

17. Sarah Bradford, *Harriet Tubman, the Moses of Her People* (1886; reprint, Bedford, Mass.: Applewood Books, 1993), 15. Hereafter cited as Bradford, *Moses.*

18. See Bradford, *Moses.* Harkless Bowley explains that one of these was his grandmother, his mother's mother, who was sold south. He explained that his mother was Harriet's niece, but "mother always called Aunt Harriet Sister Harriet." Harkless Bowley to Earl Conrad, August 24, 1939, Tubman Collection, Schomburg Center.

19. Touart MSS, 3.

20. See family trees available at the Harriet Tubman Home and at the Seward House, both located in Auburn, New York. In 1886 Sarah Bradford claimed that Harriet had three living siblings who all had been rescued from slavery by her and were still residing in the North. See Bradford, *Moses,* 108. I am also indebted to Pauline Copes Johnson for information offered to me in conversations over the years.

21. Charles Blockson, *The Underground Railroad* (New York: Prentice-Hall, 1987), 89.

22. Touart MSS, 7.

23. Marie Jenkins Schwartz, *Born in Bondage: Growing Up Enslaved in the Antebellum South* (Cambridge, Mass.: Harvard University Press, 2000), 76.

24. See Frances Anne Kemble, *Journal of a Residence on a Georgian Plantation in 1838–39* (New York: Harper & Brothers, 1863), 251.

25. Henry Stewart's account may be found in John Blassingame's *Slave Testimony: Two Centuries of Letters, Speeches, Interviews, and Autobiographies* (Baton Rouge: Louisiana State University Press, 1976), 414–16. Blassingame does not identify Henry Stewart as Tubman's brother in this volume. Although Dorothy Sterling in *We Are Your Sisters: Black Women in the Nineteenth Century* (New York: W. W. Norton, 1984) cites Tubman's brother as a source, she does not identify him by name.

26. Blassingame, *Slave Testimony,* 414.

## CHAPTER TWO: COMING OF AGE IN THE LAND OF EGYPT

1. Megan McLard, *Harriet Tubman and the Underground Railroad* (Englewood Cliffs, N.J.: Silver Burdette Press, 1991), 27.

2. Walter Johnson, *Soul by Soul: Life Inside the Antebellum Slave Market* (Cambridge, Mass.: Harvard University Press, 1999).

3. Schwartz, *Born in Bondage,* 143.

4. Benjamin Drew, *A North-side View of Slavery* (1856; reprint, New York: Negro Universities Press, 1968), 20.

5. A handful of texts cast Patty Cannon, the wife of a Delmarva slave trader, in the role of the mastermind behind this crime ring, a mysterious figure who, it was claimed, had gypsy origins. See Ted Giles, *Patty Cannon: Woman of Mystery* (Easton, Md.: Easton Publishing Company, 1965).

6. Prosecution of those who kidnapped blacks was hampered considerably by the inadmissibility of black testimony in courts. Carol Wilson, *Freedom at Risk: The Kidnapping of Free Blacks in America, 1780–1865* (Lexington: University of Kentucky Press, 1994), 31.

7. The Easton newspaper reported, "This woman is now between 60 and 70 years of age, and looks more like a man, but old as she is, she is believed to be as heedless and heartless as the most abandoned wretch that breathes." Mowbray and Rimpo, *Close-ups,* 56.

8. Rumor abounded that she had poisoned herself rather than face a jury. Her melodramatic end spawned a number of fanciful texts, full of fables as much as facts. See for example: *Narrative and Confessions of Lucretia P. Cannon* (1841); George Alfred Townshend, *The Entailed Hat* (1884); R. W. Messenger, *Patty Cannon Administers Justice* (1926); Ted Giles, *Patty Cannon: Woman of Mystery* (1965).

9. Bradford, *Moses,* 17.

10. Telford Memoir, 4.

11. Earl Conrad, *Harriet Tubman* (Washington, D.C.: The Associated Publishers, 1943), 10.

12. Telford Memoir, 5.

13. Ibid.

14. Testimony of Dr. Anthony Thompson, Dorchester County Chancery, Case 249, October 7, 1853, Maryland State Archives.

15. See *The Freedman's Record* (New England Freedman's Aid Society) 1 (March 1865) and W. J. Walls, *Harriet Tubman Home, Its Present and Its Future* (privately published, n.d.).

16. See Jane Scott, *Between Ocean and Bay* (Centreville, Md.: Tidewater, 1991).

17. She prayed for his conversion to Christianity, which indicates that he was not "saved" or was dissolute.

18. Albert J. Raboteau, *Slave Religion: The "Invisible Institution" in the Antebellum South* (New York: Oxford University Press, 1978).

19. The Bucktown Village Store is now a heritage tourist site.

20. Telford Memoir, 5.

21. Ibid.

22. Ibid.

23. Interview with John Creighton, Dorchester County, Maryland, December 3, 2002.

24. See *Narrative of the Life of Frederick Douglass, an American Slave, Written by Himself* (1845), ed. David W. Blight (Boston: Bedford Books, 1993), 40.

25. Thompson bought his land for $17,000 — offering $5,000 down and taking out a mortgage for $12,000. He was required to pay back $2,000 every six months, or he would default and lose his property and investment. Interview with J.O.K. Walsh.

26. Both Ben and Rit appear in the 1850 census, along with twenty-five male slaves and fewer than ten women and children. Interview with J.O.K. Walsh.

27. Harriet explained that she lived on Thompson's estate for two years before her escape, which would indicate that she moved with her parents to Poplar Neck. Because Thompson had more than one home — one in Cambridge, in Dorchester County, and another at Poplar Neck, in Caroline County — the exact location can never be determined, but it seems likely that Harriet would have been at Poplar Neck, especially as she is described being in the same place as her mother in a reliable account of her departure from slavery.

28. Conrad, *Harriet Tubman*, 31.

29. Calvin Mowbray, *The Dorchester County Fact Book* (Silver Spring, Md.: Family Line, 1981), 36.

30. Thomas P. Slaughter, *Bloody Dawn: The Christiana Race Riot and Racial Violence in the Antebellum North* (New York: Oxford University Press, 1991), 13.

31. Ibid., 37.

32. Ibid., 17.

33. Barbara Jeanne Fields, *Slavery and Freedom on the Middle Ground: Maryland During the Nineteenth Century* (New Haven, Conn.: Yale University Press, 1985), 28.

34. Catherine Clinton, "Ella Baker," in *Portraits of American Women*, ed. G. J. Barker-Benfield and Catherine Clinton (New York: St. Martin's, 1991; reprint, New York: Oxford University Press, 1998), 589.

35. Kay Najiyyah McElvey, "Early Black Dorchester, 1776–1870," Ed.D. diss., University of Maryland, College Park, 1991, 321.

36. This venality was reinforced when Atthow Pattison's relation Gourney Crow Pattison contested the division of the Brodess estate and entered a complaint in chancery during October 1853. Pattison believed that "Rittia" and her offspring should be returned to him after they reached the age of forty-five, as he was the primary beneficiary of the estate. The Dorchester County Court ruled against Gourney Pattison. See Touart MSS. The court's verdict may have highlighted that Rit was legally entitled to her freedom by the terms of Atthow's will. It may have been with this judgment that Harriet Green Ross was granted her freedom but her husband was allowed to "purchase" her for a nominal amount, to insure legal emancipation.

37. Bradford, *Moses,* 110.

38. Ibid., 26.

39. Ibid., 24.

40. Ibid., 29. Tubman was more likely to have taken her cue from Elazar ben Yair, the Jewish Zealot leader at Masada, who chose death over captivity in A.D. 73, rather than from Virginian Patrick Henry.

## CHAPTER THREE: CROSSING OVER TO FREEDOM

1. Bradford, *Moses*, 31. There are conflicting accounts about whether the name Harriet was used before her flight, but certainly "Araminta" was abandoned after 1849.
2. Jermain Wesley Loguen, *Reverend J. W. Loguen, as a Slave and as a Freeman* (Syracuse, N.Y.: J.G.K. Tuair & Co., 1859), 333.
3. In 2003 the only known copy of a Tubman runaway advertisement (now in possession of the Bucktown Village Foundation) was recovered from a Dorchester County dumpster. Interview with Jay Meredith, September 2003. The full text reads: "THREE HUNDRED DOLLARS REWARD. Ranaway from the subscriber on Monday the 17th ult., three Negroes, named as follows: HARRY, aged about 19 years, has on one side of his neck a wen, just under the ear, he is of a dark chestnut color, about 5 feet 8 or nine inches hight; BEN, aged aged about 25 years, is very quick to speak when spoken to, he is of a chesnut color, about six feet high; MINTY, aged about 27 years, is of a chesnut color, fine looking and bout 5 feet high. One hundred dollars reward will be given for each of the above named Negroes, if taken out of the State, and $50 each if taken in the State. They must be lodged in Baltimore, Easton, or Cambridge Jail, in Maryland. Eliza Ann Brodess. Near Bucktown, Dorchester county, Md. Oct. 3d, 1849. The Delaware Gazette will please copy the above three weeks, and charge this office."
4. See Peter T. Nesbett and Michelle Dubois, eds., *Over the Line: The Art and Life of Jacob Lawrence* (Seattle: University of Washington Press, 2000).
5. The full text reads: "$500 Reward! Runaway from subscriber on Thursday night the 4th inst., from the neighborhood of Cambridge, my negro girl, Harriet, sometimes called Minty. Is dark chestnut color, rather stout build, but bright and handsome. Speaks rather deep and has a scar over the left temple. She wore a brown plaid shawl. I will give the above reward captured outside the county, and $300 if captured inside the county, in either case to be lodged in the Cambridge, Maryland, jail. George Carter, Broadacres, near Cambridge, Maryland. September 24, 1849." Lawrence claimed he was copying a text: see Ellen Harkins Wheat, *Jacob Lawrence* (Seattle: University of Washington Press, 1991), 34. I would suggest it is from Lawrence that writers for children have given Tubman the childhood name "Minty," rather than from the mention found in an 1853 Dorchester County chancery case.
6. Conrad, *Harriet Tubman*, 37.
7. Interview with J.O.K. Walsh.
8. Quakers Jacob and Hannah (Wilson) Leverton had lived for years in Caroline County near Hunter's Creek. J.O.K. Walsh, *A Brief Overview of the Impact of the Chesapeake Bay on the Conduct of the Underground Railroad* (Denton, Md.: Caroline Economic Development Corporation, 2002), 8.
9. Interview with J.O.K. Walsh.
10. Arthur was exposed for his part in smuggling slaves northward in 1857. He was forced to flee his home in Caroline County and to resettle in Indiana, where his stepmother, Hannah, would later join him. Interview with J.O.K. Walsh.
11. Wilbur H. Siebert, *The Underground Railroad* (1898; reprint, New York: Arno Press, 1968), 56.
12. R. C. Smedley, *History of the Underground Railroad* (Lancaster, Pa., 1883), 249.
13. *The Freedman's Record* 4, no. 9 (September 1868), 142.
14. Bradford, *Moses*, 114–15.
15. Ibid., 37.

16. Brenda Stevenson, ed., *Journals of Charlotte Forten Grimke* (New York: Oxford University Press, 1988), 85.

17. James A. McGowan, *Station Master on the Underground Railroad: Life and Letters of Thomas Garrett* (Moylan, Pa.: Whimsie Press, 1977), 6.

18. William A. Breyfogle, *Make Free: The Story of the Underground Railroad* (Philadelphia: Lippincott, 1958), 19.

19. Douglas R. Egerton, *Gabriel's Rebellion: The Virginia Slave Conspiracies of 1800 and 1802* (Chapel Hill: University of North Carolina Press, 1993).

20. See Michael Johnson, "Denmark Vesey and His Co-Conspirators," *William and Mary Quarterly*, third series, 58 (October 2001), 915–76. See also Douglas R. Egerton, *He Shall Go Out Free: The Lives of Denmark Vesey* (Madison, Wis.: Madison House, 1999).

21. Kenneth Greenberg, ed., *Nat Turner: A Slave Rebellion in History and Memory* (New York: Oxford University Press, 2003).

22. See Kenneth Greenberg, ed., *The Confessions of Nat Turner and Related Documents* (Boston: Bedford Books, 1996).

23. His polarizing quality was evident in the twentieth century when William Styron published his novel *The Confessions of Nat Turner* (1967), which provoked continuing debates over Turner's role and legacy. See both the documentary *A Troublesome Property* (California Newsreel) and Greenberg, ed., *Nat Turner*.

24. Greenberg, ed., *Nat Turner*, 79.

25. Ibid., 101.

26. On page 15 of his biography, Earl Conrad has Harriet Tubman "[hanging] upon every bit of information that trickled into Bucktown about Nat Turner's exploit." As Tubman was likely six years old at the time, her interest in this topic was perhaps within Conrad's imagination, which is not to say Turner's legacy did not shape Tubman's childhood, but that throughout the book, Conrad makes hyperbolic speculations.

27. T. Stephen Whitman, *The Price of Freedom: Slavery and Manumission in Baltimore and Early National Maryland* (Lexington: University of Kentucky Press, 1997), 61.

28. Mary N. Robinson, "Sidelights on Slavery," *Lancaster County Historical Society* 15, no. 5 (1911), 138.

29. Calvin Fairbank, *Reverend Calvin Fairbank* (1890; reprint, New York: Negro Universities Press, 1969), 32.

30. *Five Hundred Thousand Strokes for Freedom: A Series of Anti-Slavery Tracts by the Friends of the Negro*, Leeds Antislavery Series, no. 68 (London: W. & F. Cash, 1900).

31. Bradford, *Moses*, 46.

32. Ward, *Autobiography*, 9.

33. Rev. Philo Tower, *Slavery Unmasked* (Rochester, N.Y.: E. Darrow & Brother, 1856), 245.

34. Ibid.

## CHAPTER FOUR: IN A FREE STATE

1. See *The Cries of Philadelphia* (Philadelphia: Johnson & Warner, 1810).

2. Wilson, *Freedom at Risk*, 10–11.

3. Gary B. Nash, *Forging Freedom: The Formation of Philadelphia's Black Community, 1720–1840* (Cambridge, Mass.: Harvard University Press, 1988), 142–43.

4. Blockson, *Underground Railroad,* 58.

5. Eber M. Pettit, *Sketches in the History of the Underground Railroad* (1879; reprint, Westfield, N.Y.: Chautauqua Region Press, 1999), 51–52.

6. Herbert Aptheker, ed., *A Documentary History of the Negro People in the United States* (New York: Citadel, 1951), 1:66.

7. J. Smith Futhey and Gilbert Cope, *History of Chester County, Pennsylvania* (Philadelphia: Louis H. Everts, 1881).

8. Many blacks were put off by the austerity of Quaker worship, as one African American confessed: "I wanted to hear singing. Sometimes I wanted to hear preaching, but was disappointed." Benjamin Quarles, *Black Abolitionists* (New York: Oxford University Press, 1969), 72. Even black converts chafed at the segregationist practices of formal Quaker worship. In Philadelphia, African American Quaker Sarah M. Douglass overheard one of her white fellow worshippers at the Arch Street Meeting admonish another white who was about to sit down next to her, "This bench is for black people." The black Quaker woman finally abandoned her Jim Crow pew and stopped attending Quaker meeting rather than sit alone. Ibid., 73.

9. Russell Weigley, *Philadelphia: A 300-Year History* (New York: W. W. Norton, 1982), 352.

10. Ibid., 352, 354.

11. Groups had an average membership of ninety, with annual dues of three to five dollars. See Quarles, *Black Abolitionists,* 101.

12. New York City was particularly dangerous because "the notorious Blackbirds, a gang of poor whites, many of them recent immigrants, earned money by delivering fugitives and sometimes free blacks into slavery." African American leader Henry Highland Garnet's family home was invaded by the Blackbirds. His father and mother escaped, but Garnet's sister Eliza was kidnapped. James Horton, *Free People of Color: Inside the African American Community* (Washington, D.C.: Smithsonian Press, 1993), 64. David Ruggles despaired, "My depressed countrymen, we are all liable." Aptheker, ed., *A Documentary History,* 1:160.

13. See Wilson, *Freedom at Risk.* See also Julia Foote, *A Brand Plucked from the Fire,* in William L. Andrews, *Sisters of the Spirit: Three Black Women's Autobiographies of the Nineteenth Century* (Bloomington: Indiana University Press, 1986), 166.

14. Loguen, *Reverend J. W. Loguen,* 12. See also Blassingame, *Slave Testimony,* 396, 403.

15. Wilson, *Freedom at Risk,* 97.

16. When Scottish reformer Fanny Wright came to town in 1829 and not only railed against slavery but preached a doctrine promoting the social equality of the races, she contributed to an outbreak of mob violence. W.E.B. DuBois, *The Philadelphia Negro: A Social Study* (1899; reprint, Philadelphia: University of Pennsylvania Press, 1996), 27.

17. John Runcie, "'Hunting the Nigs' in Philadelphia: The Race Riot of August 1834," in Kenneth Kusmer, ed., *Black Communities and Urban Development in America, 1720–1990* (New York: Garland, 1991), 2:277.

18. Ibid., 278–79.

19. Weigley, *Philadelphia,* 296.

20. Wilson, *Freedom at Risk,* 101.

21. Julie Winch, *Gentleman of Color: The Life of James Forten* (New York: Oxford University Press, 2002), 150.

22. Theodore Hershberg, "Free Blacks in Antebellum Philadelphia: A Study of Ex-Slaves, Freeborn, and Socioeconomic Decline," in Kusmer, ed., *Black Communities,* 2:248.

23. Nash, *Forging Freedom,* 278.

24. Weigley, *Philadelphia,* 352.

25. The only skilled trade that African Americans in Philadelphia dominated was catering. One observer commented: "When a few years ago we saw none but blacks, we now see nothing but Irish." Hershberg, "Free Blacks," in Kusmer, ed., *Black Communities,* 2:255.

26. Stanley Campbell, *The Slave Catchers: Enforcement of the Fugitive Slave Law, 1850–1860* (Chapel Hill: University of North Carolina Press, 1968), 11.

27. Ibid., 12.

28. Ibid., 14.

29. Gary Collison, *Shadrach Minkins: From Fugitive Slave to Citizen* (Cambridge, Mass.: Harvard University Press, 1997), 30.

30. Campbell, *Slave Catchers,* 54.

31. Garrett to Garrison, December 5, 1860. Larry Gara, *The Liberty Line: The Legend of the Underground Railroad* (Lexington: University of Kentucky Press, 1961), 104.

32. Collison, *Shadrach Minkins,* 31.

33. Richard J. M. Blackett, "Freedom or the Martyr's Grave: Black Pittsburgh's Aid to the Fugitive Slave," *Western Pennsylvania Historical Magazine* 6 (1973), 126.

34. Campbell, *Slave Catchers,* 64.

35. Ibid.

36. *Frederick Douglass's Paper,* November 27, 1851.

37. Jane H. Pease and William H. Pease, "Confrontation and Abolition in the 1850s," *Journal of American History* 58 (1972), 928–29.

38. Ibid., 929.

39. *National Anti-Slavery Standard,* September 5, 1850.

40. Harriet Jacobs, a fugitive slave from North Carolina living underground in New York City, complained she annually felt the need to keep indoors when "snakes and slaveholders made their appearance." Collison, *Shadrach Minkins,* 76.

41. See Monique Patenaude Roach, "The Rescue of Jerry Henry: Antislavery and Racism in the Burned-Over District," *New York History,* spring 2001. I am indebted to Monique Roach for allowing me to read an advance copy of her piece, which, when published, was cowinner of the 2002 Kerr History Prize.

42. Three times for assault and battery against a woman, the same woman — which would indicate he had a violent streak and unwisely and repeatedly suffered run-ins with the law. Roach, "Jerry Henry," 148.

43. Ibid., 149.

44. Albert J. Von Frank, *The Trials of Anthony Burns: Freedom and Slavery in Emerson's Boston* (Cambridge, Mass.: Harvard University Press, 1998), 22.

45. Ibid., 26. Each year, on October 1, Syracuse activists commemorated "the Jerry Rescue" with a memorial celebration. A statue was erected in the late twentieth century to honor this historical event.

46. *Five Hundred Thousand Strokes for Freedom,* Leeds Antislavery Series, no. 63, 2.

47. Bradford, *Moses,* 31.

## CHAPTER FIVE: THE LIBERTY LINES

1. See Jim Haskins, *Get On Board: The Story of the Underground Railroad* (New York: Scholastic Press, 1993), 1, and Rush Sloane, "The Underground Railroad of the Firelands," *Firelands Pioneer* (Sandusky, Ohio, 1888), 6–7. For discussion of this story, see Gara, *Liberty Line,* 173–74.

2. Pettit, *Sketches,* 35–36. The exact phrase "underground railroad" is said to have first appeared in Chicago's *Western Citizen* in 1844. See Gara, *Liberty Line,* 144.

3. Marianna G. Brubaker, "The Underground Railroad," *Lancaster County Historical Society* 15, no. 4 (1911), 96 . See also Loguen, *Reverend J. W. Loguen,* v.

4. Gara, *Liberty Line,* 58.

5. Brubaker, "Underground Railroad," 115.

6. Interestingly, Levi Coffin objected to these methods as well. See Blockson, *Underground Railroad,* 142.

7. Emerson Klees, *Underground Railroad Tales with Routes Through the Finger Lakes Region* (Rochester, N.Y.: Friends of the Finger Lakes, 1997), 92.

8. In 1848 two slaveholders from Maryland charged Garrett and John Hunn with aiding and abetting fugitives. When the circuit court met at New Castle, Delaware, Roger B. Taney presided. Taney would later join the U.S. Supreme Court, serving as Chief Justice and overseeing the infamous Dred Scott decision. Garrett was found guilty and the court decided to make an example of him, imposing a $5,000 fine, which financially ruined him. Yet Garrett refused to discontinue his antislavery crusade or abandon the UGRR. The sheriff reportedly admonished: "I hope, Mr. Garrett, you will take warning by this punishment, and never violate the laws again!" Garrett replied: "Friend, if thee should see a fugitive slave in want of help to-day, thee will please send him to me!" See *The Liberator,* October 14, 1853. William Still forwarded an account of this 1848 incident to Harriet Beecher Stowe, who incorporated the tale into *Uncle Tom's Cabin* (1852).

9. Siebert, *Underground Railroad,* 10.

10. William Parker of Christiana had to destroy his letters from fugitives when white authorities showed up. See Siebert, *Underground Railroad,* 10.

11. One Pennsylvania abolitionist was "rather proud of being a son of a Revolutionary soldier, as well as having been both an agent and a conductor on an Underground Railroad." See Gara, *Liberty Line,* 168.

12. H. U. Johnson, *From Dixie to Canada: Romances and Realities of the Underground Railroad* (Orwell, Ohio: H. U. Johnson, 1896).

13. Richard J. M. Blackett, *Beating Against the Barriers: Biographical Essays in Nineteenth-Century Afro-American History* (Baton Rouge: Louisiana University Press, 1986), 7.

14. Gara, *Liberty Line,* 45.

15. See Siebert, *Underground Railroad,* chapters 4 and 6.

16. Alexander Ross became famous after Tubman arrived on the scene. Ross left his Ontario home in 1856 to spread the gospel of the UGRR directly within the South. Ross infiltrated communities, beginning with Richmond in 1857, worming his way into the confidence of locals, until he was able to find a group of trustworthy slaves to meet with and share information. He would offer advice in clandestine meetings with blacks, an incredibly risky proposition. If he could find immediate volunteers for flight, he would supply them with knives, compasses, and money for their journey. Or at times Ross would accompany the fugitives to the first UGRR station for transport northward, or perhaps even accompany the

group all the way to Canada. Ross was intrepid, traveling to Nashville (Tennessee), Charleston (South Carolina), Augusta (Georgia), Huntsville (Alabama), and Vicksburg (Mississippi). See Alexander M. Ross, *Recollections and Experiences of an Abolitionist* (Toronto: Rowell and Hutchinson, 1875). Another abductor, John Parker, became famous locally in Ohio; his role was not widely known until the contemporary era. See *His Promised Land: The Autobiography of John P. Parker*, ed. Stuart Sprague (New York: W. W. Norton, 1996).

17. James Harris Fairchild, "The Underground Railroad," *Western Reserve Historical Society* 4, no. 87 (1895), 101–2.

18. Blockson, *The Underground Railroad*, 142.

19. Siebert, *Underground Railroad*, 169.

20. Quarles, *Black Abolitionists*, 164. When Boston's Park Street Church refused to allow Torrey's memorial, the Tremont Temple instead was crowded with hundreds paying tribute.

21. See Siebert, *Underground Railroad*, 159.

22. Fairbank, *Reverend Calvin Fairbank*, 18.

23. William Thompson recounted: "I knew a man at the South who had six children by a colored slave. Then there was a fuss between him and his wife, and he sold all the children but the oldest slave daughter. Afterward, he had a child by this daughter, and sold mother and child before birth. . . . Such things are done frequently in the South." Drew, *A North-side View*, 96. See also Quarles, *Black Abolitionists*, 15.

24. Such as Ohio black John Parker. See *His Promised Land*.

25. Haskins, *Get On Board*, 31–32.

26. Ibid., 31–33.

27. See Ann Hagedorn, *Beyond the River* (New York: Simon and Schuster, 2003).

28. Siebert, *Underground Railroad*, 118.

29. Klees, *Underground Railroad Tales*, 116–17.

30. John Stauffer, *The Black Hearts of Men: Radical Abolitionists and the Transformation of Race* (Cambridge, Mass.: Harvard University Press, 2002), 128.

31. Ibid.

32. Ralph Harlow, *Gerrit Smith: Philanthropist and Reformer* (New York: Henry Holt & Co., 1939), 274.

33. Siebert, *Underground Railroad*, 403–38.

34. Carlton Mabee, *Black Freedom: The Nonviolent Abolitionists from 1830 Through the Civil War* (New York: Macmillan, 1970), 280.

35. Laura S. Haviland, *A Woman's Life Work: Labors and Experiences* ( Chicago: Publishing Association of Friends, 1889), 133. She made a botched attempt at a rescue in 1847: See Siebert, *Underground Railroad*, 170–71.

36. There were some isolated cases of women conductors, such as Hannah Marsh of Chester County, Pennsylvania, who would take fugitive slaves to Philadelphia in her covered market wagon when she went to the city to sell produce, but these women played minor and occasional roles.

37. Pettit, *Sketches*, 34.

38. Gara, *Liberty Line*, 1. This painting now hangs in the Cincinnati Art Museum.

39. It was a great irony that Peter, William Still's brother, stumbled upon him in Philadelphia. See William Still, *The Underground Railroad* (Philadelphia, 1872), 36–38.

40. Quarles, *Black Abolitionists,* 148.
41. Ibid., 149.
42. Still, *Underground Railroad,* 135.
43. Haviland, *Woman's Life,* 195.
44. Still, *Underground Railroad,* 93.
45. William Wells Brown, *The Rising Son; or, The Antecedents and Advancement of the Colored Race* (Boston: A. G. Brown & Company, 1874), 538.

## CHAPTER SIX: THE MOSES OF HER PEOPLE

1. See Touart MSS, 3.
2. Harkless Bowley to Earl Conrad, August 24, 1939, Tubman Collection, Schomburg Center.
3. Judith Bentley suggests Bodkin's Point was the rendezvous. *Harriet Tubman* (New York: Franklin Watts, 1991), 49.
4. Ibid., 50.
5. Mary Anne Bowley reverted to the name Keziah or Kizzy when she moved back to Maryland after the Civil War. Interview with John Creighton, December 3, 2002.
6. The number of brothers on this trip and other details seem to be in dispute. See Conrad, *Harriet Tubman,* 228, footnote 7. Bentley suggests that her brother John was rescued from Talbot County (*Harriet Tubman,* 50).
7. Still worked at the American Antislavery Society from 1847, but the vigilance committee did not officially revive until 1852, and there is no mention of Tubman by name in Still's UGRR logbook until December 1854.
8. Blockson, *Underground Railroad,* 119.
9. Rosa Belle Holt, "A Heroine in Ebony," *The Chautauquan* 23 (July 1896), 461.
10. *The Commonwealth* (Boston), July 17, 1863.
11. Lillie B. Chace Wyman, "Harriet Tubman," *New England Magazine* 14, no. 1 (March 1896), 116. See also Bradford, *Moses,* 71–73.
12. Bradford, *Moses,* 39.
13. Frederick Douglass, *Life and Times of Frederick Douglass* (Hartford, Conn.: Park, 1881), 329.
14. Blockson, *Underground Railroad,* 119.
15. *The Freedman's Record* 1 (March 1865).
16. *Stories of New Jersey* (New York: M. Barrows & Co., 1938), 66.
17. Brown, *Rising Son,* 538.
18. Blockson, *Underground Railroad,* 14.
19. Brown, *Rising Son,* 536.
20. Sarah Bradford, *Scenes in the Life of Harriet Tubman* (Auburn, N.Y.: W. J. Moses, 1869), 69–70.
21. See *The Commonwealth* (Boston), July 17, 1863.
22. Bradford, *Moses,* 34–35.
23. Telford Memoir, 11.
24. Conrad, *Harriet Tubman,* 78.
25. James Freeman Clarke, *Anti-Slavery Days* (New York: John W. Lovell, 1883), 81.

26. Ibid.

27. Klees, *Underground Railroad Tales*, 107.

28. Still, *Underground Railroad*, 74.

29. Bradford, *Moses*, 43–45.

30. Conrad, *Harriet Tubman*, 63. Bradford's rendition of the tale has Tubman point a pistol at the head of a fugitive and say, "Dead niggers tell no tales; you go on or die." Bradford, *Moses*, 33.

31. McGowan, *Station Master*, 130–31, 135.

32. Wyman, "Harriet Tubman," 112.

33. Smedley, *Underground Railroad*, 250.

34. Bradford, *Moses*, 86–87.

35. Telford Memoir, 10. Telford also suggested: "Many and wonderful indeed are the instances known personally to the writer where Harriet's predictions of impending danger or her forecast of other events concerning which she could have had no possible information have been literally fulfilled."

36. Ibid.

37. *The Freedman's Record* 4, no. 9 (September 1868), 142.

38. Arch Merrill, *The Underground Freedom's Road and Other Upstate Tales* (American Brook, N.Y.: Stratford Press, 1963), 20.

39. Bradford, *Moses*, 59–61. James Freeman Clarke tells the same story with some slightly different details in his *Anti-Slavery Days*, 82–83.

40. Wyman, "Harriet Tubman," 114.

41. Bradford, *Moses*, 54–55.

42. Brown, *Rising Son*, 538.

43. McGowan, *Station Master*, 142.

44. Ibid., 141.

45. Conrad, *Harriet Tubman*, 49.

46. Bradford refers to this brother as John — so perhaps he was John Henry.

47. John Chase, Peter Jackson, and Jane Kane. See Still, *Underground Railroad*, 298.

48. Bradford, *Moses*, 29.

49. Still, *Underground Railroad*, 296.

50. Blassingame, *Slave Testimony*, 414–16.

## CHAPTER SEVEN: CANADIAN EXILE

1. Harriet's brother James Isaac (and his family), her niece Mary Anne Bowley (and her family), her brother William Henry and his wife, Catherine, as well as Harriet's parents lived in St. Catharines at one time or another. Her three brothers Benjamin, Robert, and Henry (who, like James Isaac and William Henry, changed their names from Ross to Stewart) all lived in Canada at one time or another as well. Henry Stewart was still living in Canada when he was interviewed by Samuel Gridley Howe in 1864 (see notes 25 and 29, below). On a 1913 list of Harriet's relatives, four of the fourteen listed were from St. Catharines and a fifth lived in Ontario.

2. Rev. W. M. Mitchell, *The Underground Railroad from Slavery to Freedom* (1860; reprint, Westport, Conn.: Negro Universities Press, 1970), 113.

3. Michael Powers and Nancy Butler, *Slavery and Freedom in Niagara* (Niagara-on-the-Lake, Ontario: Niagara Historical Society, 1993), 12.

4. Ibid., 29.

5. Ward, *Autobiography,* 111.

6. Powers and Butler, *Slavery and Freedom,* 50.

7. Ibid.

8. For a full account see Patricia Frazier, "Niagara's Negroes Kept Vigil at Jail," *Niagara Advance, Historical Issue,* 1976.

9. Powers and Butler, *Slavery and Freedom,* 51–52.

10. Ibid.

11. Leon Litwack, *North of Slavery: The Negro in the Free State, 1790–1860* (Chicago: University of Chicago Press, 1961), 73.

12. Ward, *Autobiography,* 111. See also Pettit, *Sketches,* 43.

13. Mitchell, *Underground Railroad,* 158.

14. Ibid.

15. Jane Rhodes, *Mary Ann Shadd Cary: The Black Press and Protest in the Nineteenth Century* (Bloomington: Indiana University Press, 1998), 30.

16. Ward, *Autobiography,* 139.

17. Mitchell, *Underground Railroad,* 138.

18. Ward, *Autobiography,* 109.

19. Mitchell, *Underground Railroad,* 138.

20. Ibid., 166.

21. Rhodes, *Mary Ann Shadd Cary,* 31.

22. Maggie Parnall, *Black History in the Niagara Peninsula* (self-published, 1996).

23. Mitchell, *Underground Railroad,* 134–35.

24. *The Commonwealth* (Boston), July 17, 1863.

25. S. G. Howe, *Report to the Freedmen's Inquiry Commission, 1864: The Refugees from Slavery in Canada West* (Boston: Wright & Potter, 1864), 22.

26. See Dr. T. Mack in ibid.

27. Ibid., 36.

28. Writing in April 1857: Still, *Underground Railroad,* 135.

29. During 1864 Samuel Gridley Howe, commissioned by the Freedmen's Bureau (a branch of the U.S. government established to care for Civil War refugees and ex-slaves), undertook an investigation of conditions for blacks in Canada West. Howe, *Report,* 45.

30. Ibid.

31. Ibid., 35, 44, 45.

32. Bradford, *Moses,* 43.

33. Ibid., 48–53.

34. Rhodes, *Mary Ann Shadd Cary,* 33.

35. Ibid., 42.

36. Ibid., 98.

37. Ward, *Autobiography,* 54.

38. Drew, *A North-side View,* 31.

## CHAPTER EIGHT: TROUBLE IN CANAAN

1. Gara, "The Fugitive Slave Law," *Civil War History* 10 (1964), 238.
2. Campbell, *Slave Catchers,* 90.
3. Carol Wilson, "Active Vigilance Is the Price of Liberty: Black Self-Defense Against Fugitive Slave Recapture and Kidnapping of Free Blacks," in John R. McKivigan and Stanley Harrold, eds., *Antislavery Violence: Sectional, Racial, and Cultural Conflict in Antebellum America* (Knoxville: University of Tennessee Press, 1999), 119.
4. Von Frank, *Anthony Burns,* 133.
5. Stevenson, *Journals,* 63.
6. Ibid., 66.
7. Ibid.
8. Von Frank, *Anthony Burns,* 213.
9. Ibid., 228.
10. McGowan, *Station Master,* 141–42.
11. Ibid.
12. Ibid., 143–44.
13. Ibid.
14. Mowbray and Rimpo, *Close-ups,* 58.
15. Still, *Underground Railroad,* 57–58.
16. Ibid., 60.
17. Mowbray and Rimpo, *Close-ups,* 60. Green's sentence was commuted in April 1863, after he'd served nearly six years of his ten-year term.
18. Bradford, *Moses,* 87.
19. Still, *Underground Railroad,* 411.
20. See Frederick Seward, *William H. Seward* (New York: Derby and Miller, 1891), 2:258.
21. Patricia Johnson, "Sensitivity and Civil War: The Selected Diaries and Papers, 1858–1866, of Frances Adeline [Fanny] Seward," Ph.D. diss., University of Rochester, 1963.
22. See Alice Lucas Brickler to Earl Conrad in Tubman Collection, Schomburg Center.
23. Shirley Yee, *Black Women Abolitionists: A Study in Activism, 1828–1860* (Knoxville: University of Tennessee), 29.
24. Interview with Peter Wisbey, Director of Seward House, Auburn, New York.
25. Ibid.
26. See Johnson, "Sensitivity and Civil War," 882, 990.
27. See Katy Stewart Northrup to Earl Conrad in Tubman Collection, Schomburg Center.
28. There are mentions of Margaret as the daughter of Harriet's brother in descendants' family letters. There is no corroborating evidence of this brother or his family — but this kind of missing evidence is all too common in the reconstruction of black families in the pre-emancipation South.
29. Christopher Phillips, *Freedom's Port.*

## CHAPTER NINE: CROSSROADS AT HARPERS FERRY

1. Telford Memoir, 14.
2. Louis Ruchames, ed., *John Brown: The Making of a Revolutionary* (New York: Grosset & Dunlap, 1969), 186.
3. Ibid., 154. John Brown to Rev. James W. McFarland of Wooster, Ohio, November 23, 1859.
4. Ibid., 188.
5. At the same time, Brown was a devoted father to his growing family. Mary Brown bore her husband thirteen children between 1834 and 1854. Sadly, only six of these children survived past the age of ten, but they joined a household filled with Brown's five sons and a daughter by his first wife. Mary and John had a challenging family life; Brown's financial investments in sheep farming and the wool trade ended up in endless litigation, debt, and bankruptcy for much of Brown's adult life. Between his struggle for financial independence and his battles to liberate slaves, Brown led a very troubled life on the road to Harpers Ferry.
6. Stephen Oates, *To Purge This Land with Blood* (New York: Harper & Row, 1970), 63.
7. Ibid., 171.
8. Ibid., 186.
9. Ibid., 191.
10. Richard Warch and Jonathan Fanton, eds., *John Brown* (Englewood Cliffs, N.J.: Prentice-Hall, 1973), 36.
11. Edward J. Renehan Jr., *The Secret Six: The True Tale of the Men Who Conspired with John Brown* (New York: Crown, 1995), 161.
12. Oates, *To Purge This Land,* 245.
13. Campbell, *Slave Catchers,* 52–53.
14. Quarles, *Black Abolitionists,* 6.
15. Oates, *To Purge This Land,* 241.
16. Conrad, *Harriet Tubman,* 116.
17. Warch and Fanton, *John Brown,* 39–40.
18. I'm afraid my interpretation of Brown's views on gender departs from current scholarship; see especially John Stauffer's excellent *The Black Hearts of Men* (2002).
19. Conrad, *Harriet Tubman,* 120.
20. Christopher Looby, ed., *The Complete Civil War Journal and Selected Letters of Thomas W. Higginson* (Chicago: University of Chicago Press, 2000), 81.
21. Brown, *Rising Son,* 536.
22. *The Liberator,* July 8, 1858.
23. Oswald Garrison Villard, *John Brown, 1800–1859* (New York: Knopf, 1943), 396.
24. See *The Commonwealth* (Boston), July 17, 1863.
25. Wyman, "Harriet Tubman," 117.
26. Telford Memoir, 14.
27. Tubman, Sanborn wrote, described Brown as "Christ . . . the Savior of our people." See *The Commonwealth* (Boston), July 17, 1863.
28. Oates, *To Purge This Land,* 356.
29. Thoreau, Emerson, and Whittier all wrote passionately about Brown.

30. Oates, *To Purge This Land,* 356.

31. Paul Finkelman, ed., *His Soul Goes Marching On: Responses to John Brown and the Harpers Ferry Raid* (Charlottesville: University Press of Virginia, 1995), 218.

32. Ibid.

33. Ibid., 308.

34. Telford Memoir, 14.

35. Blassingame, *Slave Testimony,* 463.

36. Telford Memoir, 15.

37. One scholar suggests the relative she visited was a "cousin," while Earl Conrad suspects it was a younger brother, William Henry.

38. *Antislavery History of the Year of John Brown,* American Antislavery Society Annual Report (1860), 61.

39. Jean Hoefer, *New York Alive* 6, no. 3 (May/June 1986).

40. Some have suggested that a large mob was collected because someone yelled "Fire" to attract a crowd. See Hoefer, *New York Alive.*

41. Conrad, *Harriet Tubman,* 137.

42. *Troy Whig,* April 27, 1860.

43. See Bradford, *Moses,* 127.

44. *Antislavery History of the Year of John Brown,* 61.

45. *The Commonwealth* (Boston), July 17, 1863.

## CHAPTER TEN: ARISE, BRETHREN

1. *The Liberator,* August 26, 1859.

2. Stauffer, *Black Hearts,* 250.

3. *The Liberator,* August 26, 1859.

4. Rev. J. S. Lane, *Maryland Slavery and Maryland Chivalry* (Philadelphia: Collins Printer, 1858), 24.

5. Looby, *Higginson,* 81. Mowbray disputes these figures; see Mowbray and Rimpo, *Close-ups,* 59. Nevertheless, contemporaries repeated the exaggerated numbers.

6. Bradford, *Scenes,* 36.

7. John Bell Robinson, *Pictures of Slavery and Anti-Slavery* (Philadelphia, 1863), 322.

8. Ibid., 331.

9. Ibid., 322–23.

10. Ibid., 324.

11. Ibid.

12. Ibid.

13. Conrad, *Harriet Tubman,* 150.

14. Still, *Underground Railroad,* 531.

15. As Franklin Sanborn explained, suspected UGRR leaders would become targets, especially "those who, like Harriet, had rendered themselves obnoxious to the supporters of slavery." *The Commonwealth* (Boston), July 17, 1863.

16. Fanny Kemble Wister, "Sarah Butler Wister's Civil War Diary," *Pennsylvania Magazine of History and Biography* 102 (July 1978).

17. Kenneth Stampp, *And the War Came: The North and the Secession Crisis, 1860–1861* (Baton Rouge: Louisiana State University Press, 1950), 292.

18. Ibid., 293.

19. James McPherson, *Marching Toward Freedom: The Negro in the Civil War, 1861–65* (New York: Knopf, 1965), 9.

20. James McPherson, *Ordeal by Fire: Civil War and Reconstruction* (New York: McGraw-Hill, 1982), 126.

21. The president was convinced that thousands of runaway slaves who were sure to seek refuge behind Union lines should be encouraged to emigrate. When Lincoln appointed a U.S. Colonization Agent and authorized him to explore a scheme whereby coal would be supplied to the U.S. Navy at half price if "colonists" would be shipped to Chiriqui (part of present-day Panama) to work in the coal mines, black leaders protested. See McPherson, *Marching Toward Freedom*, 91.

22. Ibid., 162.

23. See *Christian Recorder*, June 8, 1861.

24. Ibid.

25. *The Liberator*, February 28, 1862.

26. Ibid.

27. Ibid.

28. L. C. Lockwood in *Christian Recorder*, November 22, 1862.

29. McPherson, *Marching Toward Freedom*, 26–28.

30. *Christian Recorder*, December 21, 1861.

31. Ibid., December 6, 1862. The article goes on: "Winter is hard by, they must have blankets and comfortable clothing or they will perish and die to our utter shame. They are now no longer brutes and chattels, but women and children; and if we do not stretch forth our arms to their relief, the curse is upon our head."

32. *The Liberator*, March 7, 1862.

33. Katharine M. Jones, *Port Royal Under Six Flags* (Indianapolis: Bobbs-Merrill, 1960), 247.

34. For an excellent analysis, see Willie Lee Rose, *Rehearsal for Reconstruction: The Port Royal Experiment* (Indianapolis: Bobbs-Merrill, 1964).

35. *Christian Recorder*, May 24, 1862.

36. The Howlands, the Sewards, and other white families helped to take care of Ben and Harriet (Ross), who were now known as Ben and Harriet Stewart.

37. Edward A. Miller Jr., *Lincoln's Abolitionist General: The Biography of David Hunter* (Columbia: University of South Carolina Press, 1997), 67.

38. General Orders No. 11, May 9, 1862, Department of the South, *The War of the Rebellion: A Compilation of the Official Records of the Union and Confederate Armies* (Washington: Government Printing Office, 1880–1901), 6:224, 240.

39. Gerald Astor, *The Right to Fight: A History of African Americans in the Military* (Novato, Calif.: Presidio Press, 1998), 22.

40. When Hunter was granted a sixty-day leave in August 1862 and headed north, it was widely assumed he would not return. But Hunter did come back to South Carolina and commanded those black troops for which he had so long agitated. See "Departure of General Hunter," *New South* (Port Royal), September 8, 1862, quoted in Miller, *Lincoln's Abolitionist General*, 114.

41. Even though Harriet left no written record of this locale during such remarkable times, many white women did: see Gerald Schwartz, ed., *A Woman Doctor's Civil War: Esther Hill Hawks' Diary* (Columbia: University of South Carolina Press, 1984); Elizabeth Hyde Botume, *First Days Amongst the Contrabands* (Boston: Lee & Shepard, 1893); and Laura Towne, *Letters and Diary of Laura M. Towne* (Cambridge, Mass.: Riverside Press, 1912). African American women also left descriptions of wartime in the Sea Islands: see Brenda Stevenson, ed., *Journals of Charlotte Forten Grimke* (New York: Oxford University Press, 1988), and Susie King Taylor, *Reminiscences of My Life in Camp with the 33rd U.S. Colored Troops, Late the S.C. Volunteers* (Boston, 1902).

42. McPherson, *Marching Toward Freedom*, 114.

43. Bradford, *Moses*, 103.

44. See Charles P. Wood Manuscript, Pension Files, National Archives, Washington, D.C. Hereafter Wood MSS.

45. Brown, *Rising Son*, 536.

46. Wood MSS.

47. Paul E. Steiner, *Disease in the Civil War: Natural Biological Warfare in 1861–1865* (Springfield, Ill.: Charles C. Thomas, 1968), 38.

48. Bradford, *Moses*, 98.

49. Schwartz, *A Woman Doctor's Civil War*, 78.

50. Ibid., 34.

51. Ibid.

52. Looby, *Higginson*, 251.

53. J. Matthew Gallman, ed., *The Civil War Chronicle* (New York: Crown, 2000), 261.

54. McPherson, *Marching Toward Freedom*, 25–26.

55. Gallman, *Civil War Chronicle*, 213–14.

56. Freedmen's teacher H. W. Ware distinctly remembered the voice was a woman's voice, while Higginson recalled it was a man's voice. See Elizabeth Ware Pearson, ed., *Letters from Port Royal* (1906; reprint, New York: Arno Press, 1969), 130, and Looby, *Higginson*, 76, 77.

57. Looby, *Higginson*, 77.

## CHAPTER ELEVEN: BITTERSWEET VICTORIES

1. Lydia Maria Child, *Letters of Lydia Maria Child* (Boston: Houghton Mifflin, 1883), 160–61.

2. Conrad, *Harriet Tubman*, 168.

3. This at least kept Tubman from ever having any incriminating evidence on her person during clandestine missions.

4. Sterling, *We Are Your Sisters*, 245–305.

5. Conrad, *Harriet Tubman*, 172–73.

6. Ibid., 175.

7. Ibid., 171.

8. C. Peter Ripley et al., eds., *Witness for Freedom: African American Voices on Race, Slavery, and Emancipation* (Chapel Hill: University of North Carolina Press, 1993), 220.

9. Ibid.

10. *The Commonwealth,* (Boston), July 3, 1863.

11. Botume, *First Days Amongst the Contrabands,* 50–51.

12. Noah Andre Trudeau, *Like Men of War: Black Troops in the Civil War, 1862–1865* (Boston: Little, Brown, 1998), 45.

13. *The Commonwealth* (Boston), June 5, 1863.

14. Ripley, *Black Abolitionists,* 220.

15. *The Commonwealth* (Boston), July 10, 1863.

16. David S. Heidler and Jeanne T. Heidler, eds., *Encyclopedia of the American Civil War* (Santa Barbara, Calif.: ABC-Clio Publications, 2000), 4:1744.

17. Stephen R. Wise, *Gate of Hell: Campaign for Charleston Harbor, 1863* (Columbia: University of South Carolina Press, 1994), 49.

18. "If there were any among the multitude that watched the march of the Fifty-Fourth Regiment down State Street to the water side on Thursday the 28th of May who did not remember a very different scene on Friday the 2nd of June 1854 scarcely nine years before. . . . The rescuing hands of Massachusetts yeomen were restrained by bayonets and only groans and hisses, and jeers of shame and rage testified to the purpose of the people." *The Commonwealth* (Boston), June 5, 1863.

19. Clinton Cox, *Undying Glory: The Story of the Massachusetts Fifty-Fourth Regiment* (New York: Scholastic, 1991).

20. *The Commonwealth* (Boston), July 3, 1863.

21. Joseph T. Glatthar, *Forged in Battle: The Civil War Alliance of Black Soldiers and White Officers* (New York: Free Press, 1990), 137.

22. Wise, *Gate of Hell,* 89.

23. Glatthar, *Forged in Battle,* 136.

24. Cox, *Undying Glory,* 63.

25. Glatthar, *Forged in Battle,* 137–38.

26. Ibid., 138.

27. Wise, *Gate of Hell,* 95–96.

28. Ibid., 101.

29. Ibid.

30. Ibid., 113.

31. McPherson, *Marching Toward Freedom,* 191.

32. Ibid., 190.

33. Wise, *Gate of Hell,* 205.

34. Heidler and Heidler, *Encyclopedia,* 4:1745.

35. Conrad, *Harriet Tubman,* 181.

36. Ibid.

37. *The Commonwealth* (Boston), August 12, 1864.

38. Sojourner Truth, *Narrative of Sojourner Truth,* ed. Margaret Washington (New York: Vintage, 1994), xvi.

39. *The Commonwealth* (Boston), July 10, 1863.

40. One story mentions that Tubman visited Mrs. Lincoln, but there is no corroboration of this.

41. Telford Memoir, 5.

42. "Harriet Tubman Is Dead," *Auburn Citizen,* March 11, 1913. See also Sarah Bradford, *Harriet Tubman: The Moses of Her People* (New York: J. J. Little, 1901).

43. Wood MSS.

44. Ibid.

45. By 1864 many African Americans complained of discriminatory treatment, especially on the matter of furlough and medical attention. *Christian Recorder,* July 16, 1864. Black soldiers felt that injured and hospitalized white men were not only given preferential treatment, but they were released to their families' care for recuperation much more often than black soldiers.

46. Margaret Wagner et al., eds., *Library of Congress Civil War Desk Reference* (New York: Simon and Schuster, 2002), 757.

47. Ibid.

48. Wood MSS.

49. Ibid.

50. Walt Whitman, *Complete Poetry and Prose* (New York: Library of America, 1982), 1004.

51. Noah Andre Trudeau, *Out of the Storm: The End of the Civil War, April–June 1865* (Boston: Little, Brown, 1994), 392–93.

52. Another account claims Tubman was ejected from a streetcar in Washington, D.C., in March 1868. See John White Chadwick, ed., *A Life for Liberty: Anti-Slavery and Other Letters of Sallie Holley* (New York: G. P. Putnam's Sons, 1899), 208.

53. Walls, *Harriet Tubman Home.*

54. *Auburn Daily Advertiser,* January 22, 1868, 3.

## CHAPTER TWELVE: FINAL BATTLES

1. Sterling, *We Are Your Sisters,* 411.

2. *The Freedman's Record* 4, no. 9 (September 1868), 144.

3. Telford Memoir, 3.

4. Siebert, *Underground Railroad,* 189.

5. Telford Memoir, 22.

6. "Harriet Tubman Is Dead," *Auburn Citizen,* March 11, 1913.

7. Charles Harris Wesley, *The History of the National Association of Colored Women's Clubs* (Washington, D.C.: National Association of Colored Women's Clubs, 1984), 38.

8. Wood MSS.

9. Telford Memoir, 21.

10. *Baltimore News American,* October 7, 1867, 4.

11. *Baltimore Sun,* December 17, 1867, 4.

12. *Baltimore News American,* December 23, 1867.

13. Chadwick, *Life for Liberty,* 205.

14. Ibid.

15. *Auburn Daily Advertiser,* January 22, 1868, 3.

16. *The Commonwealth* (Boston), January 9, 1869.

17. Bradford, *Moses,* 139.

18. Wood MSS.

19. For example, General Saxton certifies more explicitly under a later date as follows: "I am witness to the value of her services rendered in the Union Army during the late war in North Carolina and Florida. She was employed in the Hospitals and as a spy. She made many a raid inside the enemy's lines displaying remarkable courage, zeal and fidelity. She was employed by Gen'l Hunter and I think by Generals Stevens and Sherman — and is as deserving of a pension from the Government for her services as any other of its faithful servants." Bradford, *Moses,* 142.

20. Wood MSS.

21. Telford Memoir, 19.

22. Wood MSS.

23. Mowbray and Rimpo, *Close-ups,* 63.

24. Unidentified Auburn paper, March 19, 1869. Tubman Collection, Schomburg Center.

25. Alice Lucas Brickler to Earl Conrad, August 14, 1939. Tubman Collection, Schomburg Center.

26. Bradford, *Scenes,* 112.

27. Conrad, *Harriet Tubman,* 211.

28. Bradford, *Moses,* 89–90.

29. See Cayuga County Deeds, Book 106, 51.

30. *Auburn Daily Bulletin,* October 6, 1873.

31. Ibid.

32. Mildred D. Myers, *Miss Emily* (Charlotte Harbor, Fla.: Tabby House, 1998), 134.

33. House of Representatives, 43rd Congress, 1st Session, Report 787.

34. Elliot G. Storke, *History of Cayuga County, New York* (Syracuse, N.Y.: D. Mason & Co., 1872), 211.

35. Benjamin Stewart (the name Ben Ross took after 1857) appears on the census in 1865 and 1870 but not in 1875, so his death presumably came sometime in the first half of the decade.

36. Telford Memoir, 20.

37. See Sheila Tucker, *The Township of Fleming, Cayuga County, New York, 1823–1973* (Auburn, N.Y.: Brunner, 1973).

38. Alice Lucas Brickler letter, Tubman Collection, Schomburg Center.

39. Tucker, *Township,* 21.

40. House of Representatives, 49th Congress, 2nd Session, vol. 18, pt. 1, 954.

41. Correspondence in Tubman Pension File, WC415288, National Archives, under correspondence concerning "Harriet Tubman, famous former slave."

42. *Auburn Daily Advertiser,* March 24, 1905.

43. Ibid.

44. Tubman Pension File, National Archives.

45. She had received a onetime $200 payment during the war.

46. This was indeed a dream, as money was in such short supply that in 1892 she took out a mortgage on her South Street home for $500. See Cayuga County Record, Book 24, 469.

47. Telford Memoir, 22.

48. Cayuga County Deeds, Book 106, 51. See also "Moses of the Negroes," *Literary Digest* 46 (1913), 915.

49. The Reverend E.U.A. Brooks, later superintendent of the Harriet Tubman Home, claimed the sale price was $1,250, with $250 offered as a down payment and the Cayuga County Savings Bank loaning $1,000 to Harriet as a mortgage. He also claimed she rented out the property until she donated it to the AME Zion Church, which assumed an $1,800 debt and offered Tubman a pension. An article in the *Auburn Daily Advertiser,* June 24, 1908, declared the purchase price was $1,350.

50. Holt, "Heroine in Ebony," 460.

51. Exact quote reads: "You wouldn't think dat after I served de flag so faithfully I should come to want under its folds." *New York Herald,* November 22, 1907.

52. She had provided "years of service as nurse and cook in hospitals, and as a commander of several men (eight or nine) as scouts under direction and orders of Edwin M. Stanton, Secretary of War, and of several generals." See Tubman Affidavit, January 1, 1898, Tubman Pension File, National Archives.

53. P. M. Hamer, Chief, Division of Reference, National Archives, to Earl Conrad, August 16, 1939. Tubman Collection, Schomburg Center.

54. This is echoed in contemporary America by the way in which veterans groups have resisted any rehabilitation of the reputation of actress and activist Jane Fonda. Just as Harriet Tubman could never be allowed to gain status as a "soldier" by former Confederates at the turn of the twentieth century, Fonda, nicknamed Hanoi Jane by her detractors, remains a lightning rod for conservatives into the twenty-first century.

55. House of Representatives, 55th Congress, 3rd Session, Report 1774.

56. Ibid., Report 1619.

57. Frank C. Davis, "The Moses of Her People," *New York Herald Sunday Magazine,* September 22, 1907.

58. *Auburn Citizen,* June 24, 1908.

59. Ibid.

60. Ibid.

61. *Auburn Daily Advertiser,* March 11, 1913.

62. Library of Congress, Prints and Photographs Collection, LC-USZ 62-61445.

63. Myers, *Miss Emily,* 209.

64. Ibid., 209–10.

65. Ibid., 144.

66. See *Auburn Citizen,* March 11, 1913.

67. Davis, "Moses."

68. James B. Clarke, *An Hour with Harriet Tubman* (Los Angeles: Grafton, 1911).

69. *New York Tribune,* March 11, 1913.

70. *Auburn Citizen,* March 13, 1913.

## EPILOGUE: HARRIET TUBMAN'S LEGACY

1. Simply go to Google or any other search engine on the Internet to verify that "Harriet Tubman" will produce a wide range of hits, but a significant cluster associated with spousal abuse and domestic violence shelters.

2. I remain indebted to David Blight for this information, and for his continuing support as a colleague and friend.

3. Discussions of these issues can be found at www.h-net.msu.edu. Consult the logs and use Harriet Tubman as subject keywords to trace the thread of debate.

4. See Dorothy Sterling, *Freedom Train: The Story of Harriet Tubman* (1954) and Ann Petry, *Harriet Tubman: Conductor on the Underground Railroad* (1955).

5. Bradford, *Scenes,* 7.

# Bibliography

————◄O►————

## MANUSCRIPTS

Telford, Emma. "Harriet: The Modern Moses of Heroism and Visions," as dictated by Harriet Tubman to Emma Telford, 1911, on deposit at Cayuga County Historian's Office, Auburn, New York.

Touart, Paul. "Monograph on Harriet Tubman," Maryland Historical Trust Library, Crownsville, Md.

Charles P. Wood Manuscript, Pension Files, National Archives, Washington, D.C.

## PRIMARY SOURCES

Andrews, William, and Henry Louis Gates Jr. *The Civitas Anthology of African American Slave Narratives* (Washington, D.C.: Civitas, 1999).

Aptheker, Herbert, ed. *A Documentary History of the Negro People in the United States* (New York: Citadel, 1951).

Ball, Charles. *Slavery in the United States* (New York: John S. Taylor, 1837).

Bibb, Henry. *Narrative of the Life and Adventures of Henry Bibb: An American Slave* (New York, 1850).

Blake, Jane. *Memoirs of Margaret Jane Blake* (Philadelphia: printed for the author, 1834).

Blassingame, John W. *Slave Testimony: Two Centuries of Letters, Speeches, Interviews, and Autobiographies* (Baton Rouge: Louisiana State University Press, 1976).

Brown, Henry "Box." *Narrative of Henry Box Brown* (Boston: Brown & Stearns, 1849).

Brown, John. *Slave Life in Georgia: A Narrative of the Life, Suffers, and Escape of John Brown, a Fugitive Slave, Now in England* (London: W. W. Watts, 1855).

Brown, William Wells. *The Rising Son; or, The Antecedents and Advancement of the Colored Race* (Boston: A. G. Brown & Company, 1874).

Chadwick, John White, ed. *A Life for Liberty: Anti-Slavery and Other Letters of Sallie Holley* (New York: G. P. Putnam's Sons, 1899).

Child, Lydia Maria. *Letters of Lydia Maria Child* (Boston: Houghton Mifflin, 1883).

Coffin, Levi. *Reminiscences* (Cincinnati: Robert Clark & Company, 1876).

*251*

Cooper, Thomas. *Narrative of the Life of Thomas Cooper* (New York: Isaac T. Hopper, 1832).

Craft, William and Ellen. *Running a Thousand Miles for Freedom* (1860; reprint, Athens: University of Georgia Press, 1999).

Drew, Benjamin. *A North-side View of Slavery* (1856; reprint, New York: Negro Universities Press, 1968).

Eldridge, Elleanor. *Memoirs of Elleanor Eldridge* (Providence, R.I.: B. T. Albro, 1840).

Fairbank, Rev. Calvin. *Reverend Calvin Fairbank* (1890; reprint, New York: Negro Universities Press, 1969).

Grandy, Moses. *Narrative of the Life of Moses Grandy, Late a Slave in the United States of America* (Boston: Oliver Johnson, 1844).

Green, William. *Narrative of Events in the Life of William Green, Formerly a Slave, Written by Himself* (New Haven, Conn.: published by the author, 1855).

Haviland, Laura S. *A Woman's Life Work: Labors and Experiences* (Chicago: Publishing Association of Friends, 1889).

Henson, Josiah. *The Life of Josiah Henson, Formerly a Slave, Now an Inhabitant of Canada, as Narrated by Himself to Samuel Eliot* (Boston: A. D. Phelps, 1849).

Jameson, Anna. *Winter Studies and Summer Rambles in Canada* (London: Saunders & Otley, 1838).

Johnson, H. U. *From Dixie to Canada: Romance and Realities of the Underground Railroad* (1894; reprint, Westport, Conn.: Negro Universities Press, 1970).

Lane, Lunsford. *The Narrative of Lunsford Lane* (Boston: J. G. Torrey, 1842).

Loguen, Jermain Wesley. *Reverend J. W. Loguen, as a Slave and as a Freeman* (Syracuse, N.Y.: J.G.K. Tuair & Co., 1859).

Looby, Christopher, ed. *The Complete Civil War Journal and Selected Letters of Thomas W. Higginson* (Chicago: University of Chicago Press, 2000).

Loring, James S., ed. *Memoir of Chloe Spear: A Native of Africa, Who Was Enslaved in Childhood. By a "Lady of Boston"* (Boston: James Loring, 1832).

Mitchell, Rev. W. M. *The Underground Railroad from Slavery to Freedom* (1860; reprint, Westport, Conn.: Negro Universities Press, 1970).

Myers, Mildred D. *Miss Emily* (Charlotte Harbor, Fla.: Tabby House, 1998).

Northup, Solomon. *Twelve Years a Slave* (London: Derby & Miller, 1853).

Parker, John P. *His Promised Land: The Autobiography of John P. Parker,* ed. Stuart Sprague (New York: W. W. Norton, 1996).

Pearson, Elizabeth Ware, ed. *Letters from Port Royal* (1906; reprint, New York: Arno Press, 1969).

Pennington, James W. C. *The Fugitive Blacksmith* (London: Charles Gilpin, 1850).

Pettit, Eber M. *Sketches in the History of the Underground Railroad* (1879; reprint, Westfield, N.Y.: Chautauqua Region Press, 1999).

Picquet, Louisa. *Louisa Picquet, the Octoroon; or, Inside Views of Southern Domestic Life* (New York: published by the author, 1861).

Pillsbury, Parker. *Acts of the Anti-Slavery Apostles* (Rochester, N.Y.: Clague, Wegman, Schlicht & Co., 1883).

Robinson, John Bell. *Pictures of Slavery and Anti-Slavery* (Philadelphia, 1863).

Ross, Alexander M. *Recollections and Experiences of an Abolitionist* (Toronto: Rowell and Hutchinson, 1875).

Ruchames, Louis, ed. *John Brown: The Making of a Revolutionary* (New York: Grosset & Dunlap, 1969).

Severance, Frank H. *Old Trails on the Niagara Frontier* (Buffalo, N.Y.: Matthew Northup Co., 1899).

Seward, Frederick. *William H. Seward,* 3 vols. (New York: Derby and Miller, 1891).

Siebert, Wilbur H. *The Underground Railroad* (1898; reprint, New York: Arno Press, 1968).

Sterling, Dorothy, ed. *We Are Your Sisters: Black Women in the Nineteenth Century* (New York: W. W. Norton, 1984).

Stevenson, Brenda, ed. *Journals of Charlotte Forten Grimke* (New York: Oxford University Press, 1988).

Stewart, Maria W. *Productions of Mrs. Maria W. Stewart* (Boston: printed for the author, 1835).

Still, William. *The Underground Railroad* (Philadelphia, 1872).

Thompson, John. *The Life of John Thompson, a Fugitive Slave: Written by Himself* (Worcester, Mass.: printed for the author, 1835).

Truth, Sojourner. *Narrative of Sojourner Truth,* ed. Margaret Washington (New York: Vintage, 1994).

Ward, Samuel Ringgold. *Autobiography of a Fugitive Negro: His Anti-Slavery Labors in the United States, Canada, and England* (London: John Snow, 1855).

Washington, Madison. *The Heroic Slave: A Thrilling Narrative of the Adventures of Madison Washington in Pursuit of Liberty* (Boston: Jewett and Co., 1853).

Wheeler, Peter. *Chains and Freedom; or, The Life and Adventures of Peter Wheeler, a Colored Man Yet Living* (New York: E. S. Arnold and Company, 1839).

Williams, James B. *Life and Adventures of James Williams* (1874; reprint, Nendeln, Liechtenstein: Kraus, 1973).

Wilmot, Frank. *Disclosures and Confessions of Frank Wilmot* (Philadelphia: Barclay & Co., 1860).

Wister, Fanny Kemble. "Sarah Butler Wister's Civil War Diary," *Pennsylvania Magazine of History and Biography* 102 (July 1978).

## SECONDARY SOURCES

Astor, Gerald. *The Right to Fight: A History of African Americans in the Military* (Novato, Calif.: Presidio Press, 1998).

Bentley, Judith. *"Dear Friend": Thomas Garrett and William Still, Collaborators on the Underground Railroad* (New York: Dutton, 1997).

———. *Harriet Tubman* (New York: Franklin Watts, 1991).

Blackett, Richard J. M. *Beating Against the Barriers: Biographical Essays in Nineteenth-Century Afro-American History* (Baton Rouge: Louisiana University Press, 1986).

Blockson, Charles L. *Hippocrene Guide to the Underground Railroad* (New York: Hippocrene, 1994).

———. *The Underground Railroad* (New York: Prentice-Hall, 1987).

Bradford, Sarah. *Harriet Tubman, the Moses of Her People* (1886; reprint, Bedford, Mass.: Applewood Books, 1993).

———. *Harriet Tubman: The Moses of Her People* (New York: J. J. Little, 1901).

———. *Scenes in the Life of Harriet Tubman* (Auburn, N.Y.: W. J. Moses, 1869).

Bramble, Linda. *Black Fugitives in Early Canada* (St. Catharines, Ontario: Vanwell, 1988).

Breyfogle, William A. *Make Free: The Story of the Underground Railroad* (Philadelphia: Lippincott, 1958).

Brown, Ira. *The Negro in Pennsylvania History* (University Park, Pa.: Pennsylvania Historical Association, 1970).

Campbell, Stanley. *The Slave Catchers: Enforcement of the Fugitive Slave Law, 1850–1860* (Chapel Hill: University of North Carolina Press, 1968).

Cayuga County Historical Society. *History of Cayuga County, New York* (Auburn, N.Y., 1908).

Collison, Gary. *Shadrach Minkins: From Fugitive Slave to Citizen* (Cambridge, Mass.: Harvard University Press, 1997).

Conrad, Earl. *Harriet Tubman* (Washington, D.C.: The Associated Publishers, 1943).

Cottrol, Robert, ed. *From African to Yankee: Narratives of Slavery and Freedom in Antebellum New England* (Armonk, N.Y.: M. E. Sharpe, 1998).

Davis, Elizabeth Lindsay. *Lifting as They Climb* (1933; reprint, New York: G. K. Hall, 1996).

DuBois, W.E.B. *The Philadelphia Negro: A Social Study* (1899; reprint, Philadelphia: University of Pennsylvania Press, 1996).

Egerton, Douglas R. *Gabriel's Rebellion: The Virginia Slave Conspiracies of 1800 and 1802* (Chapel Hill: University of North Carolina Press, 1993).

————. *He Shall Go Out Free: The Lives of Denmark Vesey* (Madison, Wis.: Madison House, 1999).

Fields, Barbara Jeanne. *Slavery and Freedom on the Middle Ground: Maryland During the Nineteenth Century* (New Haven, Conn.: Yale University Press, 1985).

Finkelman, Paul, ed. *His Soul Goes Marching On: Responses to John Brown and the Harpers Ferry Raid* (Charlottesville: University Press of Virginia, 1995).

Foner, Eric. *Great Lives Observed: Nat Turner* (Englewood Cliffs, N.J.: Prentice-Hall, 1971).

Foster, Frances. *Witnessing Slavery* (Westport, Conn.: Greenwood Press, 1979).

Franklin, John Hope, and Alfred Moss Jr. *From Slavery to Freedom: A Story of Negro Americans,* 6th ed. (New York: Knopf, 1988).

Futhey, J. Smith, and Gilbert Cope. *History of Chester County, Pennsylvania* (Philadelphia: Louis H. Everts, 1881).

Gallman, J. Matthew, ed. *The Civil War Chronicle* (New York: Crown, 2000).

Gara, Larry. *The Liberty Line: The Legend of the Underground Railroad* (Lexington: University of Kentucky Press, 1961).

Glatthar, Joseph T. *Forged in Battle: The Civil War Alliance of Black Soldiers and White Officers* (New York: Free Press, 1990).

Greenberg, Kenneth, ed. *The Confessions of Nat Turner and Related Documents* (Boston: Bedford Books, 1996).

————. *Nat Turner: A Slave Rebellion in History and Memory* (New York: Oxford University Press, 2003).

Harlow, Ralph. *Gerrit Smith: Philanthropist and Reformer* (New York: Henry Holt & Co., 1939).

Haskins, Jim. *Get On Board: The Story of the Underground Railroad* (New York: Scholastic Press, 1993).

Hunter, Carol. *To Set the Captives Free* (New York: Garland Press, 1993).

Humez, Jean M. *Harriet Tubman: The Life and the Life Stories* (Madison: University of Wisconsin Press, 2003).

Johnson, Walter. *Soul by Soul: Life Inside the Antebellum Slave Market* (Cambridge, Mass.: Harvard University Press, 1999).

Jones, Elias. *History of Dorchester County, Md.* (Baltimore: Williams & Wilkins, 1902).

Jones, Katharine M. *Port Royal Under Six Flags* (Indianapolis: Bobbs-Merrill, 1960).

Klees, Emerson. *Underground Railroad Tales with Routes Through the Finger Lakes Region* (Rochester, N.Y.: Friends of the Finger Lakes, 1997).

Leonard, Daisy Anderson. *From Slavery to Affluence: Memoirs of Robert Anderson, Ex-Slave* (Steamboat Springs, Colo.: Steamboat Pilot, 1927).

Mabee, Carlton. *Black Freedom: The Nonviolent Abolitionists from 1830 Through the Civil War* (New York: Macmillan, 1970).

McGowan, James A. *Station Master on the Underground Railroad: Life and Letters of Thomas Garrett* (Moylan, Pa.: Whimsie Press, 1977).

McKivigan, John, and Stanley Harrold, eds. *Antislavery Violence: Sectional, Racial, and Cultural Conflict in Antebellum America* (Knoxville: University of Tennessee Press, 1999).

McLard, Megan. *Harriet Tubman and the Underground Railroad* (Englewood Cliffs, N.J.: Silver Burdette Press, 1991).

McPherson, James. *Battle Cry of Freedom* (New York: Oxford University Press, 1988).

————. *Marching Toward Freedom: The Negro in the Civil War, 1861–65* (New York: Knopf, 1965).

————. *Ordeal by Fire: Civil War and Reconstruction* (New York: McGraw-Hill, 1982).

Merrill, Arch. *The Underground Freedom's Road and Other Upstate Tales* (American Brook, N.Y.: Stratford Press, 1963).

Mowbray, Calvin. *The Dorchester County Fact Book* (Silver Spring, Md.: Family Line, 1981).

Mowbray, Calvin, and Maurice D. Rimpo. *Close-ups of Early Dorchester County History* (1987; 2nd ed., Silver Spring, Md.: Family Line, 1988).

Oates, Stephen. *To Purge This Land with Blood* (New York: Harper & Row, 1970).

Painter, Nell. *Sojourner Truth: A Life, a Symbol* (New York: W. W. Norton, 1996).

Phillips, Christopher. *Freedom's Port: The African American Community of Baltimore, 1790–1860* (Urbana: University of Illinois Press, 1997).

Porter, Dorothy. *Early Negro Writing, 1760–1837* (Boston: Beacon Press, 1971).

Quarles, Benjamin. *Black Abolitionists* (New York: Oxford University Press, 1969).

————, ed. *Blacks on John Brown* (Urbana: University of Illinois Press, 1972).

Raboteau, Albert J. *Slave Religion: The "Invisible Institution" in the Antebellum South* (New York: Oxford University Press, 1978).

Renehan, Edward J., Jr. *The Secret Six: The True Tale of the Men Who Conspired with John Brown* (New York: Crown, 1995).

Rhodes, Jane. *Mary Ann Shadd Cary: The Black Press and Protest in the Nineteenth Century* (Bloomington: Indiana University Press, 1998).

Ripley, Peter, et al., eds. *Witness for Freedom: African American Voices on Race, Slavery, and Emancipation* (Chapel Hill: University of North Carolina Press, 1993).

Rose, Willie Lee. *Rehearsal for Reconstruction: The Port Royal Experiment* (Indianapolis: Bobbs-Merrill, 1964).

Rossbach, Jeffrey. *Ambivalent Conspirators: John Brown, the Secret Six, and a Theory of Slave Violence* (Philadelphia: University of Pennsylvania Press, 1982).

Runyon, Randolph. *Delia Webster and the Underground Railroad* (Lexington: University of Kentucky Press, 1996).

Sanborn, F. B., ed. *John Brown, Liberator of Kansas and Martyr of Virginia: Life and Letters* (1885; 4th ed., Cedar Rapids, Iowa: Torch Press, 1910).

Scheidenhelm, Richard, ed. *The Response to John Brown* (Belmont, Calif.: Wadsworth, 1972).

Schwartz, Marie Jenkins. *Born in Bondage: Growing Up Enslaved in the Antebellum South* (Cambridge, Mass.: Harvard University Press, 2000).

Sillen, Samuel. *Women Against Slavery* (New York: Masses & Mainstream, 1955).

Slaughter, Thomas P. *Bloody Dawn: The Christiana Race Riot and Racial Violence in the Antebellum North* (New York: Oxford University Press, 1991).

Smedley, R. C. *History of the Underground Railroad* (Lancaster, Pa., 1883).

Stampp, Kenneth. *And the War Came: The North and the Secession Crisis (1860–1861)* (Baton Rouge: Louisiana State University Press, 1950).

Starling, Marion W. *The Slave Narrative: Its Place in American History* (New York: G. K. Hall, 1979).

Stauffer, John. *The Black Hearts of Men: Radical Abolitionists and the Transformation of Race* (Cambridge, Mass.: Harvard University Press, 2002).

Steiner, Paul E. *Disease in the Civil War: Natural Biological Warfare in 1861–1865* (Springfield, Ill.: Charles C. Thomas, 1968).

Stewart, James B. *Holy Warriors: The Abolitionists and American Slavery* (New York: Hill & Wang, 1976).

*Stories of New Jersey* (New York: M. Barrows & Co., 1938).

Storke, Elliot G. *History of Cayuga County, New York* (Syracuse, N.Y.: D. Mason & Co., 1872).

Strother, Horatio. *The Underground Railroad in Connecticut* (Middletown, Conn.: Wesleyan University Press, 1962).

Takaki, Ronald T. *Iron Cages: Race and Culture in Nineteenth-Century America* (New York: Knopf, 1979).

Trefousse, Hans, *Thaddeus Stevens* (Chapel Hill: University of North Carolina Press, 1997).

Trotter, Joe William, Jr., and Eric L. Smith. *African Americans in Pennsylvania* (University Park: Pennsylvania State University Press, 1997).

Trudeau, Noah Andre. *Like Men of War: Black Troops in the Civil War, 1862–1865* (Boston: Little, Brown, 1998).

———. *Out of the Storm: The End of the Civil War, April–June 1865* (Boston: Little, Brown, 1994).

Van Deusen, Glyndon G. *William Henry Seward* (New York: Oxford University Press, 1967).

Villard, Oswald Garrison. *John Brown, 1800–1859* (New York: Knopf, 1943).

Von Frank, Albert J. *The Trials of Anthony Burns: Freedom and Slavery in Emerson's Boston* (Cambridge, Mass.: Harvard University Press, 1998).

Wagner, Margaret, et al., eds. *Library of Congress Civil War Desk Reference* (New York: Simon & Schuster, 2002).

Walls, W. J. *Harriet Tubman Home, Its Present and Its Future* (privately published, n.d.).

Warch, Richard, and Jonathan Fanton, eds. *John Brown* (Englewood Cliffs, N.J.: Prentice-Hall, 1973).

Whitman, T. Stephen. *The Price of Freedom: Slavery and Manumission in Baltimore and Early National Maryland* (Lexington: University of Kentucky Press, 1997).

Wilson, Carol. *Freedom at Risk: The Kidnapping of Free Blacks in America, 1780–1865* (Lexington: University of Kentucky Press, 1994).

Winch, Julie. *Gentleman of Color: The Life of James Forten* (New York: Oxford University Press, 2002).

———. *Philadelphia's Black Elite: Activism, Accommodation, and the Struggle for Autonomy, 1787–1848* (Philadelphia: Temple University Press, 1988).

Wise, Stephen R. *Gate of Hell: Campaign for Charleston Harbor, 1863* (Columbia: University of South Carolina Press, 1994).

Yee, Shirley. *Black Women Abolitionists: A Study in Activism, 1828–1860* (Knoxville: University of Tennessee Press, 1992).


## ARTICLES AND DISSERTATIONS

Blackett, Richard J. M. "Freedom or the Martyr's Grave: Black Pittsburgh's Aid to the Fugitive Slave," *Western Pennsylvania Historical Magazine* 6 (1973).

Brubaker, Marianna G. "The Underground Railroad," *Lancaster County Historical Society* 15, no. 4 (1911).

Dixon, Melvin W. "Historical Vision and Personal Witness in American Slave Literature." Ph.D. diss., Brown University, 1975.

Gara, Larry. "The Fugitive Slave Law," *Civil War History* 10 (1964).

———. "The Professional Fugitive in the Abolition Movement," *Wisconsin Magazine of History* (spring 1965).

Hoefer, Jean. *New York Alive* 6, no. 3 (May/June 1986).

Holt, Rosa Belle. "A Heroine in Ebony," *The Chautauquan* 23 (July 1896).

Johnson, Patricia. "Sensitivity and Civil War: The Selected Diaries and Papers, 1858–1866, of Frances Adeline (Fanny) Seward," Ph.D. diss., University of Rochester, 1963.

Leslie, William R. "The Pennsylvania Fugitive Slave Act of 1826," *Journal of Southern History* 12 (1952).

McElvey, Kay Najiyyah. "Early Black Dorchester, 1776–1870." Ed.D. diss., University of Maryland, College Park, 1991.

Miller, Anne Fitzhugh. "Harriet Tubman," *American Magazine* 74, no. 4 (August 1912).

Pease, Jane H., and William H. Pease. "Confrontation and Abolition in the 1850s," *Journal of American History* 58 (1972).

Robinson, Mary N. "Sidelights on Slavery," *Lancaster County Historical Society* 15, no. 5 (1911).

Sloane, Rush. "The Underground Railroad of the Firelands," *Firelands Pioneer* (Sandusky, Ohio, 1888).

Wayne, Michael. "The Black Population of Canada West on the Eve of the American Civil War: A Reassessment Based on the Manuscript Census of 1861," *Histoires Sociale/Social History* 28, no. 56 (November 1995).

Wilson, Carol. "Active Vigilance Is the Price of Liberty: Black Self-Defense Against Fugitive Slave Recapture and Kidnapping of Free Blacks," in John R. McKivigan and Stanley Harrold, eds., *Antislavery Violence: Sectional, Racial, and Cultural Conflict in Antebellum America* (Knoxville: University of Tennessee Press, 1999).

Wyman, Lillie B. Chace. "Harriet Tubman," *New England Magazine* 14, no. 1 (March 1896).

# Index

Preliminary Emancipation Proclamation, 159

*Present State and Condition of the Free People of Color of the City of Philadelphia* (1838 study), 52

*Prigg v. Pennsylvania* (1842), 54

Protection Society of Maryland, 51

Proudfoot, Reverend Mr., 106

*Provincial Freeman, The* (journal), 107–8

Purvis, Robert, 47, 52, 64, 66, 75

Quakers (Society of Friends), 66, 231*n*8
 aid fugitives, 35, 57, 59, 63–64; George Washington's complaint, 39; HT helped by, 36, 70, 90, 93
 segregate worship, 233*n*8
 slaveholders expelled from, 48

racism, 51–53, 62
 in Canada, 105–6
 Nat Turner and, 42
 and race riots, 51–52, 100
 segregation: of dead soldiers, 184; Jim Crow, 215, 233*n*8; in public schools, 49; in Quaker worship, 233*n*8

*Ram's Horn, The* (abolitionist periodical), 126

Rankin, John, 70

Ray, George, 207

Reconstruction, 189, 193, 215

religion, 20–21, 30–31
 independent black churches, 49–50
 and redemptive faith, 16, 39
 of slaveholders, 24, 48
 and slavery/antislavery, 35, 125

Remond, Sarah Parker, 56

Republican Party, 116, 141, 194, 195, 204, 207

Revolutionary War, 7, 8, 64–65, 99
 free blacks in, 25; Crispus Attucks, 175

Rhode Island
 slavecatcher law, 54
 UGRR in, 72

Richmond, Virginia
 black conspiracy in, 41, 171
 Civil War battle for, 153, 187

Ripley, Ohio, as UGRR hub, 70

Roach, Monique Patenaude, 234*n*41

Robinson, John Bell, 142–44

Rochester, New York, safe house in, 64, 84

*Rochester Advertiser,* 55

*Rochester-Democrat,* 192

Ross, Alexander, 235–36*n*16

Ross, Araminta. *See* Tubman, Harriet

Ross family, 21, 22
 after Brodess's death, 31–32
 name changed to Stewart, 115
 *See also* Stewart, Benjamin and Harriet, *and* Stewart (formerly Ross) *entries*

Ruggles, David, 233*n*12

Rush Library and Debating Society, 49

Russell, Martha, 111

safe houses. *See* Underground Railroad (UGRR)

St. Catherines, Ontario, 98, 104, 105–6, 108, 145. *See also* Canada

Salvation Army, 200

Sanborn, Franklin, 173
 HT's letters to, 171, 180
 quoted, 83, 127, 132, 134, 168, 242*n*15

Sanitary Commission, U.S., 186

Saxton, General Rufus, 158–59, 160, 164, 180, 196, 213

Scott (Georgia slaveowner defied by slave), 13

Scott, Dred, 117, 235*n*8

Scott, John (slave), 43

Scott, General Winfield, 147

Sea Islands, 150, 152
 dialect spoken on, 156
 *See also* Beaufort, South Carolina

"Secret Six," 127

Sedgwick family, 207

segregation. *See* racism

Senate, U.S., 202, 208

Seward, Frances (William's daughter), 200

Seward, Frederick, 201

Seward, William, 119, 120, 127, 204, 208, 213
 HT buys house from, *x,* 115–16, 201, 203
 and HT's finances, 193, 195, 200–201, 243*n*36

Seward, Mrs. William (Frances Miller), 116, 119, 120, 243*n*36

Seward House (Auburn, New York), 228*n*20

Shaw, Colonel Robert Gould, 174–79

Sherman, General William Tecumseh, 247*n*19

Shiloh, Battle of, 153

Shimer, Anthony, 201

Siebert, Wilbur, 192

Simcoe, Lt. Governor John Graves, 99

Simmons, Charles, 164

slavecatchers. *See* fugitive slaves

# About the Author

Catherine Clinton earned her undergraduate degree in Afro-American Studies from Harvard University in 1973, her M.A. in American Studies from the University of Sussex in 1974, and her Ph.D. in history from Princeton University in 1980. She has taught history and African American studies at Harvard, Brown, and Brandeis and held visiting chairs at the University of Richmond, Baruch College of the City University of New York, and the Citadel. She has written and edited over a dozen books, including *The Plantation Mistress* and *Fanny Kemble's Civil Wars.* Clinton is a former president of the Southern Association for Women Historians and is currently a member of the executive council of the Society of American Historians. She lives in Riverside, Connecticut, with her husband and two sons.

# About the Author

# HARRIET TUBMAN

———◆———

## THE ROAD TO FREEDOM

Catherine Clinton

A Reading Group Guide

# A CONVERSATION WITH CATHERINE CLINTON

*Harriet Tubman's name is probably familiar to many Americans who know little or nothing about the details of her life. Why did you decide to write a biography of Tubman?*

I first encountered Harriet Tubman in elementary school, like many American schoolchildren. I was in public schools in Kansas City in the 1960s and read a book about her exploits with the Underground Railroad.

When I went to Harvard as an undergraduate and majored in Afro-American Studies, Tubman's name was conspicuously absent from the curriculum. And then when I was teaching in the Afro-American Studies Department at Harvard in 1991 and was asked to write an encyclopedia article on Tubman, I was shocked to discover that the last adult biography of her had been published in 1943. So I decided that Tubman was too important a figure to be treated so shabbily; she was a person long overdue for a major biography. I wanted to liberate her from the children's shelf — to have her take her rightful place alongside George Washington, Abraham Lincoln, Martin Luther King, and other American heroes.

*What were some of the difficulties you faced in gathering information about Tubman?*

Because Tubman was illiterate, even after her flight to freedom in 1849, there are no letters or diaries in her own hand to help reconstruct her long and fascinating life. We do have some of the letters she occasionally dictated, but very few have been preserved. Contemporaries who came in contact with Tubman recorded their impressions of her, in their letters, diaries, or even in published accounts. This woman known as Moses, and sometimes called the General by her admirers, was a minor celebrity within reform circles and was revered for her heroic roles in the war to end slavery.

Despite Tubman's fame, documentary evidence remains scarce, a real handicap for scholars on her trail. In the case of her Civil War pension, papers remain on deposit at the National Archives. But for so many other matters, such as birth and marriages, and even in the case of her death certificate, documents are unreliable or unavailable.

One shining exception: although several accounts record her escape to freedom as taking place in 1849, it wasn't until 2003 that a document turned up verifying this fact. A local preservationist on the Eastern Shore of Maryland dove into a dumpster and discovered a discarded run of nineteenth-century newspapers that included an 1849 issue of the Maryland *Cambridge Democrat*. This paper carried an advertisement placed by Tubman's owner, Elizabeth Brodess, offering a reward for recovery of "Minty" (Tubman's birth name was Araminta). It was the first documented proof of her historic flight to freedom. So "evidence" about Harriet Tubman's life is still turning up.

*While researching the book, was there anything you learned about Tubman's life that you found particularly surprising?*

I remain deeply troubled that although there is a growing movement to celebrate March tenth (the date of her death in 1913) as Harriet Tubman Day, there is no national monument or appropriate tribute to this American hero. The National Park Service has undertaken a study, but at present both a historical organization near her birthplace in Dorchester County, Maryland, and the Harriet Tubman Home, at Auburn, New York, her final resting place, are underfunded and understaffed. Because Tubman was such a dynamic figure during her own lifetime — and nearly forty children's books in print attest to her continuing popularity — this neglect is both surprising and sad. Again, it was one of the reasons I undertook *The Road to Freedom*.

*How has the field of African American studies been changing and growing in the last few decades?*

Certainly there has been no more dynamic development than the emergence of voices of African American women in fiction and literature, in documentary collections and narratives, in history and in contemporary culture. From Toni Morrison's Nobel Prize to Henry Louis Gates Jr.'s forty-volume edition of the Schomburg Library of Nineteenth-Century Black Women Writers (1988), to Darlene Clark Hine's *Black Women in America: An Historical Encyclopedia* (1993), we are witnessing a great renaissance, signaling unlimited horizons. If we can just move these revolutions out of the academy and into the streets, think of what America might become.

I know Harriet Tubman has been an inspiration to students for generations and will continue to be so. My work on her has inspired me to pursue the lives of other neglected figures, such as Susie King Taylor (the only black woman to write a memoir of her service with black Union troops during the Civil War) and Frances Rollin Whipper (who wrote a biography of Martin Delaney, the only black commissioned officer in the U.S. Army during the Civil War, and may be called the first African American woman historian). I hope not just that a hundred Harriets will bloom in the next generation of academic scholarship, but that we will find out more and more about the lost black women in the American past, and recover them for our generation and those who come after.

*What can modern women in particular learn from Tubman's life?*

Tubman proves the lesson that just one person can make a difference in life: Araminta Ross (Tubman's birth name) defied slaveholders' dictates and fled to freedom to become the Moses of her people and a hero for the ages. Much was accomplished during her formative years. But equally instructive, Tubman's faith in God and her faith in herself encouraged her to always continue struggling for justice. She built her own local charity in Auburn, New York, during her later years and was a revered resource within her community.

We can honor her memory by heeding her example: each of us can reach out and try to make a difference. This was Tubman's impulse at every stage of her life and is an important message for us today.

American women, whatever their station in life, whatever their limits or opportunities, look to their families, their neighbors, their churches and schools, their legislatures and leaders, demanding changes for the better against a rising tide of indifference. This is a message of hope and humanitarianism.

*What kind of discussions would you like this book to inspire?*

Tubman refused to be defined by the prejudice society assigned to her blackness, to her womanhood. She was a proud black woman who loved and honored her family, her people, and her nation.

Tubman's patriotism was something that never went out of fashion. She did not believe in her country "right or wrong," but believed it was her right to attack the wrongs around her. She spent her energies demanding that America live up to its ideals of "liberty and justice for all." The road to freedom begins by believing in these ideals and by having the courage to, as Harriet always advised, "keep going."

# QUESTIONS AND TOPICS FOR DISCUSSION

1. Discuss the ways in which the life of Harriet Tubman helps us understand the impact of slavery on our nation.

2. Why do you think it has taken so long for scholars to investigate the history of the Underground Railroad? Can you think of other important moments in U.S. history that have not been studied as carefully as their significance merits?

3. What kinds of sources are available to document the experience of those who participated in a clandestine network like the Underground Railroad, or to chronicle the exploits of those guided to freedom as fugitives?

4. Harriet Tubman was a daring, singular, and independent individual. How did she cope with her need for love and companionship, acceptance and appreciation?

5. In what ways does this book change your perception of the limits and possibilities for African American women in American history?

6. Discuss how Harriet Tubman's conception of family shaped her life experience.

7. Is there any indication of how Harriet Tubman measured her own successes or failures throughout her long life?

8. Tubman preached a philosophy of hating the sin but forgiving the sinner. What can we learn from her inspiring example?

9. Tubman was always proud of her Civil War service, even though for more than thirty years she was denied a pension. Why did it take so long for her role in this important conflict to be acknowledged?

10. If you could go back in history and ask Harriet Tubman just one question, what would it be?

11. How can a book about past events help us understand race relations today?

12. In what ways can we honor this woman's memory and legacy today? What would be a fitting memorial, a proper tribute to Harriet Tubman?

## CATHERINE CLINTON'S SUGGESTIONS
## FOR FURTHER READING

*Passages to Freedom: The Underground Railroad in History and Memory*, edited by David W. Blight

*The Underground Railroad* by Charles L. Blockson

*Shadrach Minkins: From Fugitive Slave to Citizen* by Gary Collison

*The Liberty Line: The Legend of the Underground Railroad* by Larry Gara

*Front Line of Freedom: African Americans and the Forging of the Underground Railroad in the Ohio Valley* by Keith P. Griffler

*Beyond the River: A True Story of the Underground Railroad* by Ann Hagedorn

*Station Master on the Underground Railroad: The Life and Letters of Thomas Garrett* by James A. McGowan

*Delia Webster and the Underground Railroad* by Randolph Runyon

*North Star Country: Upstate New York and the Crusade for African American Freedom* by Milton C. Sernett

*We Are Your Sisters: Black Women in the Nineteenth Century*, edited by Dorothy Sterling

*His Promised Land: The Autobiography of John P. Parker, Former Slave and Conductor on the Underground Railroad*, edited by Stuart Sprague

*Black Women Abolitionists: A Study in Activism, 1828–1860* by Shirley J. Yee